We are the same

We are the same;

It's the details that differ.

An overview of behavioral style,
motivation and predictability.

Marcel Elfers

Cover artwork: Marcel Elfers
From left to right: Gary Ridgway, Elliot Rodger, and Jodi Arias

Figure 25, 26, 45, 50, 51
Courtesy Kimon Iannetta, author "Danger Between the Lines".

ISBN-13: 978-1507653609
ISBN-10: 1507653603

Printed by CreateSpace, an Amazon.com Company
Available from Amazon.com

For

Kimon Iannetta

My mentor, guide, and inspiration

Acknowledgments

I wish to thank
my friends who inspired me to write about behavioral styles, motivation, and predictability.

I wish to thank
acquaintances and strangers, who eloquently revealed consistencies in behavioral pathways.

I wish to thank
the late Don Riso and Russ Hudson, who recognized and defined behavioral patterns in broad terms.

I wish to thank
alcohol for reducing judgment and social inhibitions revealing core characteristics with minimal reservation and stunning clarity.

Most importantly, I thank
my wife, Elaine, for patiently standing beside me.

Who should read this book

Behavioral Pathways describes how motivation and behavioral styles develop from a childhood perspective to maturity. There are nine basic early perspectives pervasive throughout our lives leading to nine progressive behavioral patterns. These patterns are distinct and recognizable.

To recognize these patterns helps to understand yourself and others.
It has many applications:
- parenting: relationship dynamics to build cohesive family units
- businesses: precision personnel placement, position assignments
- relationship dynamics: home, school, work
- and last, but not least: personal growth.

First and foremost, *Parents* should read this book. Understanding yourself, your relationship dynamics with your partner and children, is an advantageous tool to advance existing relationships.

To learn to recognize these patterns is helpful for certain professions dealing with the general public. For instance:
- threat analysis: law-enforcement officers, parole officers, prison guards, detectives, private investigators, bounty hunters
- justice system: lawyers, judges, law-enforcement
- school system: teachers, administrative personnel, students
- mental health workers: psychologists, social workers, counselors
- medical professionals: doctors, nurses, rehab personnel
- profilers: graphologists, negotiators, textual analysts
- coaching staff: sports team cohesion

In brief, it applies to anybody with a personality.

Author's Note

Many of the story lines are real while others are fictional. People, who placed themselves in a position of public awareness, have been used to link behavioral style to their Type. Although the general public might have strong opinions regarding certain public figures, the author used such examples only because they are well-known. Other real stories based on non-public individuals have fictional names to protect their privacy.

Before we read on, we have to realize each Personality Type can be male or female. The use of "he" and "she" is random. We can behave in a healthy, average, and unhealthy manner. A healthy person will integrate many good qualities and have good social skill to cooperate with others. We don't have to worry about healthy people as they allow others to be part of their lives.

It is more important to recognize those *with average and unhealthy levels of functioning,* and the material in this book focuses on those individuals for two reasons. First, at average and unhealthy levels, we exaggerate our normal behavior which makes Type recognition much easier. Second, we need to identify their patterns in order to influence them with integrity toward better and healthier relationships.

It is my hope the reader will recognize themselves and others in these behavioral pathways. This brief synopsis of behavioral styles, motivation, and predictability is accurate in broad terms, but not in the details. It will take time and studying efforts to become competent and accurate in Type recognition and behavioral predictability. However, you will receive a tremendous pay-off. Once you recognize these patterns, you will be able to emphasize strengths and de-emphasize weaknesses in yourself as well as others. You will be able to influence others positively, promote friendships, gain cooperation, create alliances, and achieve social standing.

About the Author

Marcel Elfers was born in Haarlem, the Netherlands, and moved to the United States in the mid-eighties. After a work event involving a handwriting sample, he was instantly hooked on discovering the link between emotional impacts on writing behavior. It would become a life long journey.

After graduation and moving to the United States, he worked as a Physical Therapist for fifteen years. During his medical career, he observed handwriting behavioral styles and matched them with known author behavioral characteristics. Over time, he also noticed patterns in word selection and sentence construction revealing motivation and perspective. These were frequently consistent with writing behavior.

In his quest to write a book about danger signs in handwriting, he bought "Danger Between the Lines" by Kimon Iannetta. She contacted him and extended an invite for an on-line handwriting discussion forum. She was impressed with his skills, became his friend and mentor. It was Kim who encouraged him to study the Enneagram.

Marcel Elfers developed a systematic approach to behavioral profiling through written communication. He integrates handwriting analysis, perspective analysis, and behavioral pattern recognition. This triad turned out to be accurate, inexpensive, and efficient.

Kim Iannetta also encouraged him to start using his skill sets in professional settings for behavioral profiling through written communication and questioned document examination.

In her recommendation letter to introduce him to the profiling world, she wrote: *"He is observant, objective, and systematic in his approach. He builds a foundation for compelling conclusions regarding the behavioral characteristics of the author."*
"He illuminates with a riveting insight into the hidden motivations and likely behavior of suspects."

Although his observant and inquisitive nature has always been the primary driver behind his need to understand the link between action and intent, it was Kimon Iannetta who inspired him to push his boundaries. He cannot thank Kimon enough for being his mentor, guide, and inspiration.

His journey into behavioral style, motivation, and predictability has come to succinct and distinct conclusions. Teach what you need to know the most[1], or write a book. This book has been written for you and is added to your legacy as the premier behavioral profiler through written communication.

Marcel Elfers is available for speaking engagements, behavioral profile consultations, threat assessments, and Precision Personnel Placement. He provides training with online and onsite courses.

---

[1] "Illusions, the Adventures of a reluctant Messiah" Richard Bach.

Contents

Introduction

"We are the same; it's the details that differ" reflects on all of us operating from nine distinct perspectives, while we emphasize specific behavioral characteristics.

The cover drawing implies this is about criminality as Elliot Rodger, Gary Ridgway, and Jodi Arias are all known for murders. Nothing is further from the truth and we are very much like them. Most of us have inhibitions preventing us from overstepping an unacceptable boundary, yet, it takes a small change in perspective to move forward and do the unthinkable.

We are born with natural abilities, are influenced by our environment, and learn to deal with conflict. How we cope develops into a progressive habitual pattern driven by our key perspective and key need. The five areas influencing this pervasive pattern are (1) role model identification, (2) perceived childhood message, (3) favored defense mechanism, (4) thinking style, and (5) behavioral and social style. This develops into a *distinct, consistent,* and *therefore an identifiable* behavioral pattern.

I was born and raised in Haarlem, the Netherlands, and immigrated to the United States in 1986 as a Physical Therapist. As a teenager, I worked on a small dairy farm and learned to communicate with animals through non-verbals. The farmer, "Ome Nic", unwittingly had a major influence on my young life. He taught me by example and asked to consider his questions about animal behavior. Being observant and inquisitive, I was intrigued and read "Man Watching" by zoologist Desmond Morris. It was clear to me non-verbal communication is more reliable and even more revealing than verbal communication.

"Actions speak louder than words."

I made my first link between non-verbal behavior, motivation, and handwriting behavior as a teenager: *A young man, on his first day at work, was asked to sign a shipping document. He hesitated for a full minute, and then made many cross-out lines through which he signed his name. I instantly realized his emotional connection between hesitation and his signature. I said, "You don't want to sign, do you?"*

Figure 1: Self-negation

The young man replied: "No, I don't. I don't know whether the shipment is complete or not. Will I have to pay for a possible shortage?" His thought process and understandable uncertainty made him sign his name illegibly.

Handwriting reveals behavioral characteristics that I further developed by matching behavioral patterns and writing behaviors of healthcare professionals in patient charts. I discovered patterns in word selection and sentence construction in mid-1990. Handwriting analysis and perspective analysis turned out to be powerful tools to reveal behavioral style, motivation, and aid predictability.

In an ever-changing and technology-driven world, it is imperative to adjust and incorporate new interactive skills into our private and professional lives. Behavioral Pathways provides insights into ourselves, others, relationship dynamics, and develops compassion allowing us *to influence with integrity.*

By recognizing behavioral styles, and an awareness of motivation, we can emphasize strengths, de-emphasize weaknesses, and strengthen relationships. In the end, this reason alone makes it worthwhile studying, understanding and recognizing the nine Behavioral Pathways.

Although we all benefit from understanding perspectives and motivations, some professions will benefit more from insights in Behavioral Pathways:
- Law-enforcement for threat assessment, profiles, and improving interviewing techniques, negotiations
- Lawyers seeking behavioral profiles for offenders and juror screening
- Mental health workers providing assistance to others
- Educators by understanding relationship dynamics and how we process information
- Human resources for personnel placement

My studies initially focused on understanding the motivation behind criminal behavior. I always believed an ordinary person can suddenly find himself in hot water[2] and end up in prison as a felon. Others seem to have no boundaries from a young age and develop into career criminals. Why is that?

Behavioral Pathways applies to all of us regardless of background or culture. This all too brief and contemporary summary has been written to make Behavioral Pathways accessible to professionals and non-professionals alike.

---

[2] read "The Lucifer effect" by dr. Philip Zimbardo.

Your judgment says more about you than the one you judged. - Unknown

1. Intent

My initial focus has been on criminal behaviors, but my basic interest has always been to ascertain the *motivation behind behavioral choices*. We frequently judge an isolated action instead of intent. The mother who tells her seven-year-old Santa Claus exists and the CEO, who willfully sells a faulty product for profit, are both deceptive. Their motivations are vastly different. At what point a non-criminal becomes a felon is based on a vague boundary between socially acceptable and non-acceptable choices that hinge on action, intent, and circumstance.

"Judge intent instead of action."

In 2014, Elliot Rodger posted alarming videos online, including his final "Retribution video". His divorced parents were aware of his psychological difficulties and helped him with mental assistance. About three weeks prior to his final act, he was visited by law-enforcement at his apartment. Elliot wrote in his Manifesto, *"The police interrogated me outside for a few minutes, asking me if I had suicidal thoughts[3]."* After the deadly shooting, the Santa Barbara County Sheriff explained the officers left because he was *"articulate, polite, and timid"*. It is unfortunate; they did not realize his demeanor *was the biggest red flag.*

When we heard about the Santa Barbara shooting, we were introduced to a spree killer and judged an isolated event. But *nothing happens in a vacuum.* He was known to get angry with kissing couples and threw his coffee on girls at a bus stop. We don't punish coffee throwers because the action causes no physical harm, however, the intent and disregard for others' rights is far

---

[3] Elliot Rodger in his Manifesto "My twisted world" p. 134

more serious than we care to admit. He felt entitled to express himself with contempt, and slowly but surely reset his boundaries. And boundaries tend to be progressive in nature, and with a change in perspective, the attached behaviors may escalate. When we are introduced to a singular event like coffee throwing, is there a way to figure out what happens next, if there is going to be an escalation? And how will this escalation be expressed?

We always behave, whether good, bad or indifferent. No matter what we do, or don't, we reveal ourselves constantly and consistently. It was my mission to find consistencies in behavioral styles and reveal the motivations behind them. Pattern recognition, progressive boundaries, and motivation exposure lead to behavioral predictability. The answer to *"Is there a way to figure out what will happen next?"* is yes, but only to a certain extent.

I am providing a platform[4] to recognize consistencies in nine distinct behavioral pathways driven by nine well-defined perspectives as defined by the Enneagram. These patterns have their origin in our childhood experiences, are perspective-consistent, and recognizable. I call this natural progression *Behavioral Pathways*. Although anyone can make different choices in details, we will notice consistencies in perspective and recognize them through symmetries in behavioral patterns. And so,

"We are the same; it's the details that differ."

After 30 years of studying behavioral profiling through written communication, the actions of Elliot Rodger motivated me to write this all too brief synopsis with this question in mind: *Could this spree killing have been prevented?*

---

[4] This platform is an all too brief summary of the Enneagram.

1.1 Distinct and consistent

Our brain is arranged into three evolutionary levels and is one of the main reasons for our ability to survive and thrive. The simplest brain function is the *reflex* level like the knee jerk reflex. There is one stimulus and one possible response. The highest brain level is *conscious thought* and is where we evaluate everything. In between reflex and conscious evaluation lies *automation*.

Habit is an extremely important mechanism in our lives. We would not be able to survive without the ability to do things on an automated level. A child learning to walk pays strict attention to how to keep balance during the next step. Once balance and stepping forward are mastered, repeated and automated, we can walk and talk at the same time. The walking is automated whereas the talking is on a conscious level. A child learning to write focuses on letter formation but is unable to pay attention to context. Once letter formation is automated, we can pay attention to what we want to say. How we write is automated and what we write is conscious thought. And therefore,

> ## *"We can only do one thing at the same time on a conscious level.[5]"*

We are all very familiar with this concept. It becomes evident in our first two weeks on a new job. We come home far more fatigued than usual, and there is a good reason for that. We spent much more energy on things that used to be familiar and automated. We must find out where the bathrooms are; figure out the temperament of our colleagues and their positions; the shortest way to the parking lot; whether the door is automated or not, etc.

There is an amusing test you can do to prove we can only do one thing at the same time on a conscious level. Next time you walk side by side with someone who talks, you steer him toward an obstacle. As you get closer, and the talker starts to notice the problem, he must find a walking solution to avoid it on a conscious level. For that brief moment walking will be on a conscious level and talking is temporarily suspended.

---

[5] Dr. Ben van Cranenburg, neuro-science lecture 1985

Pickpockets and magicians make full use of this phenomenon. Pickpockets distract you with a bump, and while you are preoccupied with your assessment of "what happened" and busy recovering your balance, you don't notice your wallet is being stolen. Magicians make full use of beautiful women who walk in the direction they want you to look and hide the real action.

We remember the first time we stepped into a car and learned to drive. We didn't know the position of the turn signal or how it worked, or to switch on the high beam. How about the feeling of the steering wheel? How far must we reach for other accessories like air vents, radio, and windshield wipers? Since we initially pay conscious thought to all these new experiences, we pay less attention to traffic.

On a side note: Cell phone usage has dramatically increased over the years and talking on the phone while driving skyrocketed. The more involved we are in a conversation, the less attention we can pay to traffic.
Talking on the phone requires much more attention than talking with a passenger. You spent more energy to evaluate the non-verbals of a friend you don't see. It is much easier to read non-verbals with a passenger who will also allow the driver to pay attention to traffic when needed. Texting requires even more conscious attention, and we have to take our eyes of the road to look at the phone. According to the National Safety Council, at least 28% of vehicle crashes are caused by texting and cell phone use[6].

We will always assess circumstances from our personal perspective and cannot deny our basic needs. Our responses will be consistent with our point of view, fears, and needs. We must pay conscious attention to our environment and decide *what to do.* And that means one thing: *How* we respond is far more automated than we like to believe. In other words, we repeat the same behaviors over and over again. Simply said,

"We do what we know best."

Therefore, Behavioral Patterns are consistent and distinct for two reasons:
1. Consistent: Behavioral and Social Styles are more automated than we realize or care to admit.
2. Distinct: We must be true to ourselves and remain consistent with our perspective; protect our key fear and express key needs.

---

[6] source: www.enddd.org

1.2 Manipulation, domination, and control

Chess is a strategy game originally developed as a training tool for generals to teach tactical maneuvering. Over time, the war game with four military divisions (infantry, cavalry, elephantry, and chariotry) matured into the current day pawn, knight, bishop, and rook set.

Chess has three distinct phases: the Opening-game, the Mid-game, and the End-game. John Douglas, former FBI profiler, wrote about a progressive pattern in criminal behavior and labeled them as *manipulation, domination, and control*. Douglas described a gradual shift in the balance of power, where the manipulator gains control, and the target loses choice. During the manipulation phase, the manipulator hides his real intentions and gains cooperation of his target. In the dominance phase, the manipulator pursues cooperation more aggressively, and the target is compelled into cooperation, but still feels he is in charge of his choices. In the control phase, the target no longer has a choice, and the manipulator is the primary decision maker. He applied this to criminals but, like chess, it's everyday life.

Ted Bundy is arguably one of the most notorious and well-known serial killers, and his pattern was distinct.
- *Manipulation: pretending to be injured, and ask for assistance.*
- *Domination: once he reached his car, he dropped his keys. The victim felt compelled to pick them up and he hit her unconscious.*
- *Control: he moved his unconscious victim to an isolated place.*

Chess, life, and criminals, we all follow the same pattern. In life, we behave in our normal way, and manipulate or attempt to influence others to get what we want through cooperation. During stress, we exaggerate our normal behaviors and dominate. Then we seek control by forcing our will onto others. At the end of our rope, we give up and do the opposite of what we know best.

Our behavioral pathway follows a distinct pattern. We are born with natural abilities and are influenced by our environment. Early in life, we identify with one or both role models, develop a perspective and defense mechanisms, and mature to a habitual social style and behavioral style.

As life moves on, our perspectives will reach a point where we no longer feel comfortable with the choices we make. Discomfort is the stimulus behind our personal boundary and is different for everyone. Therefore, when we evaluate an isolated incident, we must find out what behaviors preceded the event and what motivated the action. Boundaries are progressive, and patterns build an expectation of future behavioral choices. But where will a boundary end when a person never feels uncomfortable?

Behavioral Pathways is a wonderful tool for teachers. It's a tool to understand motivation behind behaviors. This develops compassion and provides insight to re-direct unwanted behaviors. Such holds true for any interpersonal relationship, including parent-child and work relationship dynamics. Behavioral Pathways is a valuable tool for law-enforcement. The pathways, combined with known previous behavioral choices, provide a degree of behavioral predictability. It reveals strengths and weaknesses that can aid investigations and provide direction during interrogations.

In July 2014, I read about the hunt for the Tulsa serial rapist and recognized his potential pathway. I alerted Tulsa PD to compare their composite sketch with known serial burglars, shoplifters, and purse snatchers. The rapist's pathway is known to be prone to kleptomania. The offender became less careful, more erratic, and hyperactive. An increase in visible police presence could force the manic and panicked offender into making errors. Desmond Campbell fled the scene of his last victim, crashed his car into a pole on the highway, and was hospitalized with head injuries where he eventually died. Later, I learned the DA was in the process of charging him with ten sexual assaults, seven burglaries, and six robberies.

The core of the criminal justice system is based on malice and intent. There is a vast difference between Ted Bundy's willful criminal activities over a long period of time versus one-time spree killers like Elliot Rodger. Although both were severely misguided, Bundy fulfilled his need to own women, be in charge, and repeated his grisly deeds in a natural progressive pattern from childhood to adulthood. Elliot Rodger, who also progressively reset his boundaries, acted out of desperation. He was so desperate, he was willing to kill and kill himself.

It is my hope the grieving parents of Elliot Rodger will find some solace realizing Elliot was unable to cope with his self-created perspective. He focused excessively on others who had what he did not (Introjection[7], Envy). He felt entitled and perceived himself as more important than he really was.

---

[7] See Defense Mechanisms

He portrayed himself with an image of success (Identification, Grandiosity). In the end, it was Elliot who was not able to reconcile his need for admiration with the rejection received. Psychologically speaking, this was too painful to bear. The girls should admire him the way his mother did and they did not. In desperation, he symbolically eliminated those who reminded him of his inadequacies.

I hope the grieving parents of his victims and families of other victims around the world will find a way to honor those lost by remembering them for who they were and what they stood for.

I hope the parents and families of offenders find the strength to give themselves the gift of forgiveness.

I wish you courage.

"The liar's punishment is not in the least that he is not believed, but that he cannot believe anyone else." - George Bernard Shaw

2. Articulate, polite, and timid

Let's go down a never-ending list of articulate, timid, and polite sociopaths:

Konerack, a 14-year-old boy, ran naked out of an apartment while dazed and confused by drugs. A neighbor saw the boy and called police. Upon their arrival, she and her cousin got into an argument, while Jeffrey Dahmer calmly explained that Konerack, his "19-year-old lover", drank too much. Police entered Dahmer's badly reeking apartment but did not see the skulls and acid vats. They believed Jeffrey because he was *"well-spoken, intelligent, and very calm"*.

Theodore R. Cowell was charismatic, handsome, and articulate. These were excellent social qualities to have, including winning the trust of victims. The judge, handing down his death sentence, told Ted Bundy: *"You'd have made a good lawyer, and I would have loved to have you practice in front of me, but you went another way partner."*

Jodi Arias, convicted of the murder of Travis Alexander, is image-oriented, beautiful and charismatic. During her 18 days on the stand, she gave the prosecutor a run for his money. She was calm, cool, and collected, sparred with him as an equal and tried to make a fool of him. She rested her chin on her hand with middle finger extended in an act of contempt and defiance.

Gary Ridgway was married, quiet, and trustworthy. He worked his job during the day and hunted the strip at night. He picked out the most vulnerable and lured them with cash to an isolated place. After the sex act, he killed the girls he didn't like. He told law-enforcement: *"I thought I was helping you to get the dirt off the streets."* [not verbatim]

Casey Anthony, acquitted of the murder of her almost 3-year-old daughter, is widely believed to have been involved in her death. She lied for 31 days to her parents about Caylee's whereabouts, seemed to party without a care in the world, and got herself a "Bella Vita" (the good life) tattoo. After lying to her parents for two years about her employment at Universal Studios, she also brought detectives to her non-existing workplace.

Dalia Dippolito, a former escort, married her client Michael Dippolito. She had him convinced of multiple financial cons. After just six months of marriage, she set her murder for hire plan in motion. The sociopath's ability to act within a range of expectations is only as good as the information you feed them. The art of a con is the illusion of control, and the undercover cop was just as skillful as the unsuspecting Dalia.

Joran van der Sloot admitted to the murder of Stephany Ramirez in 2010. He strangled her because he thought she saw private computer files. In full view of police, Van der Sloot calmly took a cab and drove off. Joran is also the primary suspect in the Natalee Holloway disappearance. He is serving time in Peru.

Ariel Castro kidnapped, imprisoned, and sexually abused three young girls for ten years. Josef Fritzl imprisoned and fathered children with his daughter. For twenty-four years, he enslaved her in a bunker below his home. For them to deceive family and friends this long, they must be logical, methodical, and emotionally detached.

Elliot Rodger, Jeffrey Dahmer, Ted Bundy, Jodi Arias, Gary Ridgway, Casey Anthony, Dalia Dippolito, Joran van der Sloot, Josef Fritzl and the list goes on. They all feel entitled, are assertive, insistent, are blind to failure and *have the innate ability to detach emotions from their actions.*

There will be no last.

"The best predictor of future behavior is relevant past behavior."

- Dr. Phil

3. The best predictor

The Enneagram is a dynamic organizational structure based on existing theories of psychology providing an easy-to-use working model to identify behavioral styles and motivation. The late Don Riso, later assisted by Russ Hudson, made an important contribution with their *Continuum of Traits*. They not only recognized specific characteristic sequences in behavioral patterns and the motivation behind them, they also succeeded to define and describe them with great clarity.

"We are the same;"

From Jeffrey Dahmer and Gary Ridgway to Ariel Castro, Jodi Arias, and Elliot Rodger. They are all well-mannered, assertive and insist on getting what they want. They present themselves in a positive light, remain calm, cool and collected. In duress, they still manage to make their point politely. Their behavioral styles have common characteristics and are recognized through simple observations. They are the same and deteriorated in a similar fashion.

From Ted Bundy[8] to Desmond Campbell, the Tulsa serial rapist. They are assertive, insistent, opportunistic, impatient, hyperactive, and failed to see their personal limitations. Campbell wrapped his car around a pole fleeing the scene of his last victim. In his hyperactive and manic state, he fled the crime scene impulsively and lost control of his car.

---

[8] Biographies in brief can be found in addendum one

Both Bundy's and Campbell's crime sprees ended with them being out of control, manic and erratic. They are the same and deteriorated in a similar fashion.

Freddie Mercury, Robin Williams, Ted Bundy, and Desmond Campbell are the same. They grew up with the same early perspective, key fear, and key need resulting in a distinct Behavioral Pathway, including "Gluttony".

As we will see, Type Seven is a child growing up with a real or perceived lack of emotional nurturing resulting in the key fear of deprivation. They reduce their anxieties by pursuing the next thrill, fun, and joyous experience. Their fear is "I am missing out". Their observable behaviors include busy-bee agendas, boundless energy, and a "constant on-the-go" attitude. They are impulsive, energetic, and overdo things resulting in excessiveness. Type Seven artists can, for instance, have "over-the-top" attires, which remind us of Liberace and Elton John. Gluttony is overcompensation for their real or perceived lack of nurturance received as a child.

"It's the details that differ."

Most people have healthy boundaries and are productive members of society. Others have great difficulty with inhibitions and overstep boundaries with ease. Patrick Jane[9], the Mentalist, to Sherriff McAllister, a.k.a. Red John: *"You are an evil, sexually perverted sociopath with pathetic delusions of grandeur. The rest is just details."*

Behavioral profiling is a systematic approach to observing and identifying consistencies in behavioral patterns. Pattern recognition, combined with uncovering the key lens of perspective, is a tool attaching motivation to behavioral characteristics. And it helps to predict potential future behavioral choices. And so, *"The best predictor of future behavior is relevant past behavior"* [10] makes perfect sense.

Samples are provided throughout the book how writing behavior, word selection and sentence construction reveal our perspective and Type. Distinct known behavioral patterns can provide us with a progressive or regressive known pattern in broad terms, and with it, support predictability.

---

[9] Patrick Jane is the lead character in the series "the Mentalist"
[10] Dr. Phil (Phillip Calvin McGraw) on many of his shows

"Integrity is when action mirrors values" - Unknown

4. Behavioral Pathway

Our Behavioral Pathway follows a distinct developmental route which has its foundation in our natural abilities (nature) and our early childhood experiences (nurture). This progression will be discussed starting from birth to adulthood.

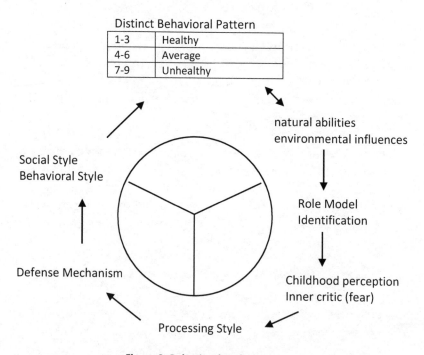

Figure 2: Behavioral Pathway

We identify with our role models in one of nine specific ways, providing us with an early, predominant and pervasive point of view. Our early perspective influences how we think. We emphasize one or two out of three intelligence centers (head, heart, gut) which, in the end favor specific defense mechanisms. From this foundation, we develop a behavioral style and social style leading to a distinct, consistent, and recognizable Behavioral Pattern.

This pattern is progressive and healthy or regressive and unhealthy.
- Childhood
  - Born with natural abilities
  - Influenced by our environment
- We identify with one or both role models
  - Identification with guide, protector, provider (F)
  - Identification with emotional nurturer (M)
- We develop an early perspective
- We see a real or perceived message
  - We develop a key fear and key need
- We develop an Information processing pattern
- We develop favored Defense mechanisms
- We meet our needs through
  - Behavioral style
  - Social Style
- And develop a distinct and consistent Behavioral Pattern
  - we are either mentally healthy, average, or unhealthy

Of course, we realize figure 2 is presented sequentially, but these processes obviously overlap, interact, and evolve in combination with each other.

4.1 Basic structure

Behavioral Pathways has a natural overlapping developmental sequence within the Enneagram. One development leads to another and to know and understand this pattern is the core concept of Behavioral Pathways and is explained with Enneagram basics.

The Enneagram is built in Triads.
- We need the same:
  - Attention, Autonomy, and Security
- We identify with one or both our role models through
  - Attachment, Frustration, or Rejection

- · nine role model identifications (+ - ~ F, + -~M,+ - ~ M/F)
- We develop a specific key perspective
  - · Nine key perspectives
  - · Key fear and key need
- Development of an Ego defense mechanism
  - · processing style weakness favors defense mechanism
- Leading to a behavioral style to fulfill a key need
  - · emphasizing compensation for key fear
- Evolution of a specific Behavioral Pattern characterized by
  - · Secure behavior: We do what we know best
  - · Stress behavior: We exaggerate what we know best
  - · Neurotic behavior: We do the opposite of what we know best

Mental health	Behavioral Pattern	Type Eight
Healthy - *Integration*	Integration with others	Compassionate
Average - *Manipulation*	Do what we know best	Self-assertion
Unhealthy - *Domination*	Exaggerate what we know best	Overwhelm
Disintegration - *Control*	Do the opposite of what we know best	Withdrawal

The right column shows the developmental behaviors of Type Eight as an example. Type Eight is a child growing up feeling vulnerable (key fear) and learned early in their lives to self-protect. They assert themselves strongly and take control (compensation). When stressed, they overwhelm others through dominance (exaggeration). Their need for control is omnipresent and affirmed with expressions of misplaced overconfidence. Once they realize they overstepped boundaries, they withdraw out of fear for retaliation (do opposite). And so, we can't help but notice, the desperate Assertive and Insistent Eight does exactly the opposite of their personal norm: Withdraw and Think.

4.2 Triads

Wants

The basic structure of the Enneagram is built on Triads. We all want the same. We want our independence (Autonomy), and do what we deem best for us in the *here and now*. We want to be appreciated (Attention) for who we are, and we project an image established *in the past*, how we want to be seen. We want to feel secure (Security) with the ones we are with; yet, we worry about what can happen *in the future*.

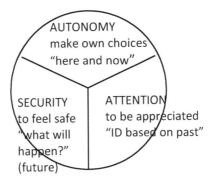

Figure 3: Core needs

The three Triads, like *the past, present,* and *future*, are inherently linked and intertwined. What we do today is the product of yesterday, and today's actions define tomorrow's choices. The thought from yesterday is a spoken word today, becomes the action of tomorrow, and habitual behavior of the future. And so, our destiny starts with "a thought".

Problems

Each Triad has a correlation with certain problem areas. The Attention seeking Triad (2,3,4) has *self-worth and shame* issues. They have the inclination to present themselves in a different light from who they really are. The presented persona, built on past experiences, is a façade and is maintained to gain personal value. "This is how I want to be seen without showing who I really am."

Figure 4: Triad and correlated problems

Type Two is positive-minded, people-oriented, and over-expresses their emotions to others (outside world), while not acknowledging their personal needs (inside world). They present themselves as being good to others but secretly seek appreciation to feel worthy of love. They think their "do-good" persona is more acceptable than who they really are.

Type Three is assertive, insistent and overstates abilities (to the outside world) and under expresses their emotions (inside world). Their inner voice doesn't acknowledge failure, tells them they are a winner while they often don't live up to their stated expectations.

Type Four is withdrawn, imaginative, and under-expresses their emotions, while rationalizing their victim role (inside world). They hope to be disco-vered or noticed. Only then will they feel personal value, because finally "someone cared". They create an internalized fantasy ID, which is not nec-essarily in line with reality.

The Security seeking Triad (5,6,7) has problems with inner guidance and feelings of support. Fear and anticipation of lack of support is a leading fac-tor for their *fears, anxieties*, and *insecurities*. They typically emphasize be-haviors linked to finding security, inner guidance, and support in order to reduce their fears and anxieties.

Type Five is withdrawn, imaginative, and fears they don't fit in social struc-tures. They think they don't have enough insight and resources to survive the outside world and retreat into their inner sanctum. They believe support is not available, or at minimum not reliable, and move into their fantasy world to solve problems, all the while avoiding the outside world. They in-ternalize problems and conflict in their minds where they feel safe.

The Five's dichotomy becomes "my thoughts are safe; the outside world is not safe". And, therefore, Fives hone in on, and are acutely aware of their environment in their need to observe, predict, and feel safe.

Type Six is dedicated, reliable, and fear their own guidance (inside world) while seeking and relying on advice outside themselves (outside world). Like all Primary Types (3,6,9), they internalize and externalize their fears. They internalize conflict to avoid outside threats (like a Five), and come into action to prevent internal anxieties (like a Seven), which in turn create new fears just to internalize those fears once again. The Six seeks guidance by relying on a strong authoritative figure or entities in their lives to reduce their anxieties.

Type Seven is assertive, insistent, and fears their inside world. They barge into activities and busy bee agendas by seeking the next exciting experience and thrills. In doing so, they appear confident and fearless. Yet, their fear lies in their internalized world. Sevens escape their inner world by staying active in the outside world by relentlessly seeking happiness in activities. Acquisition of new experiences substitute the lack of emotional nurturance received in the past. Sevens become anxious at the moment they are not pre-occupied with new activities.

The Autonomy seeking Triad (8,9,1) typically has issues with *relating to others* and *anger*. They adhere to personal standards, live in the here and now, and set boundaries between themselves and the outside world.

Type Eight is assertive, insistent, and focuses on the outside world. They resist and deny the world by trying to control it. Their need to self-protect becomes an action against the world. They expend energy in an outgoing, forceful, and domineering manner.

Type One is dedicated, reliable, and focuses on internalized boundaries to protect personalized standards. They spent enormous amounts of energy to suppress anger and tension. Ones internalize boundaries and build pent up anger and tension.

The Nine, like the other two Primary Types, have both internalized and externalized boundaries. They set boundaries with the outside world not to get hurt and internalized boundaries to maintain their peaceful and relaxed state.

4.3 Nature and Nurture

The debate about Nature or Nurture is far from over and might never be resolved. As long as we remember it is always about what we are born with (Nature) and how we are influenced by our environment (Nurture). For emphasis purposes; it is always Nature *and* Nurture instead of the most commonly asked question: Nature *or* Nurture.

Our journey from birth to adulthood starts here: We are born with natural abilities and are influenced by our environment.

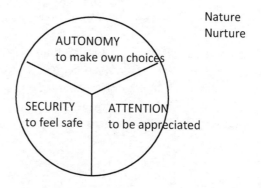

Figure 5: Nature and Nurture

A Nature and Nurture example is language. The spoken word is nothing more than a sound pattern. A child is born with natural abilities such as hearing, imprinting of sounds, pattern recognition, and recollection of sound patterns. The appropriate application of sound patterns becomes language. Whether the child learns to speak English, Dutch or Spanish depends on their environmental influences. We have the same natural abilities, and our environment emphasizes, or de-emphasizes, such natural abilities. Which sound patterns are experienced, mimicked and passed on to the next generation depends entirely on what environment you grow up in.

4.4 Role model identification

During our formative years, we identify with our role models in one of nine ways. We develop a psychological bond (+ attachment), create psychological distance (- frustration) or are unable to bond or distance (~ rejection) ourselves completely from our role models.

		Withdrawn
9	+M/F	feels attachment to both role models
4	- M/F	feels frustration with both role models
5	~ M/F	feels rejected by both role models
		Assertive
3	+M	feels attached to emotional nurturer
7	-M	feels frustrated by emotional nurturer
8	~M	feels rejected by emotional nurturer
		Compliant
6	+F	feels attached to guidance and support
1	-F	feels frustrated with guidance and support
2	~F	feels rejected by guidance and support

The role models are typically the father and the mother, but there are many substitutes available. The meaning of (F) is the role as a guide, protector, and provider and (M) is the role as an emotional nurturer. There is no doubt these roles overlap, are interchangeable and support each other.

Typically, the Father (F) is a guide, provider, and protector in a child's life. The Father should direct the child toward independence away from the nurturing mother. He should provide the child with socially acceptable strategies to cope with his or her environment. Guidance can be provided by anyone or anything. Although the patriarchal role model takes the lead role in providing guidance and protection, a child might reject directions received from the father, or can be frustrated with guidance from entities like cultural suppression and religion.

The emotional nurturer is typically the Mother (M), and she should mirror the child's behaviors to make them feel accepted and safe. She should give the child a sense of self and personal value. Emotional identification is frequently with the Mother, but any person can be a substitute. For instance, a grandfather can be the emotional nurturer for a grandchild. A teenage sister can provide guidance to a younger sibling.

It could even be entities like cultural support and religion. Again, (M) and (F) means identification with whomever or whatever supplies nurturance and guidance.

A child with a positive identification (+ 3,6,9) bonds with and feels attached to what the role model represents. A child with a negative identification (- 1,4,7) is frustrated and psychologically distanced themselves. Lastly, children with an ambivalent identification (~ 2,5,8) did not psychologically bond nor separated themselves from their role models. Identification combined with other environmental influences develops into a pervasive perspective and will shine through for the rest of our lives as the "Main Theme".

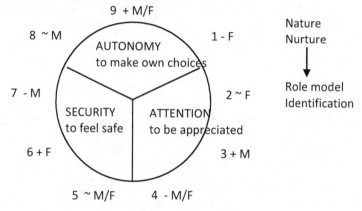

Figure 6: Role model identification

Most parents are not aware how a child identifies with them. Parents view their actions from an *intention* perspective, whereas the child evaluates their *actions*. The child's lack of life experience renders them not capable of assessing parental intent. Even as adults, we are prone to judge isolated events or the actions of others instead of the patterns of intent preceding such actions. The parental action does not necessarily meet the child's immediate needs or expectations and confuses them.

A mindless humiliating act can have a major and lasting impact on an immature, inexperienced, and impressionable child. This influences their perspective of the world, their personal value system and changes how they view themselves and their role models.

A father throws a brick at his seven-year-old son. He needed stress relief and deliberately missed, but the child felt his life was endangered and expendable.

40

With the child unable to adequately express perspectives, the parent is unable to understand how the child identifies with them.

A one-year-old, who is barely able to keep his balance, struggles toward a hot fireplace. He has no idea why he should not touch it, nor the danger he is in. The parent fears he will lose his balance and burn himself. He picks him up and halts his progress toward the fireplace. The child just wants to explore his environment and views his need and the parent's inhibiting action as a discrepancy. The child assessed the action but does not see intent.

And so, a child's perspective will not be in line with parental intentions. Irritations, discontent, annoyances, dissatisfaction, frustrations, and ultimately anger, are awaiting the parent-child dynamics.

His mother swallowed a full bottle of pills in front of him in a potentially fake suicide attempt. The child realized he could not count on those he depends on. His perspective is "I am dependent, and you are not trustworthy". And so, this can be freely translated into "the world is unpredictable, unsupportive, and unreliable". He does not psychologically bond, nor separate himself entirely from his role models.

A child grows up with a mentally abusive mother, and she psychologically distanced herself. Mother was not a reliable source of nurturance and did not provide her with personal value. In her formative years, she learned to provide her own nurturing by aggressively pursuing fun and joyful experience. These needs are essentially "nurturance substitutes".

A child grows up with her biological mother and step-father, who did not favor the child. She felt unloved and learned she would receive attention, love, and appreciation by being good to the step-father. In her early teens, she learned her biological father denied her existence, furthering her core belief system she is unloved and unwanted. For the rest of her life, her modus operandi became "I must be good to you first before you will appreciate me" and does not develop healthy boundaries.

Nine perspectives

A child's natural inclinations provide an early behavioral style, while childhood experiences provide an initial point of view. Through parental identification, we receive a real or perceived message. It is how the child interprets what he sees, hears, and feels, regardless of parental intent. Such first impressions are the strongest, the most memorable and inclined to be pervasive well into adulthood. It becomes the *main theme* throughout our lives, is our core motivational influence and can be recognized in how we behave and verbally express ourselves. Anything and everything tells a story of perspective, and we cannot help but reveal ourselves. It's how we engage, shake hands, keep our desk, dress, chosen tattoos, hair-do, hygiene, etc. There are nine identifications with our role models leading to nine basic core perspectives and therefore nine basic Types.

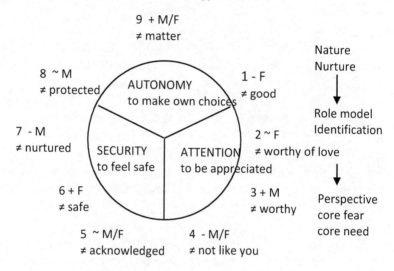

Figure 7: Perception and key fear

And so, each child develops a key perspective and sees themselves from a distinct foundation. As adults, with life experience and self-knowledge, we will be able to describe ourselves with just a few words. Many people will recognize themselves in the words below that resonate with them[11]:

	perspective	tends to be / sees themselves as
1	not good enough	reasonable, objective, sensible, modest, prudent, moderate
2	unworthy of love	loving, caring, selfless, thoughtful, warm-hearted
3	not worthy	admirable, desirable, attractive, charming, poised
4	unlike you	sensitive, different, unique, gentle, quiet, honest with self
5	not acknowledged	perceptive, smart, inquisitive, insightful, playful, unusual
6	not safe	dependable, trustworthy, self-doubt, skeptical, cautious
7	not nurtured	enthusiastic, free-spirited, adventurous, spontaneous
8	feels vulnerable	strong, assertive, action-oriented, robust, direct, resourceful
9	I don't matter	relaxed, peaceful, stable, easy-going, kind, gentle

---

[11] see addendum "Resonating key words"

*Yours truly is a Five and fourth of six children. Fives grew up with an ambiva-
lent identification with both parents. I did not bond nor reject them. By and
large, I felt unacknowledged, which makes Fives feel like a burden. They did
not fit in the family unit. The naturally withdrawn and imaginative Five compensates by providing the family unit specialty knowledge; a niche if you
will. They hope they will be acknowledged through knowledge, and believe
this way they will fit in. By offering knowledge, they assume they are not a
burden. Therefore, Fives link self-esteem to competence. As adults, this perspective shines through as Fives feel they don't fit in and are not accepted by
the world. This perspective has consequences because acquiring specialized
knowledge requires time which Fives consider their most valuable asset.
Fives feel easily intruded upon and have distaste for intruding on others.
Fives seek intellectual pursuits and become researchers, scholars, and pro-
fessors. It is no surprise, you are reading a book about behavioral analysis,
perspective analysis, and handwriting analysis. How is that for a niche?*

The child's role model identification and perspective develops into a key
fear. It's a void that needs to be filled and we compensate for. And so, our
fear leads to a key need. Over time, how we deal with our environmental
influences becomes our norm. Remember, we all *want and own the same
characteristics of all Types* in varying degrees. It's the emphasis on a key
perspective, a key fear, and key need that reflects on our Type, and is
expressed in motivation and behavioral choices.

The biggest human fear is uncertainty and overcoming uncertainty is the
most significant human trait. Our core fears are all variations of not being
appreciated for who we are. We were denied a core perspective or felt rejected about something we valued. This established early in our childhood
and becomes our key fear we need to compensate for.

	childhood perception: key fear	Perspective: key need - *filling a void*
1	I am not good enough	I must be better, even perfect
2	I am unloved nor appreciated	I must earn your love and appreciation
3	I am not worthy	I must excel to feel worthy
4	I am insignificant without identity	I must distinguish myself
5	I am inadequate, incompetent	I must provide a niche, be competent
6	I am not safe and have self-doubt	I must do what is expected of me
7	I am not taken care off, deprived	I must acquire new exciting experiences
8	I am vulnerable	I must be in control
9	I do not really matter	I must be amicable, agreeable

Of course, as children we develop a key perspective and deal mostly with our role models. Our role models taught us how to treat them and as adults we project our childhood perspective onto the world as a whole. Essentially, the world becomes our role model substitute. We tell ourselves, "treat others the way you want to be treated" and that is a valid point. Reality is, *"We treat others the way we were treated."*

1. Ones felt criticized and criticize others
2. Twos felt unloved and seek to be loved
3. Threes felt admired and seek admiration
4. Fours felt insignificant and seek significance
5. Fives felt unacknowledged and seek acknowledgment
6. Sixes have self-doubt and doubt others
7. Sevens felt not nurtured and seek nurturance
8. Eights felt vulnerable and seek control
9. Nines felt inconsequential and seek tranquility

The world as a role model substitute:
A child grows up feeling unloved and not appreciated by her father. She learns to be good, loving and caring to earn love and appreciation. As a teenager, she rebels and hooks up with the first boy saying "I love you." Her perspective is "to be good", and she gives him what he wants. The first boy is also more likely Assertive, increasing the chance of being a "bad boy." The relationships do not last long, and she is replaced by the next thrill in line. She now feels unloved and used as well. And so, the cycle continues.

A child grows up with unconditional support by his mother but feels the praise received is not earned. He learns to work hard to earn praise and to feel worthy. He links his self-esteem to task performance. In order to feel good about himself, he must excel and be better than others. Anything less makes him feel like a disappointment and attacks his self-esteem. Praise received for a task done in the past is no longer satisfying. He must push his boundaries to do better than before. As an adult, he will be ambitious and competitive needing to be admired by the world around him. Just like his doting mother did.

A child grows up with self-doubt and learns to feel more secure with the protection and guidance provided by her father. He becomes the role model she feels safe and strong with. She learns to rely on his guidance and, as an adult, on outside guidance in general. She may become dependent on those she believes are in the know. She will follow rules of authority figures or entities and overestimate their actual value.

In a discussion with a 1w2, who is naturally intuitive and compliant to the rule to "better the world", the following question was asked: *"Aren't the main theme perspectives subject to change? We grow up, mature, let go of things, adopt another perspective etcetera. Aren't circumstances crucial to our evolution and perspectives? After all, we have free will and choice".*

I replied with, *"No, the main themes do not change, and are pervasive throughout our lives. Of course, we develop and learn to cope in either healthy or unhealthy ways, but the main theme remains the same. And yes, we have free will and choice. However, our choices have a tendency to be consistent within the perspective of our main theme. We have no choice, but to live up to our key perspective and key needs. Nor can we deny our key fears. As an analogy, if you prefer tea and wine as the main theme, you are not suddenly going to change to coffee and beer. Your free choice is which tea and wine you prefer.*

For example, a child perceived the guidance provided to him as flawed. It may have been inconsistent, too harsh, too strict or too self-righteous. Maybe a Father enforced personal standards without considering alternatives. Their perspective became "I am not good enough", and resulted in the key need "I must be better". Maybe the child noticed the church enforced unyielding rules he was expected to live by, but at home, they did not live by those standards. They learned to compensate by creating a new set of rules and setting personal standards.

The Type One child will believe only they know right from wrong based on their self-created personal standards. Since not everyone shares their standards, they also come to think others will not know right from wrong unless they are told by them. Their main theme forces them to improve themselves and the world because, from their early childhood perspective, things can always be better. This perspective is not just the child's norm based on their identification with guidance (-F). In their adult life, they will project this view onto the world as a whole. Their payoff is, "If I am perfect, I won't be criticized like my dad (church etc.) always did". In layman's terms, they are the moral gatekeepers and "right-fighters". At average levels of mental functioning, they adhere rigidly to their opinions, ignore gray areas, and enforce personal standards onto others.

	Key fear	Key need	Main theme	Pay off
1	I am not good enough	I must be better, even perfect	I want to improve the world and make it perfect	When I am perfect, you won't criticize me
2	I am unloved and not appreciated	I must earn your love and appreciation	I want to be loved and appreciated	When I am good to you, you will love me
3	I am not worthy	I must excel to feel worthy	I want to earn admiration	When I perform well, you will admire me
4	I am insignificant, do not relate	I must distinguish myself	I want to be different and unique	When I am different, you will notice me
5	I am inadequate nor acknowledged	I must provide special knowledge to be acknowledged	I want to be knowledgeable and adequate	When I am knowledgeable, you will acknowledge me
6	I am not safe and have self-doubt	I must do what is expected of me	I want security through guidance and reassurance	When I do what is expected of me, I feel secure
7	I am not taken care off and feel deprived	I must seek pleasant and exciting experiences	I want to have freedom and happiness	When I acquire new experiences I avoid anxiety
8	I am vulnerable	I must be in control	I want to be self-reliant	When I am self-reliant, I don't depend on you
9	I do not matter	I must be amicable, agreeable	I want harmony, peace, and quiet	When I am amicable, I avoid confrontation

A child grows up in Foster care. On his 18th birthday, he is kicked out of the house and replaced by another foster child. His foster parents did not nurture, nor protected him adequately. He felt vulnerable and felt the need to protect himself; he learned to take control. He is direct and blunt and superficially connects with others. He is a Type Eight.

A father was never the same after mother passed away. He became emotionally distant, and the child felt unloved and under-appreciated. She learned to earn daddy's love and appreciation. She is a Type Two.

A child feels his parents pay only attention to his siblings and envies these relationships. Naturally withdrawn and introspective, he concluded "there must be something wrong with me." He emotionally distances himself by playing video games, and takes on the role of super-heroes rescuing others. He is symbolically representing what he needs the most. He is a Type Four.

Nine Types

It is important to realize that no Type is better than another Type. Each Type brings their core perspective to the table and views issues and tasks from their specific angle. Therefore, a healthy mix of Types is beneficial for any group. Of course, individual attributes might be culturally more desirable, but that will vary from culture to culture. Still, a balance in different Types will keep excessive traits in check in a natural manner.

Type variety is a necessity especially in businesses and organizations. To recognize each individual's natural abilities and points of view is extremely helpful. We can assign positions to match natural strengths. We then create a natural fit and allow core perspectives and strengths to shine.

	Strength	Relates to	Position e.g.
One	Fairness	ethics, quality control	compliance department
Two	Empathy	meet needs of others	marketing, fundraising
Three	Perseverance	promotion, competitive	marketing, sales
Four	Originality	impact on others	research, product needs
Five	Discernment	expertise, innovation	consultation, innovation
Six	Loyalty	team cohesion, rule adherence	policies, procedures
Seven	Spontaneity	optimism, action-oriented	team manager
Eight	Candor	confidence, vision	team leadership
Nine	Tolerance	negotiation abilities	HR department

Imagine a team with only Eights, and a struggle over who should be in charge might develop. A group of only Fives might not be productive as they focus on inventing and developing products.

Clearly, we need variety in any organization. When a competitive Three clashes with a bossy Eight, the Nine will keep order and negotiate the peace. The One provides direction what to do and the Six checks the policy and procedure manual. In the meantime, the Five stayed out of such fights and developed a new product, while the Four discusses with the Five what the end product should be like. Each Type has a natural role to play. It's best to complement each other and form cohesion in work relationship dynamics.

Wings

Rest me to point out nobody is a pure Type, and the healthier we are, the more we integrate healthy qualities other Types emphasize. The Types next to our own Type have influence on your Type. A Type Three is flavored by Type Two and/or Type Four and the one with the strongest influence is called your wing. A Three can be a "Three-wing-Two" (3w2) or a "Three-wing-Four" (3w4).

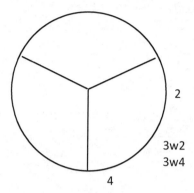

Figure 8: Type and wing

As we will elaborate in the descriptions of the individual Types, each Type has their personal core perspective. They see themselves in a certain way and describe themselves accordingly. The Wing flavors our core perspective. An excellent analogy is, "If olive oil is a Type, then garlic infusion is its wing. Oil remains oil, but the garlic flavors it". The influence of the wing can either emphasize or de-emphasize existing traits of your core perspective. At other times, the traits of your Type and wing are in conflict with each other.

Two	Three	Four
Positive, people-oriented Social to be needed	Assertive, insistent Social to be admired	Withdrawn, imaginative Solitary, individualistic

Type Three sees himself as admirable, attractive, charming, and desirable. A Type Three-wing-Two (3w2) adds the flavor of Type Two to the Three. Twos see themselves as loving, caring, selfless, and warmhearted. The Two perspective not only flavors the Three's view, it enhances their social and charming perspective. Both have a need for people. Threes need to earn admiration; Twos need to earn love and make themselves needed. Both Three and Two need people for their own sake. They tend to be charming.

A Type Three-wing-Four (3w4) is flavored by the traits of the Four. Fours see themselves as self-aware, emotional, impressionable, and intuitive. Again, the Three is social as they must earn admiration. After all, "what is a hole in one without an audience?" The Four is in search of his identity and withdraws from others and socialization. They seek Attention by being emotionally unavailable, in the hope to be noticed. The outgoing Three and the introversion of the Four are in direct contrast with each other. An unhealthy 3w4 has inner conflict. The Three's perspective makes them feel they should be admired, and their Four point of view is one of rejection and depression.

Elliot Rodger, a 3w4, wrote extensively about this inner conflict in his 2014 Manifesto. He was not alone in his perspective.

4.5 Information Processing

We process information through three intelligence centers: "heart, head, and gut". It turns out, each Type processes information in a distinct pattern. The Primary Types (3,6,9) emphasize two processing centers, while the Secondary Types (2,4,5,7,8,1) for the most part use one center which in turn is impacted, both positively or negatively, by a secondary center.

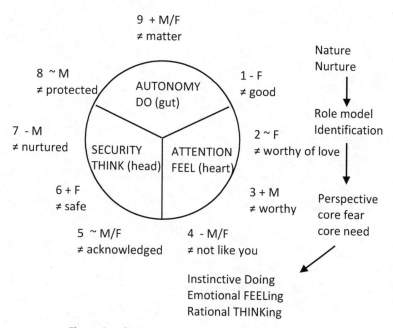

Figure 9: Information processing styles

The Three processing centers are:
- Instincts (Do)
  · gut reaction, instinctive, response immediacy
- Emotions (Feel)
  · heartfelt, subjectivity, emotional intensity
- Reasoning (Think)
  · head, reasoning, abstract thinking, measured responses

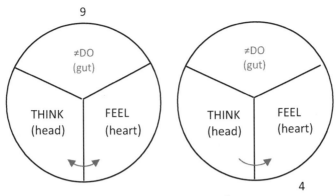

Figure 10: Processing Style

The Primary Types (3,6,9) process information in the two Triads furthest removed from them and disconnect the Triad they are in. For instance, a Nine is inclined to process information rationally and emotionally. Instinctive doing is frequently under-developed. They have a hard time expressing themselves with clarity as objectivity and subjectivity clashes. Indecision leads to procrastination.

The Secondary Types (2,4,5,7,8,1) process information in the Triad they are in, which is supported or interfered by the Triad closest to them. The third Triad is typically least developed. For instance, a Four processes emotionally and uses abstract thinking to rationalize their feelings. Like the Nine and Five, their Instinctive doing is under-developed. Fours, like Fives, may suffer from procrastination and analysis paralysis.

Type	Primary Center(s)	Secondary	Least developed
1	Instinctive	Emotional	Reasoning
2	Emotional	Instinctive	Reasoning
3	Instinctive and Reasoning	Emotional	Emotional
4	Emotional	Reasoning	Instinctive
5	Reasoning	Emotional	Instinctive
6	Instinctive and Emotional	Reasoning	Reasoning
7	Reasoning	Instinctive	Emotional
8	Instinctive	Reasoning	Emotional
9	Reasoning and Emotional	Instinctive	Instinctive

From the Enneagram perspective, we see the Assertives (3,7,8) have reduced emotional connection with themselves and those around them.

Reduced emotionality allows them to overcome uncertainty easily and propels them forward in assertive ways. This comes over as entitlement and enables them to overstep socially accepted boundaries effortlessly.

The Compliants (6,1,2) are inclined to be instinctive and emotional. They deal with uncertainty through preconceived convictions and live by certain personal standards they feel they must adhere to. The rule adherences are "I do what is expected from me (6); I must improve until I am right (1); I must be good to others (2)." With rules in mind, either provided by themselves (1, 2) or others (6), there is no urgent need for reasoning, which in turn tends to be under-developed.

The Withdrawns (9,5,4) tend to process information rationally and emotionally. Objectivity and subjectivity mix like oil and water. They deal with uncertainty through withdrawal and overthinking problems, resulting in procrastination. Their instinctive Doing is under-developed.

The Type Seven (Assertive) perspective is "I am deprived, and I must nurture myself by persistently seeking the next exciting experience". One of their traits is they get easily and quickly bored. In his last sit down interview, Freddy Mercury (Type 7) stated to his long-time friend and manager: "whatever you do after my death, <u>don't make me boring</u>".

The Type Nine (Withdrawn) perspective is "My opinion does not matter to you" and learn to not express their preferences. They rather walk away and avoid conflict in order to find peace and serenity. When they disagree, they will look at you with a smile, think "Whatever", and roll their eyes.

The Type One (Compliant) perspective is "to improve the world". They are prone to tell others right from wrong, but fail to see gray zones and can have excessive use of absolute words. This particular One assigned herself role of the neighborhood's moral gatekeeper: *"You selfishly put your kid outside <u>every</u> day and let him be <u>nothing but</u> a nuisance and a problem to <u>every</u>one else with that noise polluting whaling he <u>constantly</u> makes!!!"*

Miscommunication
"Nothing haunts us like the things we don't say" - Mitch Albom.

We have different experiences in life and are inclined to believe others view a situation the same way we do. Nothing is further from the truth as we interpret life from our perspective and process information in distinct different intelligence center patterns. We, therefore, approach any situation from a *different angle* and *process in varying ways* and at the same time emphasize personal preferences and familiarity.

My wife is a cat lover. She drinks tea, and I am a coffee drinker. For fifteen years, I have used the same model cappuccino maker. We have a calendar with paintings of local artists. I turn it to the next month and see a painting of my ol' faithful. I say to my wife, "see that?", while nodding at the calendar. "Yes, it's our cat" she replied. Two people are looking at the same picture of a coffeemaker and a cat. Both viewed the picture from a complete different angle and emphasized their priorities. Cat or coffeemaker. And that begs the question about the reliability of eye-witnesses.

And we think others possess our strengths as well. For instance, Twos process emotionally and pay close attention to the emotional needs of others. Twos respond to and act on subtle hints others provide. Twos believe others notice hints as well. And so, Twos leave hints to get what they want and do not realize these hints go unnoticed by most other Types. They feel misunderstood because, from their perspective, they should have been noticed. Fives process rationally and preserve objectivity by detaching emotions from the facts. They focus on being competent and expect the same from others. Fives expect others to focus on abstract facts. Eights are instinctual and come into action before they think. They are dominant and respect others for being strong as well.

There seems to be, at least on average, a difference between males and females as well. Research in the early 1990's claimed the brains of women have an anatomically larger Corpus Callosum. This is the "information super highway" between the right and left hemispheres. Faster information exchange is one of the many reasons why women appear to be multitaskers. Reality is, they can only do one task at the same time but are more efficient in switching between them.

Husband must fix his broken-down car. He is engulfed in his mechanics book trying to solve the engine problem. His wife asks, "Do you want more coffee?". He is not answering, heard a sound, but a few seconds later realized it was a question aimed at him. The wife, applying her quick task switching skills to him, thinks, "If I read a book, and he asks me a question, I would answer him." Her mistaken conclusion is: He is ignoring me."

We pay more attention to what will confirm our existing ideas, and de-emphasize information that challenges our established opinions. It's a recognition factor and familiarity that plays a factor. Confirmation bias reduces reasoning and can lead to misinterpretations and false conclusions. In that circumstance, our logic might fail to support demonstrative facts. Such biases are within all Types, yet, they become a problem when such opinions are rigidly adhered to, and alternatives are no longer considered.

A low functioning Type, with inflexibility at its core, is no longer willing to integrate new information into existing ideas. Adding to an existing controversy are miscommunication and feeling misunderstood. They can be unyielding, enforce personal views, want to be reassured what they believe is true and above all blame others. And believe me, *blame is a loaded word*, because blame implies *intent*. Blame builds tension, implies guilt and culpability while, at the same time, removes responsibility from ourselves. Misunderstanding, miscommunication, and consequent controversies are bound to happen. The Types processing information similarly may agree or disagree, but at least they understand each other's point of view better. They have similar behavioral, social and processing styles.

Type Two and Five exchange
Type Eight (Chris Christie):
Core childhood perception: "I feel vulnerable."
Key fear: I fear others will hurt me
Key need: I need to be self-reliant
Key perspective: I must be in control
Average Type Eights are direct, blunt, and can become domineering.

The 2014 Ebola outbreak started in several West-African countries.
New Jersey Governor Chris Christie forced Maine nurse Kaci Hickox into involuntary quarantine.

Governor Christie (Type Eight) emphatically defended his decision to isolate a symptomless volunteer nurse on the Today show: *"Because they [CDC and medical experts] don't want to admit that we're right [Christie] and they're wrong! [CDC and medical experts]"*. The favored defense mechanism of an Eight is *Denial*, which is nothing more than pretending facts don't exist.

Inevitably, social media exchanges take place regarding the issue of voluntary self-quarantine versus involuntary quarantine. Here is some communication between a Type Two and a Type Five. Pay attention to word selection as it reveals their thinking styles. Twos process primarily emotionally and Fives foremost rationally. The Two approaches the subject from the *"I must be good to others"* point of view, whereas the Five comes from the *"I must present the facts"* angle.

Type Two:
Core childhood perception: "I am not worthy of love."
Key fear: I fear not being loved.
Key need: I want to be loved and appreciated.
Key perspective: I must earn your love and appreciation.
Twos see themselves as loving, caring, and appears to be selfless.

Type Two: *"If I was a nurse and if I came home with even the <u>tiniest chance</u> of giving someone else an awful disease... I'd self-quarantine myself for <u>at least</u> 21 days. <u>Keeping others safe </u>would be more important to me than my 'rights'. <u>Once I knew I was not a danger</u> to anyone else, then I would strive to be part of the solution..."*

Type Two's perspective "to be good" shines through. With the *tiniest chance*, I will be good to you to *protect you*. I will self-quarantine *at least* 21 days and more if I have to. Only when I know *I am not a danger* to you then will I be better by being part of the solution.

Type Five:
Core childhood perception: " I am not acknowledged, don't fit in."
Key fear: I fear being inadequate, incompetent.
Key need: I seek to be acknowledged.
Key perspective: to fit in through competence.
Fives see themselves as objective, inquisitive, and knowledgeable.

Type Five response: *"According to the CDC, this is what you <u>need to know</u>: Ebola is spread through direct contact with blood and body fluids of a person <u>already showing symptoms</u> of Ebola. Ebola is not spread through the air, water, food, or mosquitoes. And the nurse is <u>symptomless</u>. She is not a risk. Or in other words, she is as much a risk as you are. Would you like to be in-voluntarily quarantined? The overreaction to Ebola reminds me of the HIV overreaction."*

The Five response shows the Five's need be competent through objectivity and fact checking. What you *need to know* is an Ebola patient *must have symptoms* in order to spread this infectious disease. Since the nurse is *symptomless*, she is *not a risk to anyone.* Therefore to quarantine her is un-warranted and an ineffective solution.

Type Two response: *"It's [ebola research] still in its infancy. Until more re-search is available, <u>all precautions</u> should be made. Even if that precaution does nothing but <u>controls other people's fears</u> and concerns. Exactly like HIV. I would self-quarantine..."*

The Two ignores the presented facts by saying *It's still in its infancy* and is in line with their favored defense mechanism (*Repression*). The medical com-munity has known for years how Ebola spreads. In the end, the real reason comes out and is the strongest emotion of all: *fear.*

The Two's perspective is *I must be good to you,* and they process infor-mation primarily on a subjective *emotional* basis. When a stressor comes into their lives, they add *instinctive doing,* and they start acting out their emotions. Rationalization is under-developed and compromises objectivity. This is furthered by repression, instinctively denying facts, and fuels an emotional reaction like *"I self-quarantine"* because I must be good.
The Five's perspective is *I must discern and be competent,* and they fact check before they speak. They process information rationally and detach their often strong emotions to preserve objectivity. And so, two Types talk with each other from a different perspective and different thinking styles. Clearly, there is no right or wrong, but they do speak a "different language".

"Perception is reality."

The direct and blunt Governor Christie fueled his political agenda by using his natural inclinations to take charge. He is emphatic, demonstrative and showed an "I am a leader" attitude, and implied he would be a great future Presidential candidate. The subjective Two reacts emotionally and readily agrees based on personal perspective and fear. The objective Five goes on a fact finding tour, and finds out quarantine is not needed, nor useful or effective.

And so, we all vote. Governor Christie will find voters who find him emotionally believable, while others think he is ill-informed, and see him as a bully. In the meantime, Kaci Hickox agreed with both Type Two and Type Five. Like the Five, she knew the facts and knew she was not a danger to society. She became part of the solution by reducing political hysteria and sticking to the facts. After due process, a judge ruled in her favor and against involuntary quarantine. Chris Christie's popularity plummeted while general character and brashness were referred to as political liabilities.

4.6 Defense Mechanisms

A defense mechanism is a subconscious strategy to deal with difficult situations and discomfort. Its function is to maintain an idealized self-image but stunts growth at the same time by not acknowledging negative feelings or undesirable traits. We create our biggest fears ourselves by preserving an idealized self which eventually comes in conflict with our true core needs.

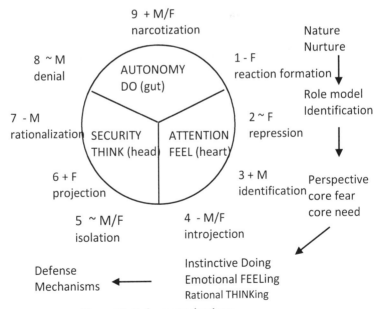

Figure 11: Defense mechanisms

Role model identification influences our processing style. Confident children move forward, assert themselves, and take less time to reflect emotionally. Others withdraw, think, reflect, and develop emotionally. How we process information will influence how we view the world around us. Some emphasize reasoning, others emotions, and lastly, some come into action without forethought. Every Type uses multiple Defense Mechanisms, and we favor defense mechanisms linked to our weakest processing style.

Types	Primary processing style	Defense mechanisms
3,7,8	Instinctive and Reasoning	Identification, Rationalization, Denial
6,1,2	Instinctive and Emotional	Projection, Reaction Formation, Repression
9,4,5	Reasoning and Emotional	Narcotization, Introjection, Isolation

The Types with emotions least developed, detached or minimally employed, *Identify* (3) with others, *Rationalize* (7) issues, or plainly *Deny* (8) the existence of facts, events or undesirable character traits. The Types with reasoning least developed, either *Project* (6) themselves onto others, *Suppress* (1) their anger by acting nice or *Repress* (2) their needs. The Types with instinctive action least developed, procrastinate by either using *Mind Numbing Activities* (9) to avoid conflict, *Internalize* their feelings (4) or *Isolate* (5) themselves to think and resolve conflict.

Although any Type can use any Defense Mechanism, each Type favors a specific one. It is the excess and prolonged use of the same mechanism that leads to rigidity and mental deterioration.

	Defense mechanism *Behavioral choice* / Deterioration pattern
1	Reaction Formation: Undesirable response is replaced by the opposite (condemnation avoidance) *Presenting amicable image suppressing inner anger.* Deterioration from undesirable response repression to counter-productive enforcing personal standards (1) to withdrawal and ending in emotional torment (4) *Typical problems: anger, impatience, emphatic certainty*
2	Repression: Providing others what you need the most (own needs avoidance) *Presenting image of selflessly helping others masking own neediness.* Deterioration from loving and caring to create dependencies to being needed (2) to counter-productive overwhelming behaviors and dominance (8). *Typical problems: clinginess, over-involvement, victim attitude*
3	Identification: Incorporating attributes of others into self-image (failure avoidance) *Presenting image of success overstating abilities while feeling like a disappointment.* Deterioration from image orientation to counter-productive grandiosity (3) to disengaging passivity (9) *Typical problems: arrogance, contempt, condescension*

4	Introjection: Internalization of environment to self (insignificance avoidance)
	Presenting image of being unique and different while feeling insignificant
	Deterioration from self-absorbed withdrawal to emotional torment (4) to coercive dominance acting like a victim (2)
	Typical problems: moodiness, irrationality, self-pity
5	Isolation: Retreating into thought and emotional detachment (emptiness avoidance)
	Searching for theoretical solutions while feeling empty and incompetent
	Deterioration from intense theorizing to useless counter-productive over-specialization (5) to being overwhelmed and scattered thinking (7).
	Typical problems: detachment, secrecy, intellectual arrogance
6	Projection: Applying own attributes to others (personal rejection avoidance)
	Presenting image of loyalty by doing what is expected suppressing personal rejection
	Deterioration from ambivalence to counter-productive over-reactions (6) to self-punishment and rage against others (3)
	Typical problems: self-doubt, impulsivity, hysterical over-reaction
7	Rationalization: Positive twists obscuring true motivation (pain avoidance)
	Presenting image of being happy and okay while feeling pain and anxiety
	Deterioration from hyperactivity to counter-productive panic-stricken (7) to punishing the world at fault (1)
	Typical problems: impulsivity, superficiality, scattered thinking
8	Denial: Negating existence of undesirable behaviors or events (vulnerability avoidance)
	Presenting image of strength while feeling vulnerable
	Deterioration from confrontation to counter-productive ruthless dominance (8) to withdrawal out of fear for retaliation (5)
	Typical problems: dominance, overconfidence, ruthless
9	Narcotization: Mind numbing activities through repetitive tasks (conflict avoidance)
	Presenting an image of harmony and peace while feeling conflict
	Deterioration from accommodating to passivity (9) to counter-productive hysterical over-reaction (6)
	Typical problems: passivity, neglectful, stubbornness

A Type Four saw a video regarding a Sports bar with forty TVs lined up. The Four commented, "I'd be completely overwhelmed." Integrating environmental aspects in a negative way to yourself is "Introjection."

A few girls go to a concert and have conflict regarding the driver's driving style. Arriving at the concert, the driver disconnected from the group and stared quietly at the band. She was angered, withdrew to avoid conflict and to think. With the band as an excuse, she used Narcotization to avoid conflict and resolve her emotions within her inner sanctum. She is a Nine.

A low-level One hates the Affordable Care Act without acknowledging any positive outcomes the Act already provided. Seven million previously uninsured are now insured. Price growth in the private sector contained, and limiting out of pocket expense, preventing people from going bankrupt based on health issues. When forced to face demonstrable facts, he quickly became irrational, belligerent, aggressive, and even threatened physical harm. Low-level Ones enforce personal standards, are irrational, and become punitive.

Needs and Defense Mechanisms

Types 8,9,1 emphasize their need for independence, and find Autonomy in different ways:

	Autonomy seeking, problems with anger, relating to others	Defense Mechanism
8	asserts emphatically and takes control *- denies they feel vulnerable*	Denial
9	withdraws avoiding conflict and self-contains *- disengages from conflict to find peace*	Narcotization
1	complies to and enforces personal standards *- suppresses anger when their standards are not met*	Reaction formation

Types 2,3,4 emphasize their need for appreciation, and find Attention in different ways:

	Attention seeking, problems with self-worth and shame	Defense Mechanism
2	complies by being good to others *- represses own needs to avoid feeling selfish*	Repression
3	asserts by portraying image of success *- pretends to be like you to gain cooperation*	Identification
4	withdraws in the hopes of being noticed *- self-evaluation to find individuality*	Introjection

Types 5,6,7 emphasize safety and find Security in different ways:

	Security seeking, problems with fear and anxiety	Defense Mechanism
5	withdraws to keep others at a distance *- presents a niche to be acknowledged and to fit in*	Isolation
6	complies by adhering to rules of authority figures *- do what is expected to feel secure and supported*	Projection
7	asserts themselves in order to not miss out *- finds the next thrill as a nurturance substitute*	Rationalization

4.7 Observable Styles

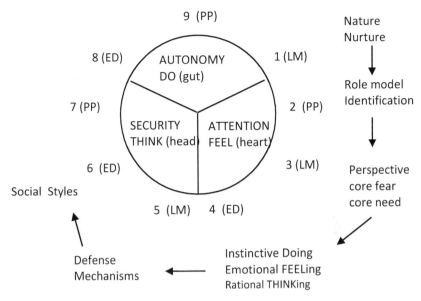

Figure 12: Social Styles

We learn to interact with our immediate environment and develop a way we present ourselves. There are three distinct styles and show how we get our needs met when frustrated.

Social Styles

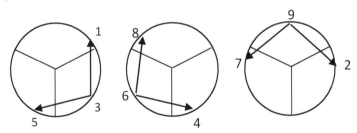

Figure 13: Social Styles

- Logical and Methodical (LM)   (3,1,5)
- Emphatic and Demonstrative (ED)   (6,4,8)
- Positive-minded and People-oriented (PP) (9,2,7)

The Logicals (3,1,5) are logical, self-controlled, and detach (3,5) or repress (1) emotions to preserve objectivity. They deal with others through reasoning and emotional detachment. They have difficulty with structure and withdraw to think.

The Demonstratives (6,4 8) are emphatic, demonstrative and want others to feel the way they do. They have problems with trusting others and expect them to mirror their concerns.

The Positives (9,2,7) are positive-minded and people-oriented. They share their optimism for positive outcomes but have issues with focusing on their own needs and exploring or integrating negatives.

The Logicals favor the following ego defensive strategies:

      3: I incorporate attributes of others to myself

      1: I am nice to others, repressing my anger and anxiety

      5: I emotionally detach and keep you at a distance

The Demonstratives have strong feelings and want others to feel the same:

      6: I am emotionally reactive

      4: I am emotionally unavailable

      8: I engage in an emphatic and direct manner

The Positives are positive-minded, people-oriented, and enjoy sharing positive experiences:

      9: I emphasize positive attributes in others

      2: I attend to the needs of others

      7: I pursue pleasure, fun, and happiness

Behavioral Styles

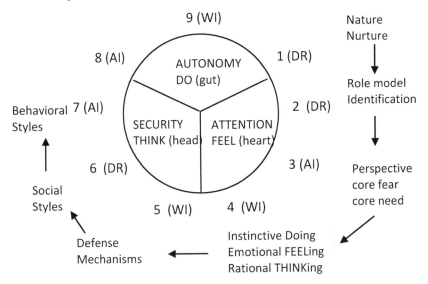

Figure 14: Behavioral Styles

The three core Behavioral Styles have similarities with Fear, Fight, and Flight reactions. These styles reflect on an underlying major perspective like "I follow rules" (fear), "I assert myself" (fight), and "I withdraw and think" (flight). These Styles reflect on how we cope with conflict and stressors.

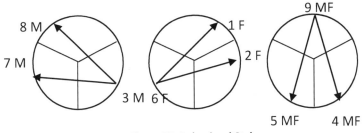

Figure 15: Behavioral Styles

- Assertive and Insistent (AI) identification with Mother
- Dedicated and Reliable (DR) identification with Father
- Withdrawn and Imaginative (WI) identification with both

The Assertives (Ego oriented: 3,7,8) place themselves in and face the world. They are independent, assertive, insistent, and have problems integrating emotions. They see themselves in a positive light and self-esteem comes from within.

Threes (attached) are covertly dependent on attention and subtly ask for praise and admiration. *(resonating key words: admirable, desirable, charming, poised).*

Sevens (frustrated) are enthusiastic, free-spirited, and need excitement in their lives. They engage the world and pursue activities with or without involvement of others. *(resonating key words: enthusiastic, spontaneous, free-spirited).*

Eights (rejected) confront the world, feel entitled to take up space, and tell themselves, "It is you that need to learn to deal with me." *(resonating key words: direct, robust, strong).*

The Compliants (Super Ego oriented: 6,1,2) are dedicated and reliable. They relate specifically to a conviction and rule adherences. They see themselves positively when they feel they are of service to others. Their self-esteem is dependent on obeying internalized standards either set by themselves (1, 2) or others (6).

Sixes (attached) affiliate with authority figures or entities to gain guidance and support. *(resonating key words: dependable, skeptical, trustworthy).*

Ones (frustrated) are servicing the world by ensuring we all know right from wrong. *(resonating key words: reasonable, prudent, objective).*

Twos (rejected) provide others with what they need the most. Everyone deserves my attention, love, and appreciation. *(resonating key words: loving, caring, selfless).*

The Withdrawns (ID oriented: 9,4,5) are withdrawn and imaginative. They don't see themselves in a positive light and withdraw from the world. They have problems matching conscious thought with subconscious feelings and are prone to procrastinate. Their self-esteem is approval dependent.

Nines (attached) withdraw into a safe inner sanctum to avoid conflict and to find their peace and quiet. *(resonating key words: peaceful, relaxed, stable).*

Fours (frustrated) withdraw to be emotionally unavailable to gain attention. *(resonating key words: sensitive, unique, quiet).*

Fives (rejected) withdraw into thought evaluating the world and solve problems. *(resonating key words: intelligent, observant, insightful).*

Our role model identification influences our thinking style, which in turn favors a characteristic defense mechanism. Our natural inclinations combined with these environmental influences evolve into a distinct and recognizable behavioral and social style.

The Assertives (3,7,8) identify with the emotional nurturer (M) and not so much with the protector and guide (F) in their lives. The Father typically is the role model providing guidance and social inhibitions. Self-esteem develops from within and emotional connectivity under-develops which allows for their assertive style. A child, who does not identify with a Father, might learn to guide themselves and might not develop appropriate social inhibitions. Their defense mechanisms are *Identification, Rationalization, and Denial* which are naturally limited in their emotional scope.

Type 3 overstates their true abilities and presents themselves as more successful than they really are (Vice: Deceit). They seek performance acknowledgment and link their self-esteem to a job well done. They willfully ignore the possibility of failure.
Type 7 is experience-oriented and stays active to avoid the anxiety of deprivation (Vice: Gluttony). They seek pleasurable experiences as a nurturance substitute. They are the busy bees with full agendas and inclined to not see their personal limitations.
Type 8 is power-seeking to mask their feelings of vulnerability (Vice: Lust). They are forceful, direct, and can be extremely blunt. They don't see the emotional impact they have on others.

The Compliants (6,1,2) identify with the protector and guide (F) in their lives. They use instinctive doing fueled by emotions and adhere to standards offered or created. With rules to live by in place, they under-develop reasoning. Their defense mechanisms are *Projection, Reaction Formation, and Repression* and reflect on limited abstract thinking.

Type 6 will do what is expected from them to avoid personal rejection (Vice: Fear). Their self-doubt makes them abide by rules provided and seeks authority approval. Exaggeration of rule following becomes overestimation of authority figures, or worse, blind obedience.
Type 1 acts nice repressing internalized anger (Vice: Wrath). They abide by self-created set of standards and do not see gray areas. Exaggeration of abiding by personal rules becomes enforcing personal standards.
Type 2 presents themselves as selfless and helpful to be loved and appreciated (Vice: Pride). Their rule is to be good to others. Exaggeration of being good can result in being over-involved and clingy. They won't acknowledge their personal needs.

The Withdrawns (9,4,5) identify with both emotional nurturer (M) and protector and guide (F) in their lives. They process through reasoning and emotions which can be in conflict. They need time to evaluate guiding principles offered to them for themselves. Their preferred defense mechanisms are *Narcotization, Introjection, and Isolation.*
All these mechanisms are reflections of withdrawal to think while delaying and reducing instinctive action.

Type 9 is agreeable and amicable to maintain peace and quiet (Vice: Sloth). Exaggeration of being amicable and agreeable can develop into passivity. They will not acknowledge personal preferences, nor express their opinions. Type 4 presents themselves as unique and different repressing insignificance (Vice: Envy). They are withdrawn and use introspection to create a personal identity and focus on that what is missing. They are blind to what they already have.
Type 5 observes to gain knowledge avoiding feeling empty and incompetent (Vice: Avarice). They withdraw and take time to develop a niche. They ignore what is in front of them and immediately available.

Logical and Methodical		Vice	Blind to
3	presents a false image	Deceit	failure to perform
1	builds pent up anger	Wrath	gray areas
5	Emotional distancing and isolation	Avarice	existing abundance
Emphatic and Demonstrative			
6	makes others feel the way they do	Fear	overestimation authority
4	holds on the negative comparisons	Envy	satisfaction with what they have
8	moves forward negating reality	Lust	impact on others
Positive-minded and People-oriented			
9	retreats in own bubble	Sloth	personal preferences
2	provides own needs to others	Pride	personal needs
7	obscuring true motives	Gluttony	personal limitations

At lower levels of functioning, the three behavioral styles broadly match the psychological personality disorder clusters. The Withdrawns (withdrawn and imaginative) match the Avoidants, who fear rejection and are reluctant to enter social relationships. The Compliants (dedicated and reliable) match the Obsessive-compulsives[12], who rely on rigid rule adherences. And lastly, the Assertives (assertive and insistent) match the Dramatic (histrionic, narcissistic, and anti-social personality disorder), who want to control their environment without feelings of guilt.

---

[12] Sue, Sue, and Sue, "Abnormal behaviors" p. 240

4.8 Behavioral Patterns

"Behavior is the mirror in which everyone shows their true image"
- Johan Wolfgang von Goethe

Behavioral Pathways is a natural progressive model which is distinct and recognizable. Each Type is prone to develop a distinct Behavioral Pattern or *Continuum of Traits*[13] based on their perspective, key fear, key need, and defense mechanisms. Most of us will function at healthy and average mental health levels whereas others, with inadequate coping mechanisms in place, might function at unhealthy or even pathological levels.

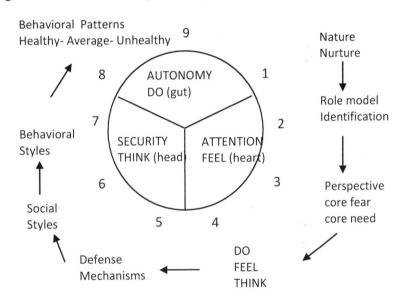

Figure 16: Behavioral Patterns

Depending on our mental health, we either cope well or don't cope well. We have our normal day to day behaviors that get us what we need. Stress unleashes the three Furies: Fear, Guilt, and Shame which are expressed as anger. Needless to say, our behavioral and social styles are much easier recognized when our behaviors are exaggerated under stress and when perspectives are more strongly expressed.

---

[13] Continuum of Traits is one of the main contributions of Riso and Hudson.

Pool Player G rattled a ball in the corner pocket. He is instantly angry, jumps up, and yells "that <u>always</u> happens to me and <u>never</u> to you!" (Type One: anger, difficulty relating to others, no gray areas, and use of absolute terminology).

Pool Player B has to make a difficult jump shot. He says "I got good news and bad news for you. The good news is I <u>always make</u> this shot. The bad news is you lose". He misses and says "Well, I <u>always make that shot!</u>" (Type Three: overestimation of personal abilities and does not acknowledge failure).

The Behavioral Pathways and consequent Behavioral Patterns are inherently linked to each other.

Childhood	Styles	Development	Behavioral Pattern
Identification with role model	Behavioral Styles assertive / insistent; dedicated / reliable; withdrawn / imaginative	Healthy *Integration*	1 <u>Integration with others</u> 2 Self-acknowledgment 3 Self-aware
		Average *Manipulation*	4 <u>Do what we know best</u> 5 Emphasize core needs 6 ego-oriented
Perceived Childhood message		Unhealthy *Domination*	7 <u>Exaggerate what we know best</u> 8 demands core needs to be met 9 Separation of others
Defense Mechanism	Social Styles logical / methodical; emphatic / demonstrative; positive / people-oriented	Disintegration: *Control*	↓<u>Do the opposite of what we know best.</u> Pathological

The Behavioral Patterns are easier recognized at *average* and *unhealthy* mental functioning because at:
- Healthy levels (1-3): we are inclusive, integrate sound qualities and blur pattern recognition
- Average levels (4-6): we do what we know best and emphasize pursuing key needs
- Unhealthy levels (7-9): we exaggerate what we know best and demand key needs to be met
- Disintegration: we do the opposite of what we know best

Strengths

We see ourselves in a specific way as we value our strengths reflected in our core needs and seen in our behavioral traits. These strengths are heartfelt and undeniable. The strengths of others are traits we can actively pursue through observation and integration.

A healthy and wholesome individual will acquire many of these healthy characteristics. Let's reflect for a moment on the wonderful qualities each Type represents: *Fairness, Relatedness, Perseverance, Originality, Discernment, Loyalty, Spontaneity, Candor and Tolerance.*

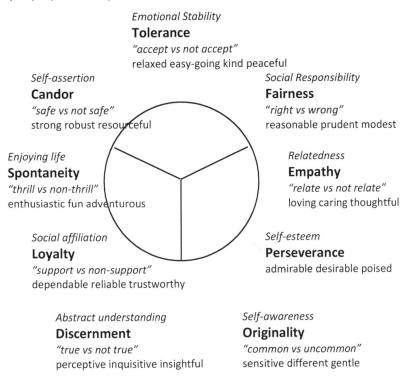

Emotional Stability
Tolerance
"accept vs not accept"
relaxed easy-going kind peaceful

Self-assertion
Candor
"safe vs not safe"
strong robust resourceful

Social Responsibility
Fairness
"right vs wrong"
reasonable prudent modest

Enjoying life
Spontaneity
"thrill vs non-thrill"
enthusiastic fun adventurous

Relatedness
Empathy
"relate vs not relate"
loving caring thoughtful

Social affiliation
Loyalty
"support vs non-support"
dependable reliable trustworthy

Self-esteem
Perseverance
admirable desirable poised

Abstract understanding
Discernment
"true vs not true"
perceptive inquisitive insightful

Self-awareness
Originality
"common vs uncommon"
sensitive different gentle

Figure 17: what we can learn from each other

Each Type can grow by observing, appreciating, and integrating traits others tend to favor. However, each behavioral trait, that comes natural to a Type, will be exaggerated under stress and can become a problem when rigidly adhered to. We are entering the realm of personality disorders[14] which is defined as long term low level mental functioning.

---

[14] Sue, Sue, and Sue, "Abnormal behavior" p. 235

The disorders are characterized by inflexibility, poor adaptation skills, nit-picking, and reduced social sustenance and credibility. They can cause substantial grief and misery for themselves as well as others. What used to be a strength has now become a weakness and unfortunately our new norm.

"Any strength in excess becomes a weakness."

At unhealthy and disintegration levels of functioning, we may lack insight and lost our orientation with reality. We cling on to our perception of reality and are generally unwilling to consider alternative explanations despite overwhelming evidence to the contrary. Consequently, we alienate others with excessive behaviors to protect our egos and rigidly adhere to our biggest fear. We present ourselves as confident and strong, however, overwhelming others shows we are insecure.

"Exaggeration is a sign of the opposite."

Type One: from fairness to enforcing personal standards.
Type Two: from empathy to creating dependencies.
Type Three: from perseverance to exploitation for personal gain.
Type Four: from original to unusual and bizarre.
Type Five: from discernment to useless over-specialization.
Type Six: from self-doubt to untrusting.
Type Seven: from spontaneity to scattered hyperactivity.
Type Eight: from candor to confrontational bluntness.
Type Nine: from tolerance to passive disengagement.

	Focal Strength	Exaggeration	Excessive = Weakness
1	fairness	correcting others	enforce personal standards
2	empathy	over-involvement	to make others dependent
3	perseverance	competitiveness	exploitation
4	originality	different and unique	unusual and bizarre
5	discernment	over-specialization	Intellectual arrogance
6	loyalty	rule adherence	authority over-estimation
7	spontaneity	variety seeking	hyper-activity
8	candor	bluntness	overwhelming
9	tolerance	passivity	disengaged

Type Traits

We have organized the nine Types into two clusters of three Style groups.

Behavioral Styles:
- the Assertives (3,7,8: Fight)
- the Compliants (6,1,2: Fear)
- the Withdrawns (9,4,5: Flight)

Social Styles:
- Logical and Controlled (3,1,5)
- Emphatic and Demonstrative (6,4,8)
- Positive minded and People Oriented (9,2,7)

Although each Type accentuates a strength (Primary Trait) born and developed from a core perspective, we cannot help but notice each Type has Secondary Traits consistent with the two other cluster Types. These traits are supported by the Wing Trait(s).

	primary	secondary	Wing(s)
1	fairness	empathy/loyalty	tolerance/empathy
2	empathy	fairness/loyalty	fairness/perseverance
3	perseverance	spontaneity/candor	empathy/originality
4	originality	discernment/tolerance	perseverance/discernment
5	discernment	originality/tolerance	originality/loyalty
6	loyalty	fairness/empathy	discernment/spontaneity
7	spontaneity	candor/perseverance	loyalty/candor
8	candor	perseverance/spontaneity	spontaneity/tolerance
9	tolerance	discernment/originality	candor/fairness

Each Type can be described with relative ease in very broad terms following the pattern of the core strengths of these groupings. For instance, a Type One emphasizes social responsibility with a focus on "right versus wrong" assessments attempting to make the world a better place (Fairness). They repress their anger when their standards are not met (Tolerance) and have Empathy for the cause of a group.

George Zimmerman was motivated to set a wrong right (Fairness). He noticed burglaries in the neighborhood (right versus wrong) and set up a neighborhood watch (Empathy for group needs). Zimmerman saw a hooded teenager in the rain. He followed Martin, called the non-emergency line and got out of his truck (Logical and Controlled).

A healthy Type One sees himself as fair, prudent, modest, and reasonable. They acquire the Spontaneity of a Seven. At average and unhealthy levels others might see them as judgmental, critical, intolerant, self-righteous, rigid, and explosively punitive.

Type Threes are success-driven. They are ambitious, competitive and blind to failure (Perseverance). They tend to say and do anything that comes to mind with disregard for social context (Spontaneity and Candor). They are cause driven (Empathy for greater good and success). They are intelligent and find ways to succeed (Originality, Perseverance, blind to failure).

Mitt Romney, the former Republican Presidential candidate, is a very successful business-man. He ran for the Presidency twice (Perseverance) and continued to be the face of the Republican Party. He made numerous questionable comments like 47% of the population is government dependent and publicly criticizing the London Summer Olympics (Spontaneity and Candor). Despite public uproar, he remained a gentleman (Logical and Controlled).
A healthy Type Three sees themselves as admirable, desirable, charming and ambitious. They acquire the Loyalty and commitment of a Six. At average and unhealthy levels others might see them as career-oriented, self-promoting, opportunistic, relentless and exploitative.

Type Fives are knowledge oriented with a "true versus not true" perspective (Discernment). They first gather the facts (Loyal to objectivity and causes), compare and weigh before they come to personal conclusions (Originality). They tend to be researchers and develop a specialty knowledge base.

Dr. Phil is the most prominent TV personality in which he promotes personal growth and relationship dynamics. He does his research first and asks many questions prior to his show. He comes to personal conclusions and uses measured responses (Logical and Controlled). He sticks to the known facts (Discernment/ Loyalty to objectivity) and is vehemently protective of his staff (Loyalty).
A healthy Five sees themselves as inquisitive, intelligent, insightful and smart. They acquire the confidence and Candor of an Eight. At average and unhealthy levels, others might see them as knowledgeable, preoccupied, provocative and eccentric.

"I am what you want me to be." - Unknown

5. Integration - disintegration

The Enneagram is a dynamic model from several perspectives:
- Any type has the characteristics of all other types and nobody is in a box. However, the emphasis on a core perspective, our core point of view on the world, determines our Type.
- Each Type accentuates a key behavioral pattern ranging from healthy to unhealthy.
- Each Type can integrate healthy traits of all other Types. This often occurs in the sequence of integration (1-7-5-8-2-4-1 and 3-6-9-3).
- Each Type can disintegrate and acquire unhealthy mannerisms of the next Type. It often ends here as unhealthy traits tend to be self-destructive (1-4-2-8-5-7-1 and 3-9-6-3).

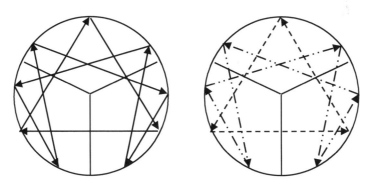

Figure 18: Integration Disintegration

The integration and disintegration patterns own a particular sequence. Each Type is inclined to make behavioral choices within the pathway of their key perspective and is reflected in the healthy, average, and unhealthy range of our mental development.

At healthy levels, we are inclusive and integrate concepts and ideas. At average levels, we manipulate to get what we want, and our behavioral style is invested in moderation. At unhealthy levels of functioning, we try to dominate and exaggerate our normal behaviors. When we disintegrate beyond the unhealthy levels, we are inclined to do the opposite what we normally do. We might no longer be in touch with reality and rigidly adhere to our principles.

Each Type can integrate the next quality skill, or mentally deteriorate. In other words, the habitually withdrawn Five acquires the confidence of an Eight. The usually bossy Eight, at unhealthy levels, will withdraw like a Five. The disintegration pattern is more important to recognize:

	Disintegration pattern
1	*From undesirable response repression to counter-productive enforcing personal standards (1) to withdrawal in self-pity while emotionally tormented (4)*
2	*From loving and caring to creating dependencies to be needed (2) to counter-productive overwhelming behaviors and dominance (8)*
3	*Deterioration from image-orientation to counter-productive competitive grandiosity (3) to disengaging passivity (9)*
4	*From self-absorbed withdrawal to counter-productive emotional torment (4) to coercive dominance acting like a victim (2)*
5	*From intense theorizing to useless counter-productive over-specialization (5) to being overwhelmed and scattered thinking (7)*
6	*From ambivalence to counter-productive over-reactions (6) to self-punishment and rage against others (3)*
7	*From hyper-activity to counter-productive panic-stricken (7) to punishing the world at fault (1)*
8	*From direct confrontation to counter-productive ruthless dominance (8) to withdrawal out of fear for retaliation (5)*
9	*From accommodating to passivity (9) to counter-productive hysterical over-reaction (6)*

Typically, a Type starts showing signs of deterioration at level 4 (average levels) of their behavioral pattern. With mental deterioration, more excessive weak traits of the next Type are acquired. The pattern is distinct and easy to remember. A mentally weak Three starts acquiring the characteristics found in the average to unhealthy Nine. The lingo used is "a Three moves to Nine". As we can see, Nine deteriorates to Six and Six to Three. The other six Types move from One to Four to Two to Eight to Five to Seven and back to One[15]. Disintegration means a Type deteriorates, becomes mentally unstable, and no longer has the confidence to know what to do.

Remember, the integration and disintegration pattern move in the opposite direction. Integration means a Type gains *confidence*; they feel assured but do not necessarily make good choices. A confident Five can act like a domineering Eight. They start to lead and become overwhelming. A confident Five, who sees another person as a hypocritical liar, can become Assertive, and bluntly set boundaries in a domineering and aggressive way.

5.1 Dynamics

The integration and disintegration pattern adds a whole new dynamic and dimension to the model and might initially confuse identifying a Type. Meeting someone with withdrawn characteristics like a Type Five does not automatically mean he is a Type Five. He could be a domineering and mentally unstable Eight, who disintegrated to Five with signs of withdrawal. Yet, mental instability would also be visible. He could be a mentally stable and an appreciative Seven and integrated to Five. The healthy Seven is harder to recognize because of the integration of socially acceptable traits. He might be a skeptical Six with a Five wing (6w5) or a melancholy Four with a Five wing (4w5). When we meet someone for the first time, we need to remain open-minded to a range of potential Types until a pattern establishes itself. It will take time to recognize the main theme perspectives, behavioral patterns, stress reactions, and the motivation behind it all.
The behavioral pattern of each Type has a distinct and consistent theme based on a key perspective. As we already know by now, each Type can function at healthy levels (1-3), average levels (4-6), and unhealthy levels (7-9). But, one thing never changes, and that is a Type's main theme: *the core perspective and the key fear and key need attached to it.* Learn to recognize this Triad and Type identification is suddenly more manageable.

For example, the world of a Type Two revolves around love. They did not feel loved and appreciated by the patriarchal role model. They give to others what they need the most themselves; to be loved and appreciated. Healthy Twos are loving, caring, and altruistic. An average Two expects a return on their "do-good" efforts and are disappointed when none is

---

[15] A handy reminder of this sequence is 1/7 = 0.1425714

received in return. They provide hints showing how good they are and then make sure others don't forget how important they are to them.

Exaggerations of normal behaviors include flattery and providing unwanted services or advice in order to be needed. They repress their anger for not receiving anything in return. The unhealthy Two won't be able to admit they do things specifically to get a return. They view that as selfish, and that is not in line with their "selfless" image presented to others. They can become manipulative and demanding to get what they need. At the lowest levels of functioning, they can become physically ill, play a victim role, and enjoy the attention they receive from being taken care off.

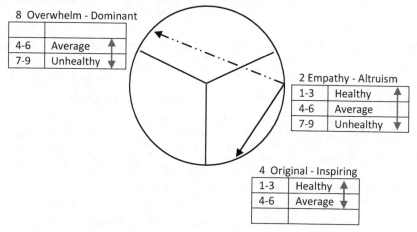

8 Overwhelm - Dominant

4-6	Average
7-9	Unhealthy

2 Empathy - Altruism

1-3	Healthy
4-6	Average
7-9	Unhealthy

4 Original - Inspiring

1-3	Healthy
4-6	Average

Figure 19: Integration: 2 to 4; Disintegration 2 to 8

The Integration pattern for the Two is toward Four. The Healthy Two has learned they don't have to be selfless all the time, acknowledge their needs and are willing to pursue them. They no longer repress negative emotions and allow themselves to vent. They shed the idea of "always being good" which is a conclusion often reached after a prolonged and exhausting period of being good and chasing love. They have become self-aware and emotion-ally honest with themselves which are naturally progressive traits highlight-ed in healthy Fours.

The Disintegration pattern for the Two is toward Eight. Disintegration is a gradual process of increased uncertainty and inability to cope with circum-stances. An insecure Two acquires traits we see in Eights starting at level 4 and integrates them with their own. The gist for the Two is to always be good to others and be selfless. Twos typically don't acknowledge their needs as they are too busy meeting the needs of others. To first accept their

76

personal needs and then asking for them to be met is very difficult for a Two. There comes a point in time they feel they have given so much without getting what they need in return, and their perspective turns into, "you are no longer worthy of me being good to you".

They now become forceful and demanding like an Eight. From this perspective, a Two becomes angered and can become violently destructive to those who benefitted from all their good deeds. The Two's aggression is typically aimed at family members, friends, and intimates who failed to meet the Two's unexpressed and often very specific needs.

Twos typically make four big mistakes. They focus on the needs of others and are in tune with the emotional meaning of non-verbals. They have a great understanding of the significance of a sniff or teary eyes within its context. Their first mistake is they assume others are just as in tune as they are. Therefore, Twos have a tendency to be indirect and only provide hints at what they want. Since others pay less attention to non-verbals, these hints are neither recognized nor understood, and their needs remain unmet because of their own doing. It behooves a Two to be more direct about their needs and speak with clarity about what they want. This goes against the grain of a Two as they need to present themselves as selfless.

Second, their perspective to "always be good and do good" allows others to be in charge of their boundaries. Twos are inclined to play different roles with different people based on the needs others have. Twos, therefore, are loving chameleons who continuously adapt to others.

To not be good to others is considered selfish which degrades their self-esteem. Thus, Twos are prone to have poor control over their boundaries, become people pleasers, and can get carried away doing things they actually don't like to do. The unhealthy Two feels unloved and unwanted. Now desperate for love, they may resort to giving the ultimate expression of love which is physical. At these unhealthy levels of functioning, they won't feel loved and wanted because they now know they are only loved back in response to their own initiative. Promiscuity becomes a real option.

The third mistake is they are convinced they are only loved if they are good to others first. At average levels, they are clingy and overly involved to earn love and appreciation. The problem with the Two initiating all their well-intended good deeds is they will not figure out whether someone loves them for who they are on their own accord. Appreciation responses are what they are; a response. But the Two will always question whether others would initiate kindness on their own and just for whom they are. Unfortunately, they probably never get that answer.

The fourth mistake the average and unhealthy Two makes is to repress negatives and apply positive twists to poor behavioral choices. In their zeal to be loved and needed, they create dependencies to make others stay. They manipulate and undermine others but will not see that as a negative. They rather focus on "how good they are" as their primary motivation, and repress their negative behaviors by rationalizing them into positive outcomes. However, others are not as forgetful about the coercive and manipulative traits. And that gets the Two into trouble.

Jerry Sandusky (1944 -) is a former football coach, who founded a non-profit charity to provide underprivileged and at-risk children. He molested young boys over a fifteen-year period and met his victims through his charity foundation. He presented himself as doing good while placing young boys in a dependent position. They had to choose between being part of the charity foundation with all the advantages or be forced back to their underprivileged lives. Sandusky manipulated the young boys into a position of dependency including his own adopted son. His son commented in televised interviews, that he did not believe Sandusky realized the gravity of his actions, nor how truly wrong he was. Sandusky has all the markings of a type Two. He was repressing negatives and applied positive twists to his actions. He has plenty of time to contemplate his life in federal prison.

She raised a family, and the children are grown up and on their own. She divorced and had nobody to take care off nor did she feel needed. She remarried a man who was willing to adopt underprivileged children. She will never admit this was for selfish reasons. "I need to give love to those who are dependent on me" in order to feel good about myself. Twos are more prone to start a second family than other Types.

It is easy to see how the Two mixes with the Eight and Four at varying levels of mental health. It is also easy to imagine these variations make Type identification initially more difficult.

Type recognition will become much easier over time. Ask pointed questions, observe and listen carefully. With the Two as an example, focus on:
- perspective: "I am always good."
- stress exaggerations: "I become overly involved and clingy."
- progressive patterns: "from being good to overly involved to a victim role to ruthless dominance."

As a reminder, the desperate Eight moved from dominance to withdrawal. The desperate Two moved from being good and kind to ruthless dominance. Each Type, at the end of their rope, tends to do the opposite of what they normally do.

5.2 Violence

Most violent offenses happen in the unhealthy mental range. Dr. Philip Zimbardo[16] shared a pattern how we slowly, but surely reset boundaries accepting new norms, see others as objects and reduce personal responsibility. Although Dr. Zimbardo described a relationship between an individual and an authority figure, we can apply the same rules to someone who sees him/herself as their own authority.

The seven steps toward evil[17] *(sub-categories added)*:
- Mindlessly taking a first small step
- Dehumanizing others
- De-individuation of self
- Diffusion of personal responsibility
- Blind obedience to authority
    - *Those who self-approve have unconditional approval*
    - *Those who depend on approval might show blind obedience*
- Non-critical conformity
    - *non-critical to social norms (self-approval)*
    - *non-critical to group norms (authority attachment)*
- Passive tolerance and indifference toward evil

In summary, our Behavioral Pathway follows a distinct natural progression: we have inborn abilities, are influenced by our environment, develop a perspective with a key fear and key need. Our role model identification leads to a thinking style, which in turn favors a defense mechanism. How we deal with conflict and stress is always expressed and observable by our behavioral style and social style.

By recognizing consistencies in behavioral style, social style, stress reactions, and defense mechanisms, we can identify someone's behavioral pathway. And with it, we have a good idea about role model identification, perspec-

---

[16] Dr. Zimbardo made an important mark with "the Stanford prison experiment" (1971)
[17] Dr. Philip Zimbardo during a TED talk

tives, key needs, key fears, and how we behave in secure and stress situations. And since we all tend to behave in one of nine distinct patterns, it is abundantly clear:

"We are the same; it's the details that differ."

Each Type owns a distinct behavioral pattern which may include violence. Some Types are more prone to aggression and violating the rights of others. Such violations occur at different levels within each behavioral pattern. Types One, Three, Seven, and Eight can be initially confrontational in the average range. Even in the unhealthy range, Types Two, Four, Five, and Nine remain more or less passive.

Since no Type is a pure Type and is influenced by their wing, any Type may have a violent inclination. Other influences like culture, group identity, socio-economic opportunity, and a need to fit in may also contribute to overstepping boundaries and violence.

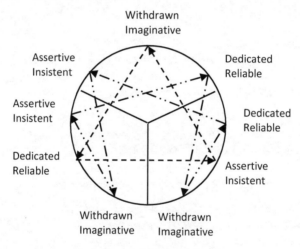

Figure 20: violation tendencies

The Disintegration model shows how the Eight moves from Assertive to Withdrawn; a Five from Withdrawn to Assertive; a Seven from Assertive to strict rule adherence of being "right" like a One. Violence happens mostly in the unhealthy range of functioning. Some Types start with confrontation while others have to be at the end of their rope before they become physically aggressive.

Although each Type can be violent, there is a distinct pattern at what point in their behavioral pattern violence occurs. Types One and Eight, both in the Autonomy Triad with difficulty relating to others and anger issues, confront first and then retreat at the disintegration level. Ones are initially critical and judgmental after which they become punitive. This is followed by withdrawal and emotional torment (One to Four). Eights are confrontational and overwhelm others with misplaced overconfidence. They then retreat (Eight to Five) out of fear of retaliation.

	Inclination	Average	Unhealthy	Disintegration
1	enforce personal standards		punitive	
2	anger toward intimates			ruthless
3	confronts others	condescending	vindictive	
4	self-punishment			
5	self-destruction			reckless
6	enforce policies			vindictive
7	do what I need		reckless	punitive
8	confronts others	domineering	ruthless	
9	self-destruction			

Type Four and Nine are probably the least in the news for violence. Fours tend to be introspective, quiet, and disappear. They are prone to hurting themselves. Nines keep the peace and in the end might become irrational. They have enormous resilience to repress and bury past hurts into the deep catacombs of their memories. Nines are seldom in the news for misbehavior. They seem to be able to take the heat and appear to effortlessly bounce back. *Narcotization*, or mind-numbing repetitive tasks, is a powerful tool to fend off crisis after crisis. Typically, not addressing the real issue goes at the cost of themselves. Maybe Riso and Hudson[18] (1996) said it best, *"Nevertheless, their ability to endure is always purchased at a price of leading an emotionally and personally impoverished life."*

The Assertives (3,7,8) are prone to *violating others through direct confrontation.* Self-approval is a core characteristic of the Assertives and their self-esteem comes from within. They feel entitled and tend to be emotionally under-developed. They can overstep boundaries with relative ease, and more so than any other Type. The unhealthy Assertives are the *Psychopaths* (3), *Narcissists* (7) and *Megalomaniacs* (8) of the world.

---

[18] "Personality Types" (1996) p. 375

Elliot Rodger (3w4) violated others through aggressive self-assertion eliminating those who reminded him of his shortcomings. *"I don't know why you girls aren't attracted to me, but I will punish you all for it."*

The Compliants (6,1,2) are *prone to violate self or others based on strict rule adherences*. They build their self-esteem and feel good about themselves when they abide by certain rules. Following rules requires less thinking, and rationalization tends to be under-developed or least employed.

Unhealthy Compliants are *Punitive* (1), play *Victim* roles (2) and are *Masochists* (6).

George Zimmerman (1w2) set up a neighborhood watch program to catch burglars. He confronted and killed Trayvon Martin because he viewed him as a burglar. Burglaries are wrong, and according to George, the hooded kid fit the bill. Type Ones initiate confrontation based on their strict rule adherence as a moral gatekeeper.

She (2w1) is a loving and caring mother and always good to her husband, but felt unnoticed and unloved for some time now. Her husband was working many hours to get his business off the ground. As a Two, she only hinted at her need for attention by cleaning the house over and over again. But he came home tired and was preoccupied trying to make ends meet. After all this time, the slightest trigger could set her off. She has been drinking, and alcohol reduced her inhibitions. The house was spotless again [Two showing you cannot do without me; creating a dependency], and now I will force you to notice how clean to house really was as you are no longer worthy of all my efforts for you. She responded with violence and destruction and tore the once clean house apart. The message was simple: Do you see me now?

The Two moved from loving and caring to being needed, to the Eight's overwhelming and destructive ways. As we can see, the loving and caring Two can become violent when they are finally at the end of their rope.

The Withdrawns (9,4,5) are least prone to violence. They first and foremost withdraw and use imagination to resolve issues and conflict.

Their self-esteem is approval dependent, and their instinctive doing is under-developed or least employed.

Unhealthy Withdrawns are *emotionally tormented* (4), *isolated loners* (5) and *disengaged from conflict* (9). When violent, they are prone to *self-destruct*. They might violate others based on a belief system or a cause and exert vicious deeds indirectly and from a distance.

Ted Kaczynski (5w4), the Unabomber, was an isolated loner, who used knowledge and expertise to violate others from a distance. He needed to gain attention for his cause as described in his thirty-five-thousand-word Manifesto. As a Five, with his core need to be acknowledged, he could not resist having his Manifesto published.

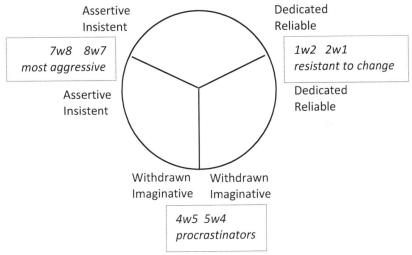

Figure 21 Type and Wing emphasis

As mentioned before, each Type is influenced by their wing. The influence of the wings is strongest where the Behavioral Styles overlap.

Types Seven and Eight are both Assertive and Insistent, which makes Types 7w8 and 8w7 the most aggressive Types.

Type One and Two emphasize dedication to rule adherence. Types 1w2 and 2w1 are the Types with strictest rule adherence, the most rigid in their opinions, and notoriously resistant to change.

Types Four and Five are both withdrawn. Type 4w5 and 5w4 reinforce withdrawal and are the most withdrawn Types. They may suffer from analysis paralysis. At average and unhealthy levels, these Types procrastinate the most.

"When you need praise, you place others in the position of judge".
- Unknown

6. Types in brief

From nature and nurture, to identification, to a key perspective, combined with processing style and defense mechanism, leading to a social style and behavioral style, ultimately developing into a distinct behavioral pattern, is what I call our *Behavioral Pathway.*

A Behavioral Pathway has a consistent theme and a natural progression. The behavioral patterns are consistent, distinct, and provide a uniform set of progressive expectations. Combining pattern expectation with known past behavioral choices leads to future *predictability.*

Healthy individuals have clarity, are inclusive of others, and flexible. They know who they are, have a strong foundation to work from, and have balance in their lives.
Average individuals become ego defensive and emphasize their personal needs. Psychological imbalance rears its head, and relationship dynamics can become strained. As we slide down this path, we seek more control over our environment. Instead of self-reflection, we become prone to take care of our own needs and at times at the cost of others.
Unhealthy individuals with inadequate coping mechanisms often display response rigidity and violations of self and others. When our outlook and consequent coping style become habitual, we no longer see our rigidity as a problem rather as our new norm. Instead of looking at ourselves in the mirror, we blame others for our issues, lash out, violate the rights of others, and are prone to use irrational views as an argument.

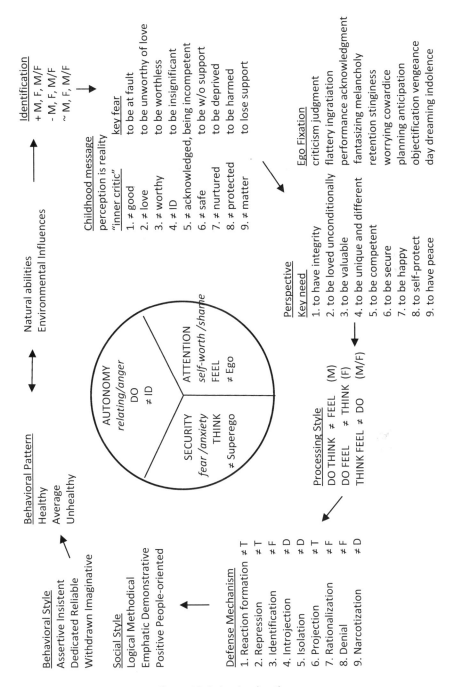

Identification
+ M, F, M/F
- M, F, M/F
~ M, F, M/F

Childhood message
perception is reality
"inner critic"   key fear
1. ≠ good   to be at fault
2. ≠ love   to be unworthy of love
3. ≠ worthy   to be worthless
4. ≠ ID   to be insignificant
5. ≠ acknowledged, being incompetent
6. ≠ safe   to be w/o support
7. ≠ nurtured   to be deprived
8. ≠ protected   to be harmed
9. ≠ matter   to lose support

Ego Fixation
criticism judgment
flattery ingratiation
performance acknowledgment
fantasizing melancholy
retention stinginess
worrying cowardice
planning anticipation
objectification vengeance
day dreaming indolence

Perspective
Key need
1. to have integrity
2. to be loved unconditionally
3. to be valuable
4. to be unique and different
5. to be competent
6. to be secure
7. to be happy
8. to self-protect
9. to have peace

Natural abilities
Environmental Influences

Behavioral Pattern
Healthy
Average
Unhealthy

Behavioral Style
Assertive Insistent
Dedicated Reliable
Withdrawn Imaginative

Social Style
Logical Methodical
Emphatic Demonstrative
Positive People-oriented

Defense Mechanism
1. Reaction formation ≠ T
2. Repression ≠ T
3. Identification ≠ F
4. Introjection ≠ D
5. Isolation ≠ D
6. Projection ≠ T
7. Rationalization ≠ F
8. Denial ≠ F
9. Narcotization ≠ D

AUTONOMY
relating/anger
DO
≠ ID

ATTENTION
self-worth /shame
FEEL
≠ Ego

SECURITY
fear /anxiety
THINK
≠ Superego

Processing Style
DO THINK ≠ FEEL (M)
DO FEEL ≠ THINK (F)
THINK FEEL ≠ DO (M/F)

Figure 22: behavioral pathways

The Behavioral Pathway model has taken shape. Each Type can be described in broad terms as follows:

Type One (*Wrath*: pent up anger)

Type One grew up frustrated with the Father (-F), and the flawed guidance he provided. It's the child who perceived they were not good enough. This became their key fear, with the consequent need to be good enough in order to avoid criticism. Ones are prone to see things black and white and don't acknowledge gray areas. They process information intuitively, which is supported by emotions. This fuels emotional reactivity and underscores emphatic certainty. Reasoning, however, is least developed. Their defense mechanism is *Reaction Formation*, suppressing their anger when others are not living up to their standards. This is a trigger to enforce personal standards, and maintain their image of being right. They are dedicated, reliable and present themselves as logical and controlled.

A healthy One is critically astute, wise, objective, and realistic. They see themselves as objective and reasonable, but others might see them as critical, emphatically certain, inflexible and punitive.

Type Two (*Pride*: in being needed)

Type Two grew up feeling rejected by the Father (~F). They perceive themselves as not worthy of love and appreciation. They are attention seeking and typically have problems with self-worth and shame. Their fear is not being loved and to fill that void they learn to earn love and appreciation. Twos are inclined to present themselves as altruistic, but don't acknowledge their needs. They process information emotionally which is subjective, and when stressed they add instinctive action. And so, they act out their emotions, while reasoning is least employed. Their defense mechanism is *Repression*, pretending not being needy while presenting themselves as selfless and helpful. They tend to be dedicated, reliable, positive-minded, and people-oriented.

A healthy Two is altruistic, empathetic, and wants the best for others. They see themselves as loving, caring, and selfless, but others might see them as overbearing, intrusive, and manipulative.

Type Three (*Deceit*: overstating abilities)

Type Three grew up with a doting mother who approved of them and feel attached to the emotional nurturer (+M). They are attention seeking, and typically have problems with self-worth and shame. They don't feel they deserve the praise and accolades they received, and perceive themselves as not worthy. They need to fill this unworthiness void and learn to excel to earn praise. Being better than others makes them feel worthy and boosts their self-esteem. Their self-esteem is linked to job performance, and they persistently seek performance acknowledgment to feel good. They become ambitious and competitive, with ultimately a need to win. They process information intuitively and through reasoning, with their emotions least developed. Their defense mechanism is *Identification*, which means they apply attributes of others to themselves, making them look like and feel like you. They create a false persona with an image of success and pretend to never to fail. They tend to be assertive, insistent, logical, and controlled.

A healthy Three is realistic, ambitious, adaptable, and socially well-adjusted. They see themselves as admirable, desirable, and charming, but others may see them as self-promoting, grandiose, opportunistic, arrogant, and exploitative.

Type Four (*Envy*: preoccupation with what is missing)

Type Four grew up frustrated with both role models (-M/F), as they perceived the lack of attention as "there must be something wrong with me". They are attention seeking, and typically have problems with self-worth and shame. They did not identify with either parent and see themselves as "I am not like them." They learn to differentiate themselves from their role models and later the world as a whole. They fill the void of being without an identity by creating their own unique and different persona, which, in turn, makes it harder to fit in. They process information emotionally supported by rationalization, while instinctive doing is under-developed. Their defense mechanism is *Introjection*, and they apply attributes of their environment to themselves. They pretend not being ordinary enforcing their false image of being unique. They tend to be emphatic and demonstrative by being emotionally unavailable. When others notice them, and come to their aid, they are fulfilled, since they are apparently worth paying attention to.

A healthy Four is self-aware, an inspiration to others, individualistic, and emotionally true to themselves and others. They see themselves as different, sensitive, and gentle, but other may see them as individualistic, moody, irrational, and depressed.

Type Five (*Avarice*: retention with what they have)

Type Five grew up feeling rejected by both role models (~M/F). They felt ignored, unacknowledged, and noticed that actions speak louder than words. They are security seeking, and typically have problems with anxiety and fears. They felt they did not fit in the family unit, and learn to observe to anticipate the world. Fives like predictability. They hope to be acknowledged by presenting specialized knowledge. They process information rationally and are predisposed to detach their emotions to preserve objectivity. Instinctive doing is generally under-developed. Their defense mechanism is Isolation, giving them time to think and ultimately overthink. They pretend not feeling empty and incompetent while enforcing an image of being knowledgeable and competent. They tend to be withdrawn, imaginative, logical, and controlled.

A healthy Five is perceptive, inquisitive, and observant with tremendous insight and understanding. They see themselves as insightful, intelligent, and smart, but others may see them as pre-occupied, eccentric, provocative, and intellectually arrogant.

Type Six (*Fear*: to be without guidance)

Type Six grew up bonding with the Father (+F). They felt supported and relied on the guidance provided. They felt anxious and not safe without guidance and support. Their greatest fear is to be without guidance and support. They are security seeking, and typically have problems with fear and anxiety. To fill the void of potentially being without support, they learn to do what is expected of them, so they fit in and feel accepted. They process information intuitively and emotionally, with abstract thinking underdeveloped. Their defense mechanism is *Projection*, as they pretend to not feel personal rejection and enforce an image of loyalty and dutifulness. They tend to be emphatic, demonstrative, dedicated, and reliable.

A healthy Six is organized, persevering, and engaging. They see themselves as dependable, reliable, and trustworthy, but others may see them as dutiful, defensive, self-destructive while overestimating authority.

Type Seven (*Gluttony*: excess acquisition)

Type Seven grew up disconnected with the Mother (-M) as they felt affection and emotional nurturance was inadequate, giving them a feeling of emptiness. Their key fear is deprivation and to fill this void they nurture themselves through acquisition of new experiences and material needs. They are security seeking and typically have problems with anxiety and fears. They find happiness in new experiences but not within themselves. They are, therefore, experience-oriented. They process information rationally fueled by intuition, with emotions least developed. Like a Three, they have limited insight into the emotional impact they have on others. Their defense mechanism is *Rationalization* presenting an image of happiness, while pretending not to be anxious. Activity pre-occupation is a way to avoid the pain and anxiety of the lack of nurturance and personal value. They tend to be assertive, insistent, positive-minded, and experience-oriented.

A healthy Seven is spontaneous, enthusiastic, and productive. They see themselves as adventurous, lively, fun, and free-spirited, but others may see them as the ones who seek too much variety, erratic, reckless and excessive.

Type Eight (*Lust*: for power)

Type Eight grew up feeling rejected by the Mother (~M), who made them feel vulnerable and unprotected. Their fear is being harmed by others or being at the mercy of others. To fill the void of feeling vulnerable, they learn to take control with an "I am gonna get you before you get me" attitude. They are autonomy seeking, and typically have problems with anger and relating to others. When stressed they have a tendency to dominate, overwhelm, and present themselves with compensatory over-confidence. They process information intuitively and rationalize after the act. Their emotional connection with themselves and others is under-developed, and like the Three and Seven, they too have little idea about the emotional impact they have on others. Their defense mechanism is *Denial*, and they pretend not feeling vulnerable by presenting themselves as strong and powerful. They tend to be assertive, insistent, emphatic, and demonstrative.

A healthy Eight is confident, resourceful, and a true leader and someone who can make others believe in them. They see themselves as strong, action oriented and assertive, but others may see them as enterprising, intimidating, dictatorial, and domineering.

Type Nine (*Sloth*: conflict avoidance)

Type Nine grew up bonding with both role models (+M/F), and their emotional and physical needs were met. But also, they felt unacknowledged and unimportant. Somehow their perspective developed into "My voice is not important to you". Their biggest fear became abandonment, loss of support or loss of connection. To fill the void of potential loss of support, they learn to be amicable and agreeable. In the meantime, they are not expressing their personal thoughts and preferences. They are autonomy seeking, and typically have problems with anger repression and relating to others. Nines are passive, and they don't feel heard since they don't express themselves readily. Anger builds and eventually needs to come out. They process information rationally and emotionally, which do not mix very well. Objectivity and subjectivity are like oil and water. It takes time to match rational thought with emotions, which results in procrastination. Instinctive doing is inherently under-developed. Their defense mechanism is *Narcotization*, showing an image of peace and harmony and pretending there is no conflict. They tend to be withdrawn, imaginative, positive-minded, and people-oriented.

A healthy Nine is emotionally stable, self-accepting and an excellent negotiator. They typically see themselves as peaceful, easy-going, and relaxed, but others may see them as passive, complacent, neglectful, and appeasing.

"You can lead a horse to water, but you can't make it drink."
                                                        - Unknown.

7. Tickle the Theme

Influencing with Integrity

I say: *"Make the horse thirsty."*

Knowing key fears and needs of a person is helpful in any interpersonal relationship and will assist in developing cooperation and gain alliances. Understanding the core needs and the focal point of attention of each Type helps to emphasize strengths and de-emphasize weaknesses. We make others feel understood by seeing their perspective first and this requires perspective analysis or main theme recognition.

Assume you are selling a car, and you are aware of the core fear and needs of a potential buyer. Suppose you have a Two as a possible car buyer who emphasizes love and appreciation. Statements, that might resonate with a Two, may be, "Your friends will love this car and enjoy the comfort of the heated seats when you pick them up to go out to dinner!"

An image oriented Three, who seeks performance acknowledgment, needs his ego tickled from a different angle. What might resonate could be a statement like "You look great in this car, and your friends will see that too! They will admire and envy you when they see you driving up their driveway."

The security seeking Five, who is constantly aware of his surroundings, might want to hear something like "Not only is this car comfortable, it is also responsive and maneuverable. There are hardly any blind spots, and you can easily see what others are doing." The indecisive Nine has no need to not differentiate themselves and what might resonate is being like someone else. A Nine might respond to "I love this car, and these are the reasons why. That is why I would buy it."

Conflict resolution

Many issues in life are approached from an antagonistic and dualistic point of view. We only have to look at any sport and dualism is at its core. The American culture encourages opposition and competition. We face each other and fight to gain superiority. When we see things from a black and white or right versus wrong perspective, we become exclusive instead of inclusive. It is the winner versus the loser attitude.

Conflict resolution is often successful when you can satisfy the hidden needs of the other person which is often related to their key needs. Successful negotiations provide win-win solutions as the parties involved get what they want and often through an all too natural compromise. Positive changes will happen when we shift from blaming others to figuring out how we contributed to the problem and then find a solution.

Often times, tension builds during conflict and tempers flare. It is always better to stay calm and actively listen, instead of pointing out how wrong someone else is. Negotiate by understanding their perspective first and then nudge them in the direction you see fit. Good negotiators come to excellent conflict resolutions because they are aware of certain required key elements.

You can influence others with integrity and allow them to make a behavioral change on their own accord. The FBI's Behavioral Change Stairway shows us five steps toward change. The core of these steps is: understand their perspective, change their perspective by presenting an alternative, and allow them a choice to act on their changed perspective.

The Behavioral Change Stairway tells us in short:
1. *Active listening*: understand their perspective and make them feel you are on track with them. Stay calm, ask open-ended questions, and use brief statements. Summarize in your own words and make them feel heard and understood. This is where understanding key fears, needs, and strengths come in handy.

2. *Empathy*: You don't only need to understand where they are coming from; you also need to feel the way they do.
Feed each Type's key need:
1. I need to be right
2. I need to be loved
3. I need to be admired
4. I need to be myself
5. I need to be acknowledged
6. I need to follow rules
7. I need a new thrill
8. I need to be in charge
9. I need to be agreeable.

3. *Rapport*: Building rapport is making others recognize you feel the way they feel. Trust has its foundation in your personal ability to deal with a situation. Rapport is a major trust building block and has its foundation in setting an expectation pattern with healthy boundaries. You need to present yourself with clarity, tolerance, and fairness and allow others to build an expectation they can rely on. They learn to see you as consistent, reliable and dependable and feel they "know how to deal with you".

4. *Influence*: After gaining trust, you can start working the problem and find solutions mutually acceptable. In order to get what you want, you must allow others to get what they want as well.

5. *Behavioral change*: By gaining trust and a change in perspective, you also changed what they want. And with it, they volunteer cooperation. You just made the horse thirsty.

This process takes time. The following techniques are helpful reminders:
a. *Stay calm*. Emotional arousal creates tension, and an antagonistic view rears its ugly head. Staying calm will also slow down the conversation providing more time to think. Effective use of pauses and speaking slowly is helpful. Nonetheless, any situation requires measured responses and assertiveness might have to be met with equal energy.
b. *Ask; don't tell*. If we tell others what we think they should do, you take their choice away. It also gives others the right to tell us what to do. By asking questions, we learn to understand their perspective, and will be able to re-direct their needs by changing their perspective.

c. *Use euphemisms*. Instead of telling others what to do, tell them what you would like to see happen. This is an open-ended way of asking while still leaving the choice to others. Questions and subtle redirections provide a sense of control over choices.

d. *Give them the last word*. By giving others the opportunity to have the last word, they feel important, "right" and like a winner.

It's Thanksgiving, and the table is set with traditional foods. The two parents, a Two and a NIne, smile at their nineteen-year-old Nine, thirteen-year-old Eight, and ten-year-old Four. The Nine's perspective is conflict avoidance. The Eight needs to take charge, and the Four withdraws to gain attention and focuses on what others have.
The children approach the well-set table; the Eight hurries up front with plate in hand, eager to get started. The Eight is naturally assertive and takes the lead role. The Four, saddened, drops his head and said "She always goes first." The Nine replies "yeah, but that is okay. Somebody has to start". The Four answers with "but what if she takes the green cupcake I want?" The Nine tells the Four to get the cupcake and get back in line. In the meantime, the Nine patiently lets others take their turn.

And so, the nineteen-year-old Nine matched the hidden need of the thirteen-year-old Eight to be in charge (Lust for power), the ten-year-old Four's need to have what others could have had (Envy for what others have), and her own need to keep the peace (Sloth or indolence to maintain support). Nines are wonderful peacekeepers and often ever so subtle ways.

"People write the way they behave and say exactly what they mean."
- Marcel Elfers

8. Handwriting is behavior

In English, we write from left to right while moving up and down. This is essentially a behavior. There is a time component in written notes as we know the starting point and final destination. A handwriting change reveals anxieties, fears, past hurts and is a reflection of our mental health. In a literal sense, we *behave* moving forward, and the ink trail left behind is like a seismographic recording. One of the beauties of graphology is, we can see an author behaving without meeting them. It is efficient, cheap, and revealing.

Written notes contain two major components. The content reveals perspectives and writing movements expose behavioral tendencies. The Behavioral Pathways within the Enneagram describe the natural development of behavioral style and motivation. We can conclude the Enneagram, handwriting analysis, and perspective analysis are a natural fit.

8.1 Freud

Freud's psychoanalytic model returns in both the Enneagram and handwriting analysis. He described the instinctive pleasure ID, the mediating realistic Ego, and the critical thinking and moral gatekeeping Super-Ego.

We are born with natural abilities and have biological needs to fulfill. We have needs like food, safety, and pleasure. We initially pursue those instinctively and without rational thought (ID). As we grow up and become consciously aware of our environment, we start to integrate environmental demands into our instinctive choices. We learn to reason and inhibit spontaneous action in order to be accepted by others (Ego).

We blend internal rules with the external demands parental guidance and later society bestowed upon us. The willingness to withhold action in the name of external inhibiting factors is what Freud described as Super Ego. In essence, this is our inner voice or our imagined internalized authority figure.

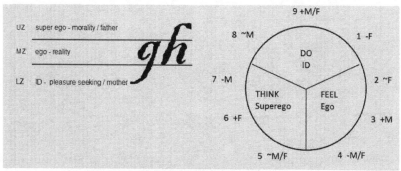

Figure 23: Freud in handwriting and Enneagram

Handwriting analysis recognizes three zones. Letters like a, e, and o are in the Mid-Zone (MZ) and so are the bodies of letters like b, g, and p.
The extensions above the Mid-Zone are the Upper-Zone (UZ) whereas the extensions below the Mid-Zone are Lower-Zone (LZ) structures.

Freud's principles are applied to handwriting, and we could argue for the Mid-Zone to be the most critical zone. It is the social zone where we experience our reality and recognize our Self. This is also where our subconscious pleasure seeking ID (LZ) connects with the moral gatekeeping conscious Super-Ego zone (UZ). Healthy individuals have balance in the three zones. In graphology, we are particularly interested in changes away from the norm and in what zone these distortions occur.

The ID, Ego, and Super-Ego principle returns in the Enneagram and recognizes, just like handwriting analysis does, the three principles interrelate and overlap everywhere. In handwriting, ID is emphasized in the Lower-Zone, and the Enneagram Types 9, 4, and 5 tend to have problems with instinctive subconscious Doing (ID). These Types might show distortions in the Lower-Zone, especially shorter and without loops.
The Superego Types 6, 1, and 2 are principled and dedicated to rule adherences. They have problems with rationalization and might exaggerate the Upper-Zone. The Ego Types 3, 7 and 8 have problems integrating their emotions and might show Mid-Zone distortions.

96

	Identifies with	Behavioral style	Freudian	Typical problems
Types 3,7,8	Mother	Assertive	Ego	≠ emotional connectedness
Types 6,1,2	Father	Compliant	Super-ego	≠ rationalization deductive reasoning
Types 9,4,5	Both	Withdrawn	ID	≠ instinctive doing procrastination

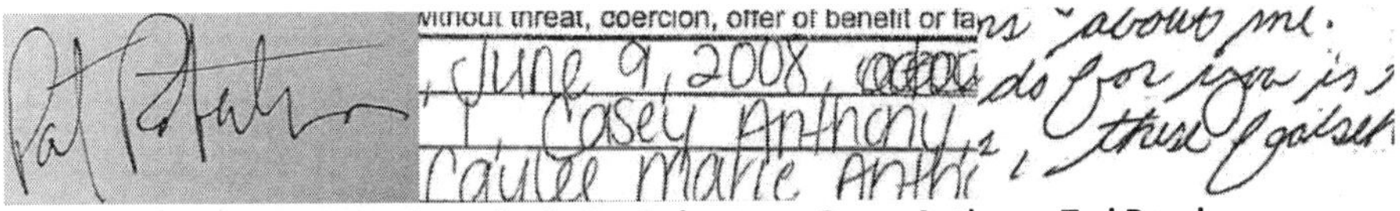

without threat, coercion, offer of benefit or fans `about me.`
June 9, 200X
I, Casey Anthony,
Caylee Marie Anth

Figure 24: Zonal emphasis Pat Robertson, Casey Anthony, Ted Bundy

As a handwriting expert, I see correlations between writing behaviors and the behavioral patterns described in the Enneagram. Pat Roberson's (Super-ego) signature shows an inflated Upper-Zone. This zone reflects on our spirituality, abstract thinking and is where we set moral principles. Overemphasis on this zone implies an above average imagination. Robertson is the evangelical Christian, who claimed Haiti was punished with an earthquake in 2010 because they had a pact with the devil dating back to the 1700's.

Casey Anthony's (Ego) handwriting emphasizes the Mid-Zone. This zone is indicative how we interact with others in our day to day life, how we see ourselves, and where we act out our moral principles. It is the zone of the "here and now". Mid-Zone emphasis implies immaturity, lack of long-term planning, and a need for immediate gratification.

Ted Bundy's (ID) overemphasized his Lower-Zone and mirrored his sexual overdrive. The biological necessities zone can be materialistic or sexual in nature. It also reflects on drive, determination, and emotional experiences from the past. His unusual high drive and determination, as shown in the long and overinflated Lower-Zone, matches his multi-state crimes, multiple escapes from prison, and his criminal past.

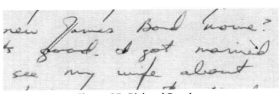

Figure 25: Richard Ramirez

Without going into too many details, we observe that Richard Ramirez was impulsive as he wrote fast with a stronger forward slant. The exaggerated length of the Lower-Zone and his t-bars denote a strong drive.

These features are frequently seen in Type 7 who felt deprived and seek to nurture themselves through new experiences. Their core need makes them enthusiastic, active, busy bees and adventurous. His heavy and longer Lower-Zone implies strong and purposeful action (ID or instinctive doing). The under-sized Mid-Zone reflects on reality imbalance(Ego - reduction of Self in Society). The oversized Upper-Zone, including the unnecessary looped d-stem and t-stem, magnifies ideations. Ramirez was naturally assertive; ego driven and in constant search for the next thrill. He became hyperactive and scattered in his thinking and overstepped boundaries through his criminal activities.

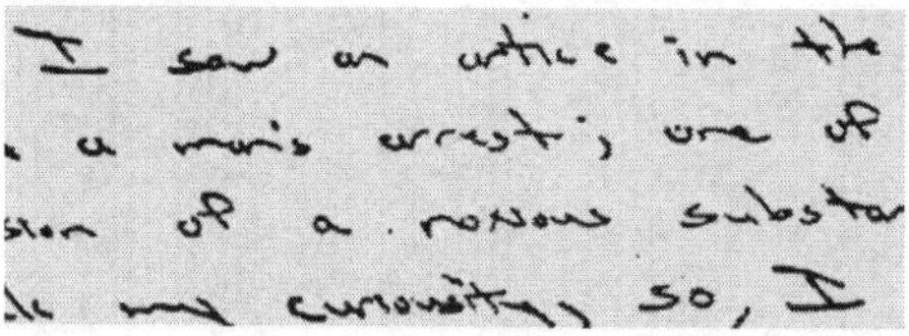

Figure 26: Timothy McVeigh

Timothy McVeigh (Type 5) was withdrawn and reserved as he wrote slowly with a backward slant. This writing shows he is a careful planner, keeps others at bay, and moves forward with caution. This is in line with reduced instinctive doing (ID). The Oklahoma City bomber made a statement for a cause (Government overreach) and attacked from a safe distance. His violence was an act of revenge against government intrusions. He cited the Waco, TX siege and the Ruby Ridge incident. Like his handwriting, he kept his distance from his target and set off a car bomb.

Another Type 5, who also felt unacknowledged and needed to be heard for his insights, is Ted Kaczynski. The Unabomber offered his view of the world through his 35,000 word Manifesto, and he too kept his distance from his victims. The Unabomber was active for many years living a nihilistic lifestyle.

Type Threes often grow up with a doting mother who approved of them. They don't feel worthy off the accolades received, feel pushed to do better and need to earn admiration by excelling at tasks. They learn to link their self-esteem to job approval and seek attention through performance acknowledgment. They learn to chase job excellence and become overly ambitious. To protect their egos, they will exaggerate what they have to offer to make them look better than they are and create an image of a "Winner". Healthy ambition can turn into competitiveness and downright exploitation. If they cannot be better than someone else, the only thing left for them is to put others down with arrogance and condescension.

They lean towards slow, deliberate and vertical writing, giving them more time to think. This reduces spontaneity and gives them sufficient time for a calculated and measured response. Type Three's vice is *Deceit*, and their handwriting shows to be logical and methodical presenting themselves with false clarity and conceitedness. They hide their true intentions behind their lack of spontaneity and calculated identities. This is called Façade or persona writing. The disconnected lettering implies *"naturalness is replaced by precision[19]"*, difficulty bonding with others, and emotional detachment.

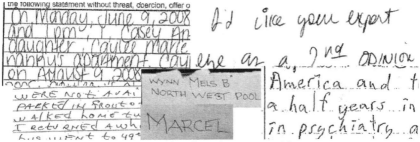

Figure 27: facade and persona writing

A Three presented an online course as if it was a college level program. He managed to charge fees similar to college fees but failed to deliver in quality. After the course, he attempted to sign students up with repetitive phone calls to make more money. He called me three times in four-week intervals with the same story line at exactly 7 pm on Tuesday nights. He stated he was in the courthouse awaiting trial against the "great Jesse Dines". Which courthouse is open at 7 pm every Tuesday night? And exactly in four weeks intervals he sits in the hallway waiting to face exactly the same "great Jesse Dines"? Threes overestimate personal abilities, do not see failure and use deception for personal gain.

A Type Three used to work at a gas station and had a gun pulled on him. He told me "I knew he was not going to shoot me because if he wanted to, he would already have pulled the trigger. So I told the guy to hang on and let me grab my baseball bat to beat the hell out of him". Threes overestimate abilities and are blind to personal failure.

---

[19] Kimon Iannetta: "Danger between the lines" (2008) p.204

Personal Pronoun I

The Personal Pronoun I (PPI) is arguably the most significant letter as it mirrors our self-image. It reflects on how we see ourselves, our self-esteem, our identification with role models, and how we interact with our environment. Significant changes from the norm can be indicative of a poor self-concept.

Figure 28: PPI's

A: the PPI slant heavily backward suggesting the author keeps his distance emotionally. The forward slant in the rest of his writing implies emotional impulsivity. The PPI has two breaks indicative of high levels of anxiety as related to self-concept. This is likely linked to a difficult upbringing. Authors like this keep others at bay (backward slant) because they don't trust to know how to deal with others. The lack of trust is probably based on parental inconsistencies (anxiety breaks in PPI).

B: The three PPIs are shaped differently. The top portion is related to identification with the nurturing role model (M) and suggests a fluctuating identification with the author's mother. This can be an indicator of ambivalence with the mother and would support Type Five and Eight (~ M/F and ~M) for instance. The PPIs drop down below the baseline and indicative of poor urge control.

C: These two PPIs vary in size while the first one drops below the baseline. The variable initial hook is related to identification with the patriarchal role model (F) and implies anxiety and frustration. This could be a trait consistent with a Type One and Four (-F and -M/F).

D: The PPI is written in a reversed pattern. This suggests an author who goes his own way and may be non-conventional.

PPI and MZi

As a general rule, positive emotions have a tendency to expand and negative emotions are likely to contract. We only have to imagine a football player scoring a touchdown, and he will jump up and down with arms up in the air. Yet, the defensive back hangs his head and shoulders. In writing, we see such expansion and contraction in letter size and slant for instance.

The Mid-Zone is the social zone where we present ourselves socially, interact with and adapt to others. The Mid-Zone i (MZi) denotes our self-concept within a social environment. The size and slant can tell very much how an author sees herself.

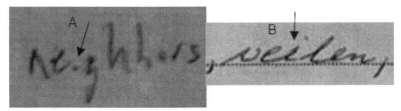

Figure 29: MZi

A: MZi is undersized, and this author wanted to disappear.
B: healthy MZi with consistent size and slant.

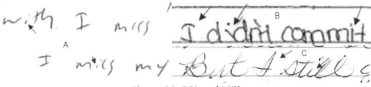

Figure 30: PPI and MZi

Combining the PPI and the MZi can tell a whole lot about an author. The PPI is our personal business shingle, if you will, and is how we present ourselves to the outside world. The MZi reveals how confident we present ourselves in social settings.
A: The PPI has a healthy size but in the second line shrinks. The MZi tends to be smaller suggesting this author is insecure with fluctuating confidence levels.
B: The PPI is undersized, and the MZi is healthy. The author presents herself more confident in public than she feels. Note the low sitting t-bar which is consistent with lower self-esteem.
C: PPI and MZi healthy size and this implies confident social skills with a healthy self-esteem. Note how the t-bar sits high confirming her self-esteem.

The M

We looked at the PPI and the MZi revealing our self-esteem and our social confidence. Another interesting letter is the M.

The letter M has three legs and two arcades, or humps. The first leg (A1) is the equivalent of the PPI (self). The second leg (A2) equates to intimates (family, friends), and the third leg (A3) to the world (others in our immediate environment).

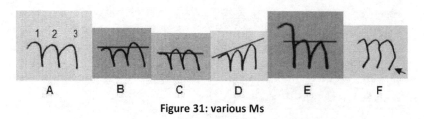

Figure 31: various Ms

The letter M shows how we see ourselves in relationship to family and the world.

A: The height of the three legs is about equal suggesting balance and harmony of self within our environment. Such authors are likely content with the position they have in the world.

B: The third leg is substantially higher than the first two and suggests an author who puts more value on society than himself or family. They might be rule followers or rely on authority figures.

C: Both the second and third legs are higher than the first and suggest the author places family and society above himself.

D: The legs are rising in height and imply self-consciousness or fear of ridicule. They are often not comfortable meeting new people and feel they are being scrutinized.

E: The first leg, "the self", is higher. This relates to self-importance and an authoritative posture. If very high, egocentricity and narcissism come to mind.

F: The backward ending is unusual and a difficult to produce stroke. In my experience, it is only seen in slow writing. Such authors are deliberate, mock others, and use sarcasm to protect their self-loathing personality. They tend to be sensitive themselves and become furious when others criticize them. They do to others what was done to them in their childhood.

In sum, the PPI, MZi, and the M can tell very much about how a person relates to their social environment, their confidence levels, and how they see they fit in the world.

8.2 Handwriting and mental health

An individual who mentally declines will deteriorate in their behaviors, including handwriting behaviors. Handwriting is a great and inexpensive tool to get the gist of the author's mental health. Writing of healthy authors is structured, disciplined and consistent.

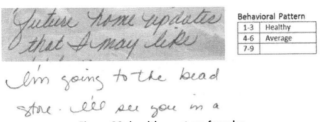

Behavioral Pattern	
1-3	Healthy
4-6	Average
7-9	

Figure 32: healthy mature females

Handwriting of unhealthy authors lack structure and is undisciplined with gross inconsistencies.

Behavioral Pattern	
1-3	
4-6	Average
7-9	Unhealthy

Figure 33: Various authors unhealthy

Excessive traits like chaotic, bizarre, pent up anger, unusual structures, anxiety, rage, or overly controlled are signs of mental breakdown and exaggeration of ego defense mechanisms and opinion rigidity comes along with it.

Twos are children growing up feeling unloved and under-appreciated by their protector, guide, and provider (~F). The patriarchal role model's job is to develop a child's independence away from the emotional nurturer; however, Twos take on the role of substitute nurturer. Twos are positive-minded, people-oriented, dedicated to being good, and reliable. They are social, warm, giving, and thoughtful. We can expect to see these character traits in their handwriting.

For instance, rising baselines and rising t-bars reflect on optimism or "positive-minded". Mid-Zone emphasis and rounded structures suggest warm social traits or "people-oriented". Steady baselines and uniformity are linked to steadiness and reliability. Twos are self-forgetting by repressing their needs, and retracing[20] can be expected.

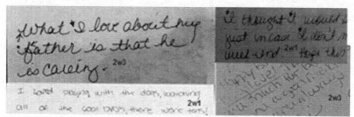

Figure 34: various Twos

The Twos, the People Pleasers, show a general Mid-Zone emphasis with many rounded features. Note the ambivalence toward the Father as shown in the PPIs and marked with arrows.

8.3 Stability and instability

In the big scheme of things, we can spot mental stability and instability through our writing. The beauty of handwriting is, you can see behaviors without meeting someone. Although we won't know what the cause for the instability is by handwriting alone, we do know whether an author is unstable or not.

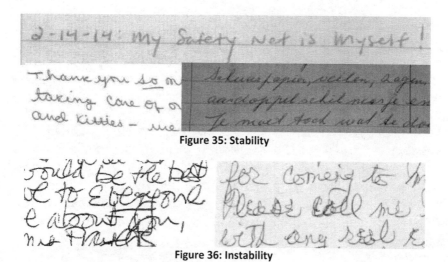

Figure 35: Stability

Figure 36: Instability

---

[20] Retracing is retracing a down stroke with an upstroke like in the h, m, n

104

Substantial variations in size, shape, slant, baseline, and unusual use of space might all be indicative of mental instability.

Bizarre Barry

I met Bizarre Barry for the first and last time at my local pool hall. He walked in with certitude, was tense and intense, and not very social. He had dark, deep-set and judgmental eyes. He challenged the pool table without introducing himself and signed up for Karaoke. His turn was up at the table, and six players had to wait for him to finish his dance with a woman he never met. When he finally arrived and started the game, he made two shots and left to sing Karaoke with gross disregard for others. For the non-pool players, this is like swiping your finger through an untouched wedding cake before the bride had a chance to cut it. The six players decided to play on without him. He came back to play pool and was perturbed telling everybody loudly "This is wrong! This is just plain wrong!" He was angered and explosive; he left the hall and was never seen again. And then I found his karaoke slip under the pool table. I was mighty pleased.

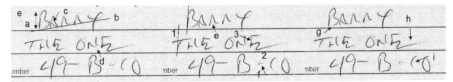

Figure 37: bizarre Barry

The handwriting behavior matched his observed behaviors and perspective. The writing is primarily in the Mid-Zone (Ego). The structures are distorted, inconsistent, and odd, implying he lacks self-discipline, self-control and difficulty channeling his energies appropriately. In other words, *"people behave the way they write."*

- a: good size Capital implies confidence, misplaced or not = matches the way he walked in
- b: upward slant baseline means optimism = matches expectation positive outcomes to his actions
- c: letter A crossbar slants down suggests dominance = matches domineering attitude
- d: gaps in letters mean poor handling of social situations = Karaoke, dancing with disregard for other players
- 1: down stroke slant variations suggests emotional instability

- e: disguised lettering implies hiding true intentions = comes to play, sings Karaoke instead
- 3: The E is a very tense and odd letter formation = strange structures, unusual thinking patterns
- 2: initial hook implies irritability = "that is wrong; that is sooo wrong".
- f: inconsistent forward strokes suggest instability = he seemed unstable in this first encounter
- g: open B bottom means hypocrisy = it's okay for him to let six players wait, but not for him to wait
- h: excess forward movement implies impulsivity = he left angry after one dance, one song, and no pool
- i: curved down strokes implies pressure from father = left with minimal criticism

Bizarre Barry's handwriting, verbal, and non-verbal behaviors were a perfect match. The writing behavior and my brief experience with him suggest he is an average Type One. Angry, entitled, demanding, and hypocritical.

As we will see later, the characteristics of an average Type One are
- autonomy seeking (took charge)
- have issues relating to others (poor social skills)
- are anger driven (intense and explosive)
- abide by strict rule adherence (his rules in right and wrong)
- tend to be critical and judgmental

Although these traits are consistent with a Type One, and he likely was, we need to remain open to other possibilities. For instance, a disintegrated Type Seven, a 2w1 or a 9w1. He was too critical for the Nine's amicable and agreeable point of view. Twos are likely to adjust to others, and his rigidity seems to exclude a Two. Type One seems, therefore, a very good option and is most likely the correct Type.

Sudden changes

Casey Anthony was acquitted of being responsible for the death of her almost three-year-old daughter Caylee. The story line was riddled with unusual excuses, far-fetched misrepresentations, and demonstrative lies. Of course, it all began when her mother, Cindy Anthony, demanded seeing her granddaughter and Casey explained that she had not seen her daughter in thirty-one days. Cindy puzzled, suspicious, and angered involved law-enforcement, and the ball started rolling.

Casey and her family wrote statements for police. Here is a portion of Casey's first page:

the following statement without threat, coercion, offer of benefit or favor by any persons whomsoever.
On Monday, June 9, 2008, between 9am and 1pm, I, Casey Anthony, took my daughter, Caylee Marie Anthony, to her nanny's apartment. Caylee will be 3-years-old on August 9, 2008. She was born on August 9,

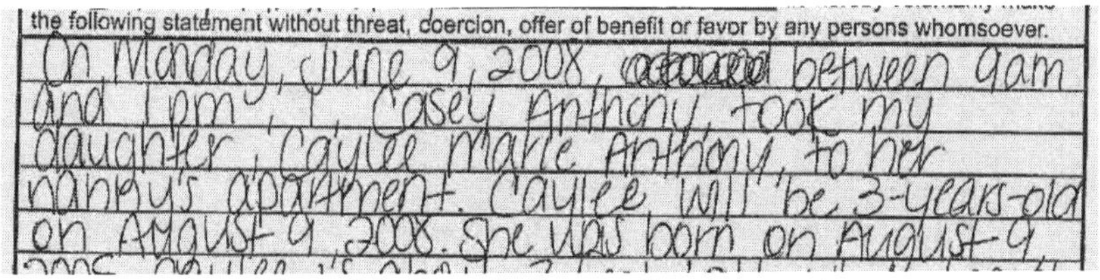

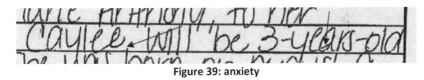

Figure 38: Casey Anthony police statement

At first glance, it looks well written, logical, and controlled. But put your detective hat on and observe the writing as behavior. Do you see anything that might be unusual or out of the ordinary?

Caylee will be 3-years-old

Figure 39: anxiety

In the fourth line, we see a sudden change in her daughter's name Caylee. The first "e" cramps up in the body and drops below the baseline. The connection stroke lost its roundness, and the second "e" floats suddenly above the baseline. In the word "years", the "e" has a sudden long and impulsive final stroke extension. In other words, Casey lost control over her penmanship and is a change from her norm. Anxiety causes sudden changes like this one, and the question is: "what was she thinking off?" Did she already know Caylee would not reach her third birthday? Or, less likely, was she anxious about her child missing for 31 days?

George Anthony, her father, made the following statement[21]:
"On July 15, 2008, at approximately 20.05 pm, my spouse (Cindy) called my cell phone. I immediately attempted to return her call, and only got her voicemail. I called our landline # and also got a voicemail. I immediately then called my son, Lee told him I would appreciate him checking on his mom, told him briefly about Casey again, and mom & I are upset. At 20.35 pm, I finally got a hold of my spouse by cell, and she asked when I would be home. I told her I would be home about 10-10.30 pm. Arriving at 9.50 pm, my spouse was in our garage, crying upset + told me that Caylee Marie (our

[21] public records

granddaughter) was missing, taken a month ago, by a person by the name of Zany. "

At first glance, the content does not seem unusual but read it again with the added underlinings:
On July 15, 2008, at approximately 20.05 pm, <u>my spouse</u> (Cindy) called my cell phone. I immediately attempted to return her call, and only got her voicemail. I called our landline # and also got a voicemail. I immediately then called <u>my son</u>, Lee told him I would appreciate him checking on his <u>mom</u>, told him briefly about (....?....) Casey again, and <u>mom</u> & I are upset. At 20.35 pm, I finally got a hold of <u>my spouse</u> by cell, and she asked when I would be home. I told her I would be home about 10-10.30 pm. Arriving at 9.50 pm, my <u>spouse</u> was in our garage, crying upset + told me that Caylee Marie (our <u>granddaughter</u>) was missing, taken a month ago, by a person by the name of Zany.

Casey did not receive the family connection ("my daughter") and is a sudden change. George subconsciously distanced himself from Casey and the question is, *"Why did he distance himself?"*
This emotional distancing is a give-away revealing his perspective and his expectation pattern regarding Casey. Apparently George expected, or at minimum included the possibility, that Casey was involved. And that means only one thing: She must have displayed other questionable behaviors prior to the disappearance of Caylee and, in his eyes, she lost her credibility. At the time of the writing, George likely expected Casey could very well be involved in Caylee's disappearance.
Casey's signature changed as she awaited trial in jail. She must have been under a lot of pressure and signing with handcuffs might be difficult. Her parents remained supportive, but Casey distanced herself from her family and resorted to first name basis only.

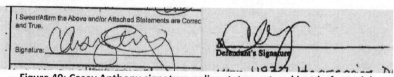

Figure 40: Casey Anthony signature police statement and just before trial

Over time, Casey Anthony's signature changed to first name only. The police report signature on the left show self-protective traits, whereas the signature during her time in jail lacks the last name and is indicative of emotional disconnect with her family.

And so, the lack of "my daughter" made clear George had his suspicions and the lack of her last name in her signature revealed her distancing perspective. There is meaning in what was not said.

Casey Anthony's handwriting and behavioral style is consistent with a Type Three. Threes are assertive, insistent, logical, and controlled. Their vice is *Deceit* through identification with others and they remain calm during stressful situations. Casey did not tell about the disappearance of her daughter for thirty-one days [blind to failure] and went as far as bringing detectives to her place of non-existing employment [Vice: Deceit]. These traits reveal overestimation of personal abilities and the expectation others are not bright enough to notice [arrogance].

8.4 Danger signs in handwriting

Many people are interested in or just curious regarding handwriting and criminality. Handwriting is certainly a behavior and, like reading non-verbals clues, needs to be interpreted within context. A non-verbal clue like crossing your arms can be a defensive posture, or the room might just be cold. Touching one's nose can be a sign of deception. As anxiety increases, the sweat glands around the nose open up and tiny sweat droplets create a temporary itch. Yet, it is a sign of anxiety and not necessarily a lie. Context is everything.

A lie detector is a misnomer as well. The measurements taken by a polygraph are recordings of changes in blood pressure, heart rate, skin conductivity or sweat gland productivity and breathing patterns. It is believed lying creates uncontrollable physiological responses secondary to increase in anxiety. Responses that change from a personal norm suggest an increase in nervousness and are probably linked to deception. The polygraph measures anxiety levels and deception is a mere interpretation within context.

There are no definite signs pointing to danger or criminality in handwriting either. However, there are writing traits implying core characteristics consistent with the potential for someone losing control and asserting themselves by overstepping boundaries. The strongest indicators are *mental instability* and *loss of perspective*.
Any handwriting trait needs to be interpreted and build on the framework of the Global View. We can integrate writing behavior (*how* they write) and

the author's perspective (*what* they wrote) with known past behavioral choices. This triad builds a reasonable expectation for future choices.

Danger signs in handwriting[22] need to be interpreted by combining traits within its context and not by stand-alone traits. There are many mitigating circumstances to be considered and it is important to not jump to premature conclusions.

Handwriting behavioral traits implying problematic behavioral tendencies are frequently excessive in nature. In general, a person, who could be considered at risk for overstepping social boundaries, could have some of the following characteristics:
- mental instability: various traits like variations in slant, baseline, spacing, inconsistent pen pressure.
- feels entitled: oversized capitals, very tall "d" and "t" stems
- assertiveness: strong forward slant, forward thrust strokes, heavy down strokes, larger capitals, good size MZi, larger PPI.
- emotional intensity: heavy pressure, repetitive overwriting, thickened periods, club strokes.
- uncontrollable urges: sudden forward slant, letters dropping below the baseline, sudden unexpected pressure variations.
- decisiveness: forceful t- bars, down-slanting crossbars, heavy stroke endings.

Mental instability
There are many handwriting traits suggesting mental instability and most of them are clearly visible. Signs like too much variation in size, slant, spacing, pressure patterns, and letter formations. At the other end of the spectrum, it can be overly controlled out of fear of losing control. Those with mental instability, stress, and anxiety are predisposed to have lesser quality coping mechanisms in place.

---

[22] Recommendation: Danger between the Lines by Kimon Iannetta

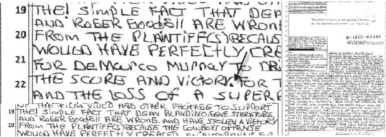
Figure 41: Overly controlled

This is the handwriting of an inmate suing the NFL over a decisive call reversal. The writing has signs of high anxiety levels, is slow and overly controlled. Note how he writes two lines per line number. He fills the whole available space in on the page. Such traits suggest he crowds others out, is controlling, domineering and unconventional. The very thick periods suggest pent-up anger. Kimon Iannetta wrote, *"Dot grinding frequently indicates resentful silence[23]"*.

The pent up anger, his attempts to control himself, and his word selection suggest he is in the Autonomy / Anger Triad and probably a Type One.

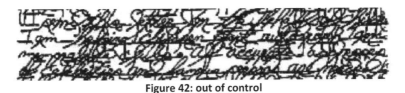
Figure 42: out of control

It is hard to believe this is actual handwriting. When you see writing this much out of control, would you invite him to babysit your child?

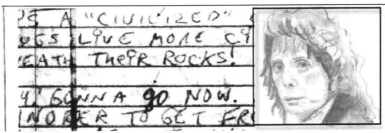
Figure 43: Phil Spector - visible variations

Phil Spector's handwriting was messy because of size, slant, pressure, and letter formation variations. The man who invented the "wall of sound" was

---

[23] Kimon Iannetta : "Danger between the Lines" (2008) p. 112-114

convicted of second-degree murder. Erratic pressure shows the author is not able to control his energy output. This is often due to uncontrollable urges implying an emotionally labile individual.

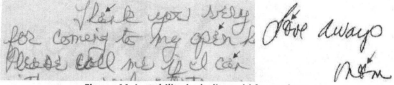

Figure 44: Instability including odd formations

Two mature females have additional structures on top of the Mid-Zone letters. The one on the left is unstable, has odd formations, and seems highly anxious. The extra structures on top of the Mid-Zone letters suggest excess imagination and potentially mixing fantasy and reality without being able to distinguish what is real or not.

Entitlement

Entitlement is in a sense self-approval. This can come in the form of high self-esteem or as over-compensation for lack of self-esteem.

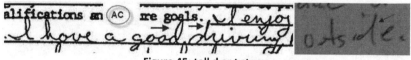

Figure 45: tall d or t stems

The letter "d" represents how we view our value system. Tall stems in the letter "d" imply entitlement. This trait might be linked to an overestimation of self-worth, over-confidence, pride and maybe arrogance. The sample marked AC is Ariel Castro, a Type Three, who imprisoned three young girls for about ten years.

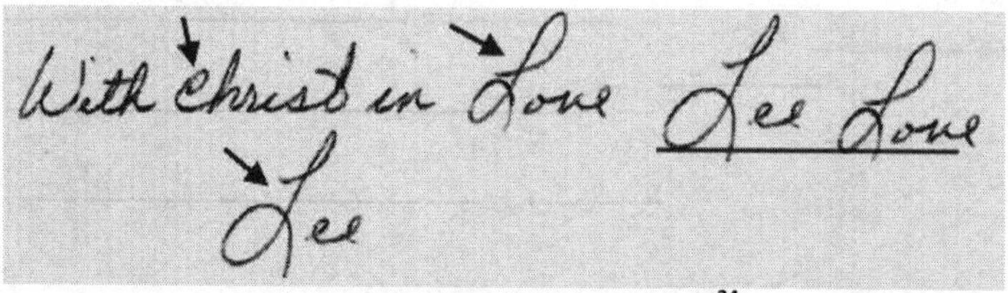

Figure 46: Aileen "Lee" Wuornos[24]

---

[24] Kimon Iannetta: "Danger between the Lines (2008) p. 273

Entitlement as compensation for low self-esteem is also a real possibility. Notice how the capital in "Christ" is much smaller than the capital in "Love" and "Lee". The name "Lee" has the largest capital of all implying self-importance. Wuornos was executed for multiple murders.

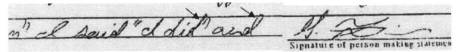

Figure 47: George Zimmerman entitlement

Zimmerman uses larger capitals in his signature, tall "d" stems, and an average size PPI. As a Type One, he failed to see gray areas and was emphatically sure Trayvon Martin was a burglar. His certainty was likely fueled by self-approval as the tall "d" stems imply.

Uncontrollable urges

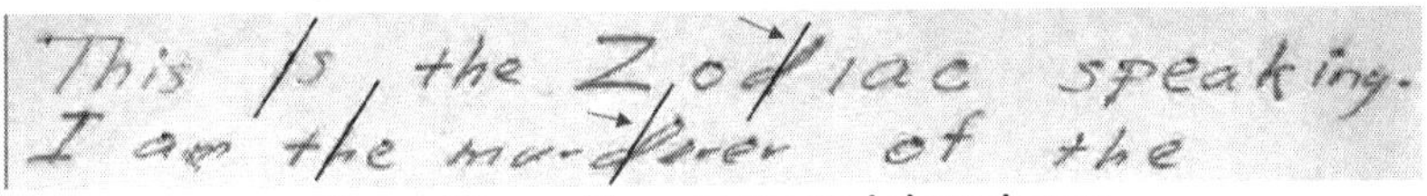

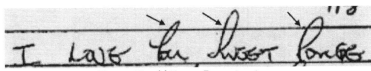

Figure 48: a sudden unexpected slant change

The Zodiac was never identified, but he suffered from sudden emotional outbursts. We see the sudden forward slant in the stem of the letter "d" which suggests a sudden loss of control. The i-dot and the period after the word "speaking" reflect on obsessiveness and pent up anger.

Figure 49: odd Upper-Zone structures

Russell Williams, the former Canadian Air Force Colonel, has been convicted of murder, rape, and forcible confinement. The odd looped structures are unexpected sweeps into the Upper-Zone and don't belong. Such distortions into the Upper-Zone imply distorted thinking patterns and strong potential for amorality.

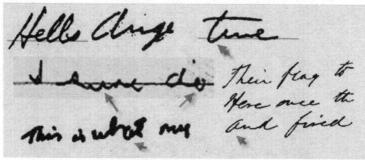

Figure 50: letters drop below baseline

Letters dropping below an established baseline, the social boundary line, may indicate unconscious and uncontrollable urges. Instinctive doing without thinking is a real possibility. Authors, whose letters overshoot the baseline boundary, might also overstep social boundaries.

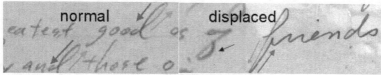

Figure 51: displaced pressure

Generally speaking, down strokes are made contracting the hand, are action oriented and should have heavier pressure than upstrokes. The upstrokes reflect on our ability to relax and let go. An author who reverses the pattern has poor control over his energy release and his personality might lack flexibility to adapt.

Extreme decisiveness

Figure 52: club strokes[25]

A letter thickening at the end looks like a club and happens when the author increases pen pressure at the end of the task. Club strokes are the result of increased mental intensity and are linked to extreme decisiveness. Try to write a t-cross bar with a really heavy ending and feel how that increases bodily tension. What if you feel that way all the time? This particular stroke,

---

[25] Kimon Iannetta : "Danger between the lines" page 101-103

when combined with signs of instability and aggressiveness might be indicative of an author capable of brutality.

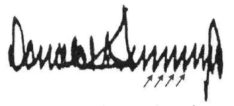

Figure 53: Angular connecting strokes

Strokes connecting one letter to the next with sharp angles where roundness is expected imply the author is disciplined, unyielding, and can be emotionally harsh and detached. The tag line "You're fired" without explanation is befitting. Donald Trump is in the Assertive group (3,7,8), and some see him as an Eight, others as a Three.

Bizarre formations

Figure 54: bizarre formation Upper-Zone and Mid-Zone

Former Air Force Colonel showed odd structures in the Upper-Zone and Mid-Zone. This suggests unrealistic ideation and social confusion. He burglarized homes, stole women's underwear and posed in them within the privacy of his home. Just remember: bizarre writing means peculiar behavior as a consequence of twisted thought processes.

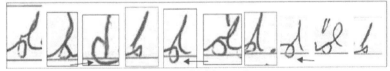

Figure 55: odd d formations

The letter "d" is of particular interest as it reflects on our personal value system. This author has very strong variations and barely writes any "d" the same. Substantial distortions, twists, and unusual formations like these are a good indication of non-conformity and mental instability. In three of the ten "d's", we also see the body of the "d" dropping below the baseline implying reduced urge control. Such authors have distorted personal views and act outside acceptable standards, norms and values.

Handwriting evaluation

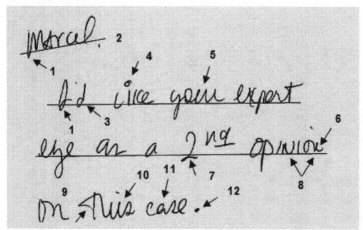

Figure 56: expertise request

This sample is of a mature male and has Mid-Zone emphasis which is our social zone or the "here-and-now zone". The writing is somewhat inconsistent in letter formation, size and spacing implying some instability. He fits the Type Three pattern by his known behaviors and there are significant traits supporting this Type, shown in *italics*.

1. The PPI drops below the baseline and suggests unpleasant subconscious urges affecting personal belief, behavior, and value system[26]. This is especially significant with the PPI and also seen in the first leg of the M, or "self". Such authors tend to overdo things in hidden and sneaky ways. *Assertive and Insistent.*

2. The baseline rise in the name implies optimism, albeit temporarily. Note the size of the capital M is smaller as compared to his PPI. *Vanity and self-importance.*

3. The "d" stem does not come down to the baseline and fell short coming back to reality. This hesitation suggests he was not forthcoming with the request. *Deception, hiding true intentions.*

4. The circular dot is unusual and draws attention like 16-year-old schoolgirls tend to do. It is a sign of emotional immaturity. *Emotional shallowness.*

5. Some words are hard to read when seen by themselves. The word "your" is clear but only within the context of the sentence. Disguised lettering is an escape route, with a "no, I didn't mean that" attitude. *Deception, ambiguity, hiding true intentions.*

---

[26] Kimon Iannetta: "Danger between the Lines" (2008) p. 157-158

6. The "n" final stroke bends inwards. This is called a "shark's tooth" and suggest covertly using other people. Such authors are intelligent, cunning, with excellent psychological insight in others and know how to manipulate for personal gain. *Deception, hiding true intentions.*

7. The number 2 is enlarged and drops below the baseline. Exaggeration is a sign of the opposite and combined with the increased spacing suggests an ulterior motive. *Deception, hiding true intentions.*

8. Inconsistent letter formation like mixing printing and cursive suggests an adaptable and flexible attitude and might mean indecision. This is seen in the "Aa" and "Nn". *Adaptability is a major part of the Three's ego-defense mechanism: Identification.*

9. The lack of pen-lift in the "t" is called a "tied structure" or a "butterfly stroke." The unwillingness to lift the pen where it should be is indicative of persistence and tenacity. *Hardworking, competitive.*
Note also how the "t-s" tend to be on the tall side. This implies vanity and pride in accomplishments. *A need to excel at tasks.*

10. The MZi tends to be larger and he feels confident in social settings. An oversized MZi suggests overstating self-importance. *Assertive, overstating abilities in public, failure blindness.*

11. The last word "case" is written smaller than the rest of the writing. The letters "ca" cramped up significantly, and the "se" mildly enlarged once again. Cramping up like this suggests a negative emotional relationship with a word and suggests there was no real case. *Deception, hiding true intentions.*

12. Letters or periods that are overwritten suggest compulsiveness and obsessiveness. Such authors have an intrusive thought causing them to repeat the stroke. A ground-in period implies irritability, tension, resentment, and pent up anger.

It turned out, the author pretended to need a second opinion as a lure to gain cooperation for personal financial gain (*Identification*). His known behaviors, handwriting, and content told me he is an average Type Three who feels entitled, is ambitious, grossly overstates his abilities, has been arrogant and condescending while hiding his true intentions.

"We teach others how to treat us." - Dr. Phil

9. Nine Behavioral Pathways[27]

"My personality is who I am. My attitude depends on who you are."
- Unknown

We always talk about what is important to us. Our thoughts become words and are expressed as behaviors. Behaviors develop into habits and determine our values. Our values convert into a progressive behavioral pattern and define our destiny.
Treating others with dignity and respect means you honor them for who they are. It is up you to find and set healthy boundaries within the confines of your personal standards. It is our willingness to acknowledge our boundaries and limitations that determine the quality and depth of our relationships.

Each relationship is mutually defined and the quality of a relationship is measured by how much the needs of those involved are met. The most important needs to be met are basic and very pervasive. These are known for each Type and are the core fears and needs. This means, we need to recognize our needs, express them with clarity and mutually define acceptable boundaries.

---

[27] Assembled from "Personality Types" Riso / Hudson (1996), other sources, and personal experiences.

Acknowledge

It is most important to acknowledge the core needs of a person as it is a compensation for a core fear. If we don't, we reinforce a childhood fear and deny the core of their being. This is painful, frustrating and antagonistic. It is important to recognize Types, their core fears and needs, so we can acknowledge each other for who we are. We can emphasize strengths and gain alliances, cooperation, and build friendships.

	fear	compensation	needs acknowledgment for
1	I am faulty	I must do the right thing	prudence, being objective
2	I am unloved	Let me take care of you	empathy, being good
3	I am unworthy	I must excel	performance, being the best
4	I am a nobody	I must be different	identity, being different
5	I am incompetent	I must be informed	competence, being smart
6	I have no support	I must be dependable	support, being guided
7	I miss out	I must have joy	acquisition, being busy-bee
8	I am vulnerable	I must be self-reliant	security, being protected
9	I don't matter	I need serenity	private space, being left alone

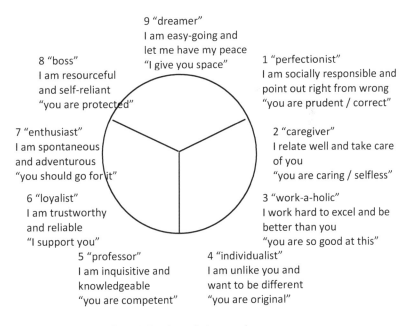

Figure 57: acknowledge needs

119

Trigger

Ego defense mechanisms are triggered when we emphasize weaknesses and do the opposite of what they need or want to hear. This is where many people unwittingly push buttons. Each Type tends to be blind to the exaggeration of their personal core fear.

	needs	blind to	fear trigger
1	to be right	gray areas	"you are dead wrong"
2	to be loved	personal needs	"you are selfish"
3	to be a winner	personal failure	"you are a loser"
4	to be different	what they have already	"you are ordinary"
5	to be informed	existing abundance	"you are incompetent"
6	to be supported	overestimation authority	"you are on your own"
7	to be happy	personal limitations	"you cannot have this"
8	to be self-reliant	impact on others	"you are at my mercy"
9	to be peaceful	personal preferences	"intrusion private space"

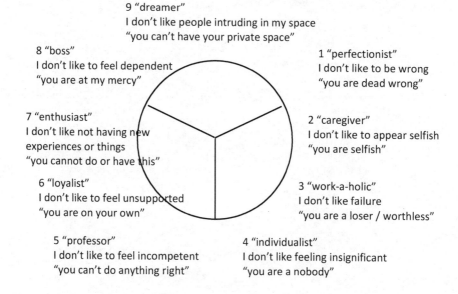

9 "dreamer"
I don't like people intruding in my space
"you can't have your private space"

8 "boss"
I don't like to feel dependent
"you are at my mercy"

1 "perfectionist"
I don't like to be wrong
"you are dead wrong"

7 "enthusiast"
I don't like not having new experiences or things
"you cannot do or have this"

2 "caregiver"
I don't like to appear selfish
"you are selfish"

6 "loyalist"
I don't like to feel unsupported
"you are on your own"

3 "work-a-holic"
I don't like failure
"you are a loser / worthless"

5 "professor"
I don't like to feel incompetent
"you can't do anything right"

4 "individualist"
I don't like feeling insignificant
"you are a nobody"

Figure 58: push buttons

120

9.1 The Assertives (3,7,8)

The Assertives identify with the matriarchal role model or an emotional nurturer. They either feel attached (3), frustrated (7) or rejected (8) by their Mother[28]. These children do not identify strongly with the father figure (guide, protector, and provider) who had less or no influence on them. Reduced guidance typically leads to under-development of social inhibitions. They are engaging, social, assertive, and insistent in getting what they want. They are instinctive doers who rationalize their actions while emotionally detached. They frequently do not understand the emotional impact they have on others and allows them to overstep social boundaries with relative ease.

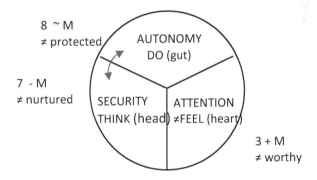

Figure 59: The Assertives

Type	Primary	Secondary	Least developed	Defense Mechanism
3	Instinctive Reasoning	Emotional	Emotional	Identification
7	Reasoning	Instinctive	Emotional	Rationalization
8	Instinctive	Reasoning	Emotional	Denial

- Assertive and insistent motivated by
    - 3 to project image of success
    - 7 to find happiness
    - 8 to take charge and be in control

---

[28] Mother (M) means "the emotional nurturer" and is the person symbolizing the matriarchal role model.

3. Attachment to approval and assertive towards others through comparisons (competitive)
7. Frustrated by deprivation and seeks aggressive satisfaction for themselves (acquisitive)
8. Rejected and vulnerable with assertive superficial connection with others (self-assertion)

The Assertives have under-developed emotional connection to self and others.
Threes deceive by presenting a false image, overstating abilities and don't see task failure.
Sevens rationalize by putting positive twists on negatives and fail to see personal limitations.
Eights deny reality, dominate, and don't see the emotional impact they have on others.

Type Three: *I am a winner*

Behavioral Pattern
Healthy: authentic, self-accepting, well-adjusted, ambitious and modest
Average: image oriented, meets expectations of others, competitive, self-promoting
Unhealthy: exploitative, arrogant and condescending.

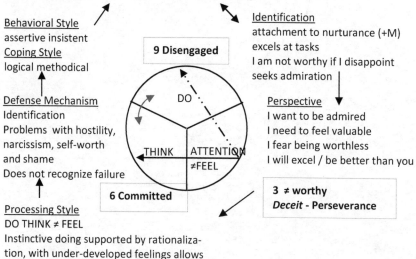

Behavioral Style
assertive insistent
Coping Style
logical methodical

Defense Mechanism
Identification
Problems with hostility,
narcissism, self-worth
and shame
Does not recognize failure

Processing Style
DO THINK ≠ FEEL
Instinctive doing supported by rationalization, with under-developed feelings allows for overstepping social boundaries

9 Disengaged

DO

THINK   ATTENTION
        ≠FEEL

6 Committed

Identification
attachment to nurturance (+M)
excels at tasks
I am not worthy if I disappoint
seeks admiration

Perspective
I want to be admired
I need to feel valuable
I fear being worthless
I will excel / be better than you

3 ≠ worthy
Deceit - Perseverance

Figure 60: Behavioral Pathway Type Three

Look!

Childhood experience: a child growing up feeling rewarded and appreciated for what they do instead for who they are. Task performance is objective and their feelings were not acknowledged. They compensate by seeking praise by excelling at jobs as a substitute for love and appreciation.

- driven, ambitious and self-promoting
- image orientated in appearance
- wants to be seen as successful by others
- insecurity when image is under pressure
- highly adaptable to avoid failure
- intelligent through exploratory achievements
- detaches emotions to complete tasks
- difficulty with emotional connection in relationships
- increased stress levels with emotional demands
- secretive and worried with those who see through them
- hardworking, discipline, structured, goal oriented

Listen!

A Type Three typically makes statements involving performance acknowledgment.

- my mother appreciated and supported me
- I work hard and play hard
- I achieve because I go for it
- Nothing can stop me
- White lies are just fine
- I am a Type A personality
- I want things and I want them now
- I am admirable
- I am a winner
- I am the best
- I don't let emotions get in the way
- I never had close friends

Type Three sees themselves as admirable, desirable, sociable, well-adjusted, and attractive. The underlying theme is performance acknowledgment. Others see healthy Threes the same but see average and unhealthy Threes as career-driven, self-promoting, deceptive, entitled, grandiose and exploitative.

Threes grow up with a positive identification with the Mother (+M). Unconditional approval leads to limited self-reflection, reduced self-inhibitions, and emotional under-development.

They link self-esteem to performance and are in search of admiration, positive regard, and performance acknowledgment. Failure to perform disappoints and makes them feel unworthy. Threes, therefore, refuse to see performance failure and must push themselves to maintain self-esteem. Repeating the same task for no praise is no longer enticing and hence, they must improve and be better than before. Type Threes tend to feel pushed toward success to maintain a sense of self.

Patrick Jane is the main character in the series the Mentalist. Sherriff McAllister, a.k.a. the serial killer Red John[29], bragged about his ability to set up a covert organization of corrupt judges, cops, and others in law-enforcement. Red John is the murderer of Jane's wife and child. The Mentalist described Red John like a Three, *"You want to brag? Go ahead. I am not gonna stop you. Is that what you have been missing? Appreciation? You want me to applaud?"*
They are attention seeking and typically have problems with self-worth, shame, arrogance, and vanity. Gross over-estimation of personal abilities reflects on grandiosity and blindness to failure. Threes grow by shedding their need for performance acknowledgment and shift from image orientation toward being appreciated for who they are.

The Three grows up with a doting mother and feels approved off. They link their self-esteem to praise and they must earn admiration to maintain self-esteem. They love to hear how well they did cutting wood for the woodstove, yet, the next year receiving the same praise for the same task is far less satisfying. Threes must satisfy their ego demands for admiration and will push their limits for bigger or better. Next year he splits wood more efficiently with a wood splitter. They constantly reset their boundaries in their everlasting search for a substitute for Mother's praise. Average and unhealthy Threes reset their social boundaries and when they are not better than someone else, they put them down through condescension. They can violate the rights of others without remorse. The final destination of grandeur is being a God.

---

[29] Two fictional characters in the series "the Mentalist".

Elliot Rodger reached an unhealthy perspective when he said, *"They [women] treated me like an insignificant little mouse, but on the Day of Retribution, I would be a God to them."*

Threes process information primarily through rationalization and instinctive action. They disconnect their emotions until after a job has been done. Their favored defense mechanism is *Identification*.
They incorporate attributes of others to themselves to gain cooperation and create alliances. They pretend to be like you and create a false persona. They are adaptable[30] and do not reveal their real motivation. Their Vice is "Deceit" or projecting and identifying with an image of a winner rather than their true self. Since self-esteem is linked to performance, they must succeed and be better than others at tasks. It's the "I am a winner" perspective and makes them hard working, competitive, and driven. Inevitably, they will fail to live up to their inflated self-image, disappoint themselves, and damage their self-esteem. The only thing left for them is to be relatively better, and they will put others down with snide remarks, pure arrogance, and a relentless condescending and vindictive posture.

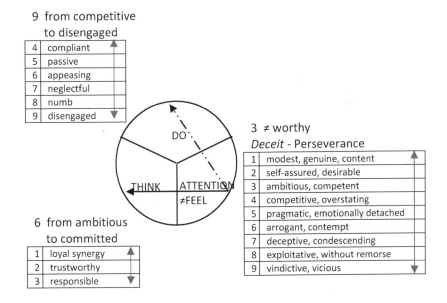

9 from competitive
to disengaged

4	compliant
5	passive
6	appeasing
7	neglectful
8	numb
9	disengaged

6 from ambitious
to committed

1	loyal synergy
2	trustworthy
3	responsible

3 ≠ worthy
Deceit - Perseverance

1	modest, genuine, content
2	self-assured, desirable
3	ambitious, competent
4	competitive, overstating
5	pragmatic, emotionally detached
6	arrogant, contempt
7	deceptive, condescending
8	exploitative, without remorse
9	vindictive, vicious

Figure 61: Type Three integration - disintegration

---

[30] "Flip Flop Romney"

Threes are assertive and insistent in getting what they want. Their approach is logical and methodical with an uncanny ability to remain calm under stress as they disconnect their emotions.

At healthy levels, Threes are authentic, self-assured, and take others into consideration. They are ambitious, adaptable, success-oriented.

At average levels, they are concerned with their image of success, prestige, and status. Ambition is replaced by competitiveness. Authenticity replaced by image-consciousness and narcissism.

At unhealthy levels, competitiveness becomes exploitation with deception at its core. A need to win at all cost leads to betrayal and vindictive violence. They disengage from themselves and their anger within, are emotionally vacant, and capable of destruction without remorse.

Threes can deteriorate from healthy ambition to competitiveness with a need to win, to exploitation and gross overstatements. From being admired to a need to be admired, to making others feel worthless. Unhealthy Threes retreat and disengage as they finally realize others are abandoning them because of their exploitation.

Type Three summarized

Type 3	Vice: Deceit	
Childhood perception	"I am not worthy" (failure means I am a disappointment)	
Key fear	I fear not being able to live up to my inflated self-image	
Key need	I earn admiration through performance acknowledgment	
Key perspective	I must excel and be better than you (Vanity)	
Styles	Assertive Insistent	Logical Methodical
Willfully ignores	Inability to perform a task	
Behavioral Pathway:	*From seeking worthiness to chasing success at all cost*	
Defense mechanism: Identification	Inserts attributes of others into self-image (failure avoidance) *Presenting image of success overstating abilities and contributions, while feeling like a disappointment.* *Typical problems: Arrogance contempt condescension*	
Healthy	"I am admired for who I am and what I do." Self-accepting, modest, gracious, authentic, ambitious, inclusive	
Average	"I must be admired for what I do." Must be the best, competitive, adapts to others to maintain façade of success, seeks status, image oriented, prestige	
Unhealthy	"I make you feel worthless." Grandiosity, gross over-representation, needs to win at all cost, exploits others, arrogant, condescending, malicious and vindictive	
Disintegration *Creating my own fears*	"My claims are unsubstantiated and they will never admire me." From driven to succeed to apathetic complacency *Others reject me because of my exploitation, and now I am truly worthless*	

D

Overestimation of personal abilities, competitiveness, and vindictiveness are part of the perspective of a Three. D is a 68-year-old pool player who is demanding and conceited. When a new young and attractive bartender arrived on the scene, he suddenly started singing and flailing to gain her attention. This was remarkable, as he displayed the same attention seeking behaviors with another attractive young lady. When he didn't get what he perceived as his turn at a pool table, he mocked a valid argument, became argumentative and derogatory. He lost the dispute, raised his fist and yelled, "I should clog you! Put your money where your mouth is, and play five dollars a ball!" The Three's need for attention, aggression, competition, and his need to produce a winner and loser clearly shines through. He still does not realize arrogance, entitlement and condescension are anti-social traits resented by others.

Odd

Type Three, Seven, and Eight all identify with the emotional nurturer or the Mother. The more intimidating Father, in principle the guiding role model, had less or no inhibiting influence on the child. Their assertive and insistent nature provides them with self-assurance and certitude, while emotional shallowness allows them to overstep social boundaries effortlessly. And so, we see the assertive Threes, Sevens and Eights frequently in the news. This can be an exploitative CEO, a fraudulent politician or a felon committing violent crimes. There might very well be a correlation between the increase in divorce rates, the rearing of children by single mothers and violence.

The criminal Type Three is particularly interesting as they are charming, friendly, hide behind a façade and do not reveal their true intentions. They are much harder to recognize and catch unless you are aware of their pattern.

David Holmes, behavioral profiler, stated in a documentary regarding Randy Kraft, *"his childhood was uneventful, his father distant, and he had a doting mother. This combination makes the child strive for attention; feel pushed and supported, tend to achieve a lot, and felt secure by the mother. This is also the background of many serial killers."* Mr. David Holmes described Type Three to a T.

The Threes are far more cunning and sneaky than the more direct and confrontational Sevens and Eights. Low-level Sevens become highly reactive and hyperactive whereas low-level Eights become domineering and demonstrative. In other words, you are forewarned by their behaviors. The Three follows an indirect and less aggressive pattern using deceit, entitlement, arrogance, and condescension as their weapons. Where Sevens and Eights are more direct and confrontational, Threes are secretive and manipulative. As far as criminality is concerned, the Assertives (3,7,8) are more frequently in the news than the Compliants (6,1,2) and Withdrawns (9,4,5). The public regularly acts with surprise when a Three is caught for their deeds. Statements like, "he is such a gentleman" and "he is one of the kindest people I know" are often expressed. Some get away with crimes for years without being noticed. People in the community will eventually find a pattern of odd behaviors as they all recognized peculiarities. These quirks and oddities did not stand out enough to actually talk about and those surrounding the Three never thought to compare their observations.

A few samples of average and low-level Threes are provided to learn to recognize the patterns. Threes feel entitled, are ambitious, competitive and work-a-holics. They are instinctive and use reasoning to back up their choices while detaching their emotions from their actions. They don't see failure as an option and overstate their abilities. Their ego defense mechanism is *Identification*, and their Vice is Deceit.

They are observant, incorporate attributes of others to themselves and act like they are like you. They tell you what you want to hear to gain support and obtain alliances. But, they do not reveal their true motivation and intentions. Threes hide behind a mask and are emotionally under-developed. Although they mimic the emotions of others, they don't understand nor feel the connection between the emotion and its context. They will say the right thing but within the wrong context or at the wrong moment. And so, others see them as a little odd, a little off, or plain weird.

Here is a typical misplaced identification attempt by a successful Three: Presidential candidate Mitt Romney told NASCAR fans wearing plastic ponchos "*I like those fancy raincoats you bought. Really sprung for the big bucks.*" He continued with, "*I have some great friends who are NASCAR team owners.*" Again, he was trying to be charming and funny but missed the boat with the joke and then separated himself from the average citizen. And so, Threes are emotionally shallow and don't understand the emotional impact they have on others.
Romney's comments completely fit the Three's personality. The NASCAR team owners are rich and his friends. It was important for him to tell others

how successful he is through association. However, he failed miserably to emotionally connect with his voters.

The Presidential candidate's visit to Britain was an utter disaster. He publicly downplayed Britain's organizational skills for the 2012 summer Olympics. Anonymous British officials told the Daily Mail Romney was worse than Sarah Palin, nicknamed him "Mitt the Twit", and "devoid of charm, warmth, humor or sincerity". And that description is the core of a Type Three.

A criminal Type Three is one of the harder Types to recognize and catch. They are friendly, calm, charming and tell you what you want to hear in a believable way. They mimic emotions of others without feeling them and act with shame without feeling shame. This makes unhealthy Threes a little odd, but most people cannot put their finger on it. This is a very common theme and one of the signs of a sociopath. As Martha Stout put it *"Often, multiple individuals will think a sociopath is "odd" / "weird" but just not remarkable enough to talk about it with each other avoiding general consensus."*

Gary Ridgway's childhood was unremarkable, yet, he remembers it differently. He reportedly was a bed-wetter into his early teens and recalls his domineering mother washing his genitals. He developed a lust towards her and recalled gazing at her while sunbathing. He had sexual fantasies and felt enraged wanting to kill her at the same time. Therefore, sex and violence were psychologically linked for him. Gary worked at Kenworth trucks and painted designs on trucks. He had a job that required "patience and neatness". He may have been precise but, according to his co-workers, something was not "quite right" about Gary Leon Ridgway.

Josef Fritzl grew up during the Nazi era which meant respect for authority and control. His mother kicked his father out of their small apartment, and Fritzl stated "I was in awe of her. Completely and totally in awe of her". The monster of Amstetten imprisoned his daughter for twenty-four years. Elisabeth was eighteen, went to bars, got drunk, and did not go to work. In his delusional state of mind, he built a cellar beneath his home and locked her up for twenty-four years. His reasoned she defied his authority and he had to control her for her own good. He raped and fathered several children and said, "it was great to have a second proper family in the cellar, with a wife and a few children". How Josef Fritzl was capable of keeping his double life from his wife and general public is hard to imagine. His wife never complained about his sex vacations to Thailand and apparently never questioned

Fritzl's absence when he celebrated birthdays and even Christmas in the underground bunker.

Dichotomy 3w4 and 4w3

Nobody is a pure type as we own all characteristics of all types in varying degrees. The Type next to your own Type with the most influence is called your wing. For instance, Type Three can have a Two or a Four wing. Type 3w2 have similarities in social traits and reinforce each other. Both are personal with good social skills. They are people-oriented, social, charming, and in tune with others.

Type 3w4 has opposing traits resulting in inner conflict. The Three is personable and needs others to reinforce their self-image through identification and task excellence. The Four applies negative interpretations to themselves and withdraws from others to cope with stress. Where the Three is assertive and insists on getting what they want, the Four withdraws in the hope somebody will notice them and help them out.

This inner conflict between assertion and withdrawal is their dichotomy. The Three's perspective is *"I am admirable"* with a propensity to overstate abilities, grandiosity, and blindness to personal failure. Their modus operandi is mixing assertiveness with taking on attributes of others to gain cooperation (Vice: Deception).

Identification: Incorporating attributes of others into self-image to gain cooperation and create alliances. Adaptable façade. From (3) image-oriented to counter-productive grandiosity to (9) withdrawal and disengagement.

The Four's perspective is "I have no significance", is withdrawn, self-absorbed, and blind to internalizing satisfaction for what they already have (Vice: Envy). Their modus operandi is withdrawal and through rationalization reinforces their negative self-regard. *"I am a nobody."*

Introjection: *Internalization of negative information while preferring to deal with self-inflicted pain rather than outside criticism. From self-absorbed withdrawal to counter-productive emotional torment (4) to coercive dominance acting like a victim (2).*

Type 3w4 is prone to self-torment by an unresolved "admiration versus insignificance" conflict. The main Type Three is assertive and insistent, with an undertone of negative self-regard. It stands to reason the unhealthy Type 3w4 is more prone to self-destruction (4) by violating others (3). The way out of this inner conflict is to destroy what reminds them of their shortcomings. Vindictive violence and suicide by cop ideation becomes an all too real possibility.

Elliot Rodger, the Santa Barbara shooter (May 23, 2014), was a Type 3w4. He expressed this dichotomy in his Manifesto.

p. 32 It made me feel an insignificant (4), unworthy little mouse. (3)
p. 53 I bet that lucky bastard (3 condescending) took great satisfaction from my envy. (Vice 4)

Transcript "Retribution video"
I don't know why you girls aren't attracted to me, but I will punish (3 vindictive) you all for it. You will finally see that I am in truth the superior one. Well, now I will be a god (3 grandiosity) compared to you. I've wanted a girlfriend; I've wanted sex, I've wanted love, affection, adoration (3 "I am to be admired"). You think I'm unworthy of it. (3 key fear).

Social media exchange

Once you start recognizing patterns, it becomes easier to spot certain Types. In an online discussion regarding the JonBenét Ramsey case, a Type Three was quickly identified.

5: Both John and Patsy were involved. The ransom note made that clear with stunning clarity. However, JonBenét was not the intended target.
3: Which completely contradicts the FACTS of the case. So.

Threes are assertive and secretive. She unnecessarily emphasized the word "facts" through capitalization without stating what facts she is referring to. Threes habitually imply things without telling you what they think. The use of "So...." is evidence of this trait. She left the conclusion to the reader without stating what her thoughts are. In this way, she can back paddle. Interestingly, her profile was also set as "private".

5: There is no contradiction with facts. The drunk driver did not intend to kill another motorist, but he did. The key word is "intent." They were both involved as the ransom note revealed but did not intend to kill their daughter. And thus, she was not willfully and deliberately targeted.

3: *Wow, you are considerably more ignorant than I gave you credit for. Just look up the Wikipedia page. The entire Ramsey family was exonerated by Boulder PD in 2008 by DNA samples. Really not sure how you missed that when doing the required research for your book, but okay.*

Type Threes process information rationally and have immediate instinctive reactions. As we can read, she processes rationally as she argues her points. The jumping to false conclusions, and acting on them without forethought, is her instinctive part. Emotional development is under-developed and is revealed with the average Three's typical arrogant and condescending tone.

3: *In 2008, THE ENTIRE RAMSEY FAMILY WAS EXONERATED (which you should know already if you wrote a book about the case, Mr. Profiler, sir). A simple glance at the Wikipedia page would have told you that!*

The capitalization is an exaggeration in an attempt to dominate. This put her in the second phase of manipulation, domination, and control. Her assumption the Five didn't know about the exoneration letter is false. The assumption a book was being written about the case is false as the Ramsey case is a mere chapter. The word "if" implies she does not believe the Five is writing a book. This is assertion and instinctively reacting at work. This Three clearly lacks insight in the Ramsey case and is not willing to consider other perspectives. And now her patronizing nature drools off the page with the "Mr. Profiler, sir". She carried on with *"a simple glance"* and basically stated minimal effort would have informed the Five. Part of the Three's modus operandi is overstatement of their abilities and inability to see personal failure. This Three believes she knows it all (lack of personal failure) and presents assumptions as facts with certitude (overstating abilities).

5: *yes, they were "exonerated" by Mary Lacy, the then DA. The wording was "no longer under suspicion" and is not saying exonerated for the murder. The letter was economically driven. An open cold case requires assigning man-hours and other resources to investigate the case. And this case will not be solved unless there is a confession.*
3: *LOL. Oh. Okay. So now you are saying that after 15 years, she suddenly felt compelled to publicly humiliate herself and the BPD by apologizing to the Ramsey family for blaming them for the murder of JonBenét? I'll be sure to pick up that book of yours.*

The *"LOL, oh, Okay"* is mocking a valid point while providing the appearance of agreement. This matches the Three's ego defense mechanism (*Identification* and condescension). The assumption the letter was *"suddenly"* written is false. This was a long time coming for Mary Lacy. The Boulder Police Department never accused the Ramseys, nor were they officially charged with a crime. They were placed under an "umbrella of suspicion" at the time. And she continued with sarcasm by saying *I'll be sure to pick up that book of yours* while she dismissed and distanced herself with the word "that".

The markers for a Three perspective in this excerpt are assertion, insistence, rationalization, instinctive doing, arrogance, condescension, secrecy, blindness to failure and overstating personal abilities. This individual is likely an average Type Three who does not realize the exchange tells more about her than the one she judged.

Anti-Social Personality Disorder
The combination of rationalization (Think) and the immediacy of instinctive action (Do) without understanding emotional impact (≠ Feel), allows the Assertives to overstep social boundaries with *remarkable ease*.
Anti-Social Personality Disorder (ASPD) is characterized by a long-standing pattern of indifference to other people's rights and unresponsiveness to their boundaries. They tend to be callous, contemptuous of the feelings of others and unsympathetic to their suffering. They may or may not realize other's frustrations, hurts, and pain; however, they don't feel what others feel. And that is the core of their indifference.
They do know right from wrong, but don't see, or should I say feel, the need to limit their behaviors. This often goes at the emotional, and at times physical expense, of others. Therefore, they may be in the news for violations of accepted social standards and blatant disregard for the rights of others.
Those in the Anti-Social Personality Disorder spectrum have *"no intervening sense of obligation based on emotional attachment[31]"*, and are considered to be without a conscience. They are hustlers taking advantage of situations to the detriment of others. They expect others to not say anything out of fear for retaliation.

Although the term Anti-Social Personality Disorder is often substituted with sociopath and psychopath, the latter two are not distinct professional labels. A sociopath is defined as a person with Anti-Social Personality Disor-

---

[31] "The Sociopath Next Door" Martha Stout page 172

der. Psychopathy is defined as any disease of the mind with emotional or behavioral problems. The terms are intermingled, yet, Anti-Social Personality Disorder is the correct term for the disorder.

Regardless what we call it, ASPD, sociopath, and psychopath are marked by over-inflated self-regard, superficial charm, poor social boundaries, and a lack of empathy.

Personality disorders always describe a *long-term behavioral pattern* which is, unsurprisingly, diagnosed later in life and often in adulthood. However, as a general rule, conduct inconsistent with accepted standards established itself already in early childhood. They progressively overstep these boundaries with age, physical abilities and increased confidence in their teenage years.

As a child, Ted Bundy tortured cats and dug holes in popular running paths. He placed spikes on the bottom of them. Young Ted talked girls into intimacy in the bushes and, after they undressed, urinated on their clothes[32]. Bundy is also suspected of the murder of 8-year-old Ann Marie Burr. He was 14 at that time.

Theodore Millon (1928-2014)[33], an American psychologist known for his work on personality disorders, described fourteen variations of anti-social behaviors. They highlight traits we find back in all Enneagram Types. We could summarize sociopathic behaviors in five broad categories emphasizing a trait overwhelmingly present:
- Narcissism: self-assured, ambitious and competitive
- Corruption: deceptive, fraudulent and exploitative
- Amorous: charming, seductive, and superficial relationships
- Superiority: self-promoting, grandiose and condescending
- Anti-social: non-conforming, socially vacant and reckless

Anti-Social Personality Disorder can be found in any average and unhealthy Type. It is reasonable to expect, the emotionally shallow Assertives will have a higher percentage of mal-adjusted personas with reduced social inhibitions amongst them.

---

[32] source: conversations with individuals who grew up with Ted Bundy
[33] source: millon.net

Threes seek admiration through performance acknowledgment. When admiration is not received, they counter with contempt, arrogance, and condescension. They can become vehemently vindictive and violent.
Sevens pursue the next ideal experience, and when it's not fulfilling, they become hyperactive, scattered, and compulsive. In their highly anxious and manic state, they can lash out at others or become self-destructive.
Eights seek to control their environment. A vulnerable Eight compensates with misplaced over-confidence, dominance, and overwhelms with an in your face attitude. They can be ruthless and destructive.

The existence of ASPD is estimated to be in between 1% and 4% of the population, and about 70% are males. The prevalence of ASPD amongst felons, politicians, and CEO's is estimated to be around 20%. Typically, extreme behaviors decline with age as physical abilities wane, hormonal influences fade, and life experience taught some form of restraint.

Robert Hare, Ph.D. made great strides in the recognition of psychopathy traits and developed a *Psychopathy checklist*. When three or more traits on the most prominent trait list are present, ASPD should be considered. Of course, we leave clinical diagnoses to mental health professionals, because any disorder is too complex and too involved to be diagnosed by laymen.

The most prominent ASPD traits to observe are:
- Failure to conform to social standards
- Failure to assume responsibility
- Lack of remorse after violating others
- Reckless disregard for safety of self and others
- Grandiosity or over-estimation of self-worth
- Glibness and superficial charm
- Need for stimulation and boredom avoidance

And some other traits requiring more time to recognize are:
- Manipulation through deceit
- Pathological lying
- Lack of empathy
- Shallow emotional affect
- No genuine interest in emotional bonding with a mate
- History of early behavioral problems

Many individuals with ASPD are difficult to recognize as they are engaging, charming, and entertaining. They have a great sense of humor, smile a lot, are social, and very likable. Their quirky wit is often interlaced with condescension:

He says, "Dr. Phil is as much a doctor as Queen Latifah is a queen." The fact Dr. Phil has a PhD in clinical psychology and received a year of post-doctor training in forensic psychology is irrelevant to him.
He loudly produced pungent flatulence, and his friends choke. He is relishing the moment and is entirely oblivious to how others are offended. And so, he grins, and toots again and again.
He calls his wife "kitchen-staff," and while all said in good humor, it does not go unnoticed most of his puns are derogatory in nature.
She visits a 50th birthday party and gift-wraps a half emptied bottle of Drambuie as a birthday gift.

They are charismatic, social, and superficial. Their emotional shallowness often goes unnoticed for long periods of time. It can take years to see through their superficial charm before recognizing pattern consistency befitting anti-social personality disorder. Their lack of concern is often unexpected, stuns most people, and can have a serious negative socio-economic impact on others.

He is 43, tall, handsome and has highlights in his hair [image oriented]. *He owns 7 acres and drove his backhoe diagonally across his wetlands* [blindness to failure]. *It got stuck and sunk as deep as the floorboard* [recklessness]. *He parked busses, boats, trucks, cars, and trash on his driveway, and refuses to abide by neighborhood standards* [failure to conform]. *He blocked the community roadway culvert to divert water away from his wetlands, and the roadway flooded. He attempted to drain and fill in wetlands against county regulations* [overestimation of abilities, failure to conform]. *Property values dropped and he added trash* [lack of remorse]. *He is in a relationship with a woman twenty years his junior matching his emotional development.* [superficiality, emotionally shallow].

Most sociopaths not only refuse to take responsibility, but they are also forthright about blaming the victim. They rationalize their behavior and won't acknowledge the role they played. Ariel Castro, who kidnapped and imprisoned three young girls as sex slaves for ten years, said *"It was their fault. They should never have gotten in my van"*.

Josef Fritzl, who held his daughter captive for over 24 years in a bunker specifically built for that purpose, said, *"I protected her from bad influences"* and *"It was great to have a second normal family downstairs."*

A common cited characteristic for sociopaths is their lack of empathy. They objectify others and are unable to place themselves in their emotional position. That makes sense as their emotional development is limited, and therefore it is hard, if not impossible for them, to imagine the underlying emotional effect they have on others. Gary Ridgway, at age 16, stabbed a six-year-old for the simple reason of curiosity: *"I always wondered what it would be like to kill someone."* He walked away laughing after he stabbed the child. He developed thoughts of violence against his mother early in his childhood. This fantasy became a curiosity and developed into an uncontrollable urge to act out.

Sociopaths have a strong sense of entitlement. They demand their needs to be met, are offensive, and either ignore or disregard the needs of their immediate environment.

He is in his fifties and hosted a party. He demanded the music to be ear-shattering loud. The party-goers protested, but he enforced his demands by throwing his pool cue on the ground. He stamped his foot and yelled "It's my party!" Some whisper, "I don't even know why I am his friend" and others rolled their eyes and left the party.

They are emotionally shallow and move forward without consideration of the needs of others, nor feel the need to obtain consent with those in their immediate circle.

He is married and bought a home for him and his wife. She did not see the home and was not asked her opinion. He started remodeling the kitchen the day before their big party. As the guests arrived, he was beaming with pride soaking in the compliments regarding his remodeling plans. He ignored his wife's expressed dismay regarding the unexpected inconveniences.

They feel entitled and feel no shame or fear. They make reckless decisions putting themselves and others at risk. They look back and say *"I am not proud of that"* and repeat the same behavior again.

He is a diehard Eagles fan and visited their Seahawks game in Seattle with his friends. He sneaked in alcohol, and the Eagles got a beating. With two minutes left, now sufficiently drunk and out of control, he stumbled down the stairs and waited at the bottom. Irritated and quickly bored, he turned around and emphatically flipped off numerous Seahawks fans. He repeatedly yelled "Seahawks Suck" at the top of his lungs. One Hawk's fan ran down the stairs and knocked him down.

Entitled, arrogant, and reckless, are characteristics that come to mind. He put himself and his friends at risk, as this incident could easily have escalated to a section wide brawl. We all have them in our midst. We all know them. It's time to recognize them.

Deception and manipulation are naturals for the true sociopath. They see deceit as a tool to get what they want and enjoy their abilities with pride. They lie with ease and don't appear to mind being caught in blatant falsehoods. Sometimes I wonder whether they know they are lying or whether their fantasies just get carried away and are no longer realistic.

The media labeled Casey Anthony as a pathological liar, and she was smug about her insincerity too. She reportedly was on the phone talking, and while she threw her phone onto the dashboard, she said *"Oh my God, I am such a good liar."* Elliot Rodger wrote, *"I registered for some classes, but only to keep up the pretense to my parents [otherwise] they would have stopped all their support for me … Thankfully, I was a good liar."*

Casey Anthony brought two detectives to her place of employment. For two years she claimed to work at Universal Studios but never did. Did she believe this herself, or did she believe that if she gave a strong appearance to work there, others would back off and just believe her?

They are assertive and relentless in their pursuit to win. Their condescension and deceitful tools are aimed at those preventing them to win.

A pool tournament director repeatedly changed the rules in an effort to disadvantage players better than him. He made false claims undermining the integrity of these players and shamelessly applied non-existing rules to those he targeted.

Emotions can be a great motivator to spring into action, but the lack of emotion is a "Get out of Jail Free" card. They allow themselves to lie

138

because they are emotionally shallow and don't feel shame. Words are meaningless to them, and their deeds can be told as if they read them from a book. They don't feel what the average person feels like a color-blind man doesn't see colors. But they do learn to compensate through observation and mimicking emotional behaviors. Since they don't feel, nor understand the emotions they imitate, their timing and context will be off. And so, others will find them "a little weird", or "little odd", but not bad enough to talk about them.

Eric Clinton Newman (3w2) is a Canadian murderer who recorded his deeds and posted them online. He even informed the media ahead of his killing spree. Some initially thought these recordings were snuff films and did not realize they were actually real. Eric had many online identities and legally changed his name to Luka Rocco Magnotta. His original claim to fame was killing cats in various ways and posting these acts on the internet. He taped kittens to a stick and drowned them. He placed kittens in a bag and sucked the air out with a vacuum. Such acts reveal his ability to overstep boundaries and his utter lack of empathy. This earned him the nickname "vacuum kitten killer". It appears the young man suffered from narcissism with traits like exaggerated self-importance, attention seeking, a need for admiration, and an inability to accept rejection.

He tried out for several reality TV shows, including a show about plastic surgery. He admitted to being a surgery addict (image oriented) citing a nose job and hair transplants. He said, *"If I didn't have my looks, I don't really have anything."* Statements like these are superficial, image-oriented and show he is rather seen for *what* he is than *who* he is. A former transgender girlfriend said, "Luka had a troubled past and was sexually abused. He would later act out these acts as an escort. He had major anger issues and hit himself on the head. He was fascinated with Karla Homolka, Paul Bernardo, and Jeffrey Dahmer." Unfortunately, he reset his boundaries once again and moved on to the unthinkable. He was on the run in Europe and bragged about his ability to evade justice.

The vacuum kitten killer caught the attention of an internet sleuthing group. They were dumbfounded by the excessive number of names and profiles he used on the internet (Three's Vice is Deceit). He antagonized this group and actively looked up their personal information. He publicly stated, *"It is fun watching people work so hard gathering all the evidence. Then not being able to name me or catch me. You see, I always win* [the Three's "I am a winner" perspective; sees this as a game].

I always hold the trump card [lack of insight in personal failure], *and I will continue to make more movies. Next time you hear from me, it will be in a movie I'm producing that will have some humans in it, not just pussies."* [Resetting of boundaries].

After about a month on the run, he was caught in an internet café in Berlin, Germany. He was looking at information about himself or busy posting in one of his many accounts. He was convicted of first-degree murder. He killed a Chinese student, dismembered him, and sent body parts to elementary schools and politicians.

On his personal website, under a picture of himself in a leather jacket, showing off his naked chest, he wrote, *"Dreams turn into reality for those who aggressively pursue them."* [Assertive and Insistent]. Since any strength in excess becomes a weakness, Eric's ambition turned into a game to be won. He will have plenty of time to rethink the value of his statement.

Sociopaths see life as a game. Patrick Jane, the "Mentalist", has been in the hunt for the murderer of his wife and child. When he finally squares off with the serial killer Red John, they both know the hunt is over.

PJ: *"So I am supposed to die, am I? After all these years, seems kind of unfair."*

RJ: *"It's totally fair. Game's over, and I won."*

PJ: *"It's not a game."*

RJ: *There's a winner and a loser; that's a game."*

Lukah Chang (3w4) is the son of Christian missionaries, who deserted the Marines. In his early twenties, he murdered a motel maid in an opportunistic attack. A year later, on the anniversary date of the first death, he attacked but failed to kill a second woman. When he was interviewed by police, he explained he wanted to know what "it felt like". He stated it felt empowering (3) to take a life and was saddened (4) at the same time since he realized life is precious. During the interview, he was calm, collected, and stared the detective straight in the eye without blinking. He said he did not really have remorse (3) as he got tired of having feelings and learned to switch them off. The detective interviewing him was stunned as he had never heard this explanation before, but this lighthearted and superficial explanation is more common than we like to believe or understand. Read the interview excerpt and notice how he rationalizes (Think) his behavior. His actions were highly instinctive (Do), and the emotional flat affect is a sure sign of an emotional disconnect (≠ Feel).

Chang's police interview:
LC: *"I saw her working, and just ... Oh, look. Target. Opportunity. Attack".*
Q: Why?
LC: *"To see how it felt."*
Q: To see how what felt?
LC: *"Taking a life."*
Q: Why?
LC: *"I was curious."*
Q: How did it feel?
LC: *"Empowering because I took a life. Saddening because I realized at the same time, life is precious."*
Q: Do you feel remorse?
LC: *"Not really. I got tired of feeling emotions and stuff like that. So I am like: All right, let's just cut that out. So I did".*

Notice he was *saddened* and *realized* that *life is precious.* A realization is rationalization, and he knows what to say but contradicts himself at the same time. If he realized life was so precious during the first murder, why did he try it again a year later? And then say in the same interview about the second attack: *"She was walking by. I noticed. Followed. Attacked."*

Contradictions and inconsistencies like these are very common in sociopaths and may be hard to detect for an untrained ear. Words are emotionally meaningless allowing them to recite phrases verbatim out of papers, magazines and movies in the right circumstance, but at the wrong moment. They know the words but not their full meaning. It's the dancer going through the motions without being able to project the emotional expression of the dance.

Lukah Chang made a vital comment as he answered the question *why?* he attacked with *"to see how it felt".* He admitted switching his feelings off and was without remorse. Yet, Gary Ridgway, who has the same flat affect as Chang, said exactly the same thing when he stabbed an 8-year-old as a teenager. With no feelings to speak off, it seems they have to find emotions through excitement, thrills, and excessive activities. They seem to commit crimes just to feel something for once and might be a similar psychological mechanism as self-mutilation. They are the adolescents who cut themselves for the satisfaction of pain. Cutters apparently prefer to feel physical pain over feeling nothing at all. They have often been severely traumatized and became emotionally stunted by pushing the hurt, fear, and pain away.

His answer to the question, *"How did it feel?"* is also revealing. He felt *empowered* which is in line with the main theme of a Type Three.
I am to be admired by doing something nobody else would do. Chang decided to kill for no other reason than curiosity, and he placed himself in the position of God *(Grandiosity)*.

Compare Lukah Chang with Elliot Rodger, who summarized his grievances and superiority in his Manifesto:

"All of my suffering...has been at the hands of...women. All I ever wanted was to fit in...but I was cast out and rejected, forced to endure an existence of loneliness and insignificance." The Santa Barbara spree killer made his decision to retaliate on Halloween weekend when he imagined that guys who are just visiting for Halloween night would be getting laid by *"those evil, slutty bitches"*. He continued with *"They* [women] *treated me like an insignificant little mouse, but on the Day of Retribution, I would be a God to them."* *"I am superior to them all. I am Elliot Rodger ... magnificent, glorious, supreme, eminent ...Divine! I am the closest thing there is to a living god."*

Most people abide by the rules of engagement but to those in the anti-social personality disorder spectrum the rules are a game. And games need a winner. Although the vast majority of sociopaths are "just" manipulative and exploitative, there is a small percentage that can be extremely vindictive, relentless, and ruthless.

Interestingly, emotional shallowness and indifference towards suffering while violating the rights of others, is only a few mental steps away for individuals with empathy. Indifference can be taught and trained. We know this very well as impressionable young men are trained as soldiers to see the enemy as less than human.
We can all fall victim to changes in our perspective and become less sensitive to meet the demands of authority figures. From a religion based Jihadist to a socio-economic driven street hustler or an ordinary student acting as a prison guard[34]. And in doing so, we reduce our emotional attachment and shift personal responsibility toward an authority figure. The entitled sociopath is their personal authority figure. For them, the lure of the dark side is ever present.

---

[34] "the Lucifer Effect. Understanding how good people turn evil" Philip Zimbardo

Type Seven: *What is next?*

Behavioral Pattern
Healthy: spontaneous, appreciative, well-rounded, grateful
Average: materialistic, variety seeking, acquisitive
Unhealthy: impulsive, narcissistic, addictive, erratic

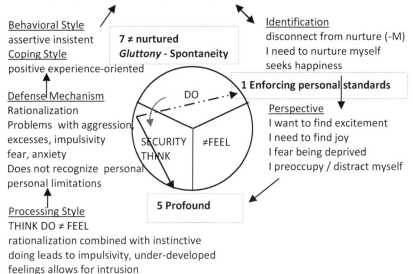

Behavioral Style
assertive insistent
Coping Style
positive experience-oriented

7 ≠ nurtured
Gluttony - Spontaneity

Identification
disconnect from nurture (-M)
I need to nurture myself
seeks happiness

1 Enforcing personal standards

DO

Defense Mechanism
Rationalization
Problems with aggression,
excesses, impulsivity
fear, anxiety
Does not recognize personal
personal limitations

SECURITY   ≠FEEL
THINK

Perspective
I want to find excitement
I need to find joy
I fear being deprived
I preoccupy / distract myself

5 Profound

Processing Style
THINK DO ≠ FEEL
rationalization combined with instinctive
doing leads to impulsivity, under-developed
feelings allows for intrusion

Figure 62: Behavioral Pathway Type Seven

Look!

Childhood experience: a child growing up with a lack of emotional nurturing. They compensate by seeking distractions through activities to reduce anxiety and pain. They seek pleasurable and fun experiences as a substitute for the missed motherly love.

- fun, spontaneous, excitable
- tends to get bored quickly
- charming, light-hearted, fun to be around with
- superiority, narcissistic tendencies
- keeps options open, ready to change direction
- changes plan when other excitement presents itself
- hard working, needs to stay pre-occupied with activities
- does not finish what was started
- superficial and difficulty with intimacy
- humorous, non-committed extrovert
- fears to be missing out

143

Listen!

A Type Seven typically makes statements involving excitement.

- My mother didn't understand me
- I want to have fun!
- I get easily bored
- I love doing things with people
- I love change
- I start the party
- There is always room for more
- I love music and dance
- I have many, many friends, but not really close friends
- I plan my day and change my plans on a whim

Type Seven sees themselves as enthusiastic, energetic, adventurous, and spontaneous. The underlying theme is anxiety avoidance by finding happiness in the next exciting experience. Others see healthy Sevens the same but may see average and unhealthy Sevens as thrill seeking, hyper-active, excessive, reckless, and even hedonistic.

Sevens grew up with a negative identification with the Mother (-M) and frustrated with inadequate emotional nurturance. It's the mother, not in tune with her child or the mother not available through work. She does not mirror the child's behaviors, gives insufficient emotional support resulting in limited personal value for the child. Naturally assertive and insistent, they learn to nurture themselves by acquiring new experiences and fulfilling materialistic needs. Their happiness lies in the next thrill, and new experiences are essentially substitutes for motherly love not received.

Their self-esteem is linked to the joy and happiness in the next experience, and so they are driven to fulfill their next desire. They typically have problems with fear, anxiety, superficiality, excessiveness, and impulsivity. Preoccupation with finding the next experience maintains self-esteem through perceived happiness. Problems arise when their under-developed emotional connection does not allow them to internalize an experience. Anxiety sets in with the lack of new experiences. Sevens grow by emotionally internalizing experiences, enabling them to relive gratification indefinitely.

Sevens process information through reasoning supported by instinctive action. Their emotional connection with themselves is under-developed. They are preoccupied with finding the next thrill. Their favored defense mechanism is *Rationalization*, and they justify their actions with positive explanations while obscuring their real motivations leading to misrepresentation.

They are prone to exaggerate and overdo things, and their Vice is "Gluttony" or a desire for new experiences, pleasure, and fun to make them feel good.

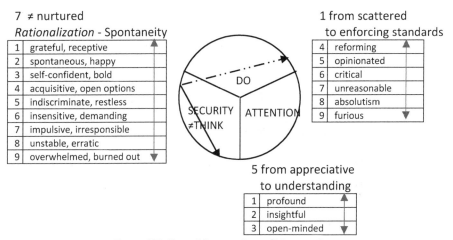

7 ≠ nurtured
Rationalization - Spontaneity

1	grateful, receptive
2	spontaneous, happy
3	self-confident, bold
4	acquisitive, open options
5	indiscriminate, restless
6	insensitive, demanding
7	impulsive, irresponsible
8	unstable, erratic
9	overwhelmed, burned out

1 from scattered
to enforcing standards

4	reforming
5	opinionated
6	critical
7	unreasonable
8	absolutism
9	furious

5 from appreciative
to understanding

1	profound
2	insightful
3	open-minded

Figure 633: Type 7 integration - disintegration

Self-esteem becomes linked to the joy from an activity instead of emotionally integrating an experience. They typically are busy bees, have full agendas, and jump from experience to experience. They are unlikely to recognize their limitations and move forward impulsively and without much forethought. Sevens can intrude on others by involving them in their drama.

Sevens are assertive and insistent in getting what they want. They apply positive twists to negatives and are people-oriented. They tend to be demonstrative and impulsive.

At healthy levels, they internalize experiences and find personal satisfaction. They are hard-working and good at many things. They appreciate what they have, enjoy life, and remain enthusiastic with every new experience.

At average levels, they have reduced internalization of experiences and are less appreciative. They compensate for their lack of nurturance by creating more and more experiences, giving them less time to internalize. Their constant chase of fun becomes a goal in and by itself and too many experiences dilute emotional connection.

At unhealthy levels, they become hyperactive, impulsive and out of control with too much on their plate. They avoid facing their anxiety and replace it with staying busy. Hyperactivity increases their anxiety, and they jump from task to task without finishing the previous one.

Type Seven summarized

Type 7	Vice: Gluttony	
Childhood perception	"You did not take care of me."	
Key fear	I fear deprivation; fear of missing out	
Key need	I want to have freedom and happiness	
Key perspective	I must gain pleasant experiences (Self-indulgence)	
Styles	Assertive Insistent	Positive-minded People-oriented
Willfully ignores	Personal limitations	
Behavioral Pathway:	*from seeking happiness to panicked escapism*	
Defense mechanism: Rationalization	Positive twists obscuring true motivation (pain avoidance) *Presenting image of being happy and okay while feeling pain and anxiety* *Typical problems: impulsivity superficiality*	
Healthy	"I have all I need." Spontaneous, appreciative, outgoing, optimistic, thoughtful	
Average	"I need to have pleasant experiences, own beautiful things." Needs variety, hyper-activity, jumps to new tasks	
Unhealthy	"I will burden you by insisting on my demands." Superficiality, reckless, impatient, restless, scattered	
Disintegration *Creating my own fears*	"My actions hurt others and they will now deprive me." From hyperactive and scattered to intolerant and punitive *Immediate and superficial gratification do not bring happiness after all.*	

J

Deprivation, a fear of missing out, narcissism, and emotional shallowness are part of the Seven's perspective. J's acquaintances were getting married. They were friends with her partner and his ex-girlfriend, but J had "no use" for the ex-girlfriend and mother of his child. She contacted the bride and groom to be and demanded to be part of all three festivities instead of two. These demands were designed to exclude the ex-girl-friend in the celebra-tions and against the known wishes of the soon to be married couple. But whose wedding is it?

Type Eight: *It's my way or the highway*

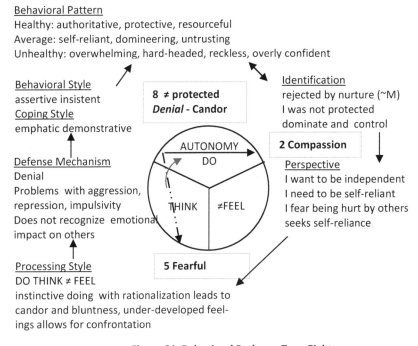

Behavioral Pattern
Healthy: authoritative, protective, resourceful
Average: self-reliant, domineering, untrusting
Unhealthy: overwhelming, hard-headed, reckless, overly confident

Behavioral Style
assertive insistent
Coping Style
emphatic demonstrative

8 ≠ protected
Denial - Candor

Identification
rejected by nurture (~M)
I was not protected
dominate and control

AUTONOMY
DO

2 Compassion

Defense Mechanism
Denial
Problems with aggression,
repression, impulsivity
Does not recognize emotional
impact on others

THINK   ≠FEEL

Perspective
I want to be independent
I need to be self-reliant
I fear being hurt by others
seeks self-reliance

5 Fearful

Processing Style
DO THINK ≠ FEEL
instinctive doing with rationalization leads to
candor and bluntness, under-developed feelings allows for confrontation

Figure 64: Behavioral Pathway Type Eight

Look!
Childhood experience: a child growing up in an environment that was unsafe and feeling vulnerable. They compensate through assertion and taking
control. Their need to be in charge may lead to conflict, disorderly conduct
and unhealthy relationships.

-   independent and self-reliant
-   intimidating, power-seeking, demanding
-   confrontational and easily angered
-   denies negatives and pretends bad behavior is non-existent
-   impulsive and overwhelming
-   self-protective and protective of the under-dog
-   appreciative of assertive, strong and direct peers
-   blames others while denying own role
-   intimacy through sex, conflict and confrontation

Listen!

A Type Eight typically makes statements involving power and control.
- I love my mother, but I am stronger than she is
- I have to protect myself, who else will?
- I protect the underdog
- You are with me or get out of the way
- I have leadership abilities
- Emotions make you weak
- I am fearless and powerful
- I like confrontation and tell others off
- I am direct and blunt
- I have an "in your face" attitude
- Rules. What rules?

Type Eight sees themselves as strong, assertive, direct, and as a protector of the underdog. The underlying theme is feeling vulnerable with a need to self-protect by controlling their environment. Others see healthy Eights the same but view average and unhealthy Eights as overly confident, over-whelming, domineering, direct, blunt, and dictatorial.

Eights grow up feeling rejected by the Mother (~M) and did not bond nor reject her. The emotional nurturer made them feel vulnerable for various reasons. Naturally assertive, they learn to become self-reliant and vehe-mently protect their personal space. Self-protection can deteriorate into constant fighting. It's the classic "I'm gonna get you before you get me" atti-tude.

Their self-esteem is linked to control. In order to feel safe, self-reliant, and protected, they must control their immediate environment. From this per-spective, they are autonomy seeking and typically have problems relating to others, anger, superficiality, and over-confidence.

They grow by not having to control everything and trusting themselves to rely on others.

Eights are highly intuitive and action oriented. They will rationalize their ac-tions after the fact and use their favored defense mechanism, *Denial*, as a tool. Denial negates or minimizes the existence of their undesirable behav-iors. They minimize being a bully to just being direct and blunt, because "you needed to hear the truth".

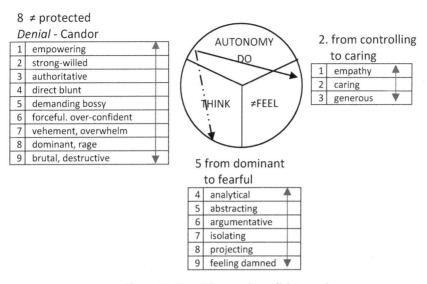

8 ≠ protected

Denial - Candor

1	empowering
2	strong-willed
3	authoritative
4	direct blunt
5	demanding bossy
6	forceful. over-confident
7	vehement, overwhelm
8	dominant, rage
9	brutal, destructive

2. from controlling to caring

1	empathy
2	caring
3	generous

5 from dominant to fearful

4	analytical
5	abstracting
6	argumentative
7	isolating
8	projecting
9	feeling damned

Figure 65: Type 8 integration - disintegration

Their emotional connection with themselves is under-developed, and they don't appreciate the emotional impact they have on others. Their Vice is "Lust", a lust for power, that is.

Eights are assertive and insistent on getting what they want. They are emphatic, demonstrative, decisive, and can fill a room by being omnipresent.

At healthy levels, they learned they don't have to be in control all the time. They can restrain their forceful presence, and their need to dominate is replaced by thoughtful and compassionate measured responses. They are confident, self-assertive, and have become natural leaders with selective appropriate force and decisiveness.

At average levels, they are forceful with limited to no restraint. They are assertive, aggressive, domineering, and can be overwhelming with misplaced overconfidence. They seek to control and force their will onto others. They are intimidating and confrontational.

At unhealthy levels, they act with unrestraint force. They have limited insight into the emotional impact they have on others, can become ruthless, vengeful, and violent.

Type Eight summarized

Type 8	Vice: Lust	
Childhood perception	"I am not protected and feel vulnerable."	
Key fear	I fear others will hurt me	
Key need	I want to be self-reliant	
Key perspective	I must be in control (Vengeance)	
Styles	Assertive Insistent	Emphatic Demonstrative
Willfully ignores	Emotional impact on others	
Behavioral Pathway:	*From self-protection to constant fighting*	
Defense mechanism: Denial	Negating existence of undesirable behaviors (vulnerability avoidance) *Presenting image of strength while feeling vulnerable* *Typical problems: dominance overconfidence*	
Healthy	"I replace control with compassion for others." Constructive, decisive, empowering, pragmatic, inspiring	
Average	"I need control out of fear being at the mercy of others." Needs to control, overwhelms, blunt, defiant, in your face	
Unhealthy	"I enforce my dominance onto you." Forceful, domineering, demanding, willfully vengeful	
Disintegration *Creating my own fears*	"I can't be in charge and fear they will now retaliate." From overly confident and ruthless to withdrawal in fear *Destruction of others leads to retaliation, and now I am at the mercy of others*	

D

Directness, bluntness, and misplaced overconfidence are part of the perspective of an Eight. D, irritated by the loud ringtone of another patron's cell phone, got up and demanded the man to switch his [expletive] phone off.

9.2 The Compliants (6,1,2)

The Compliants are dedicated and reliable, identify with the protector, guide, provider in their lives, typically the Father. They feel attached (6), frustrated (1), or rejected (2) by their guide and protector. The Compliants' self-esteem is conditional on being good or acting good. They see themselves positively when they abide by their convictions and earn their way through strict conviction adherence.

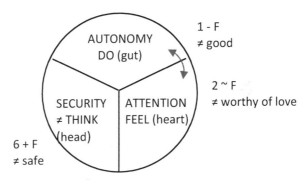

Figure 66: the Compliants

Type	Primary	Secondary	Least developed	Defense Mechanism
6	Instinctive Emotional	Reasoning	Reasoning	Projection
1	Instinctive	Emotional	Reasoning	Reaction formation
2	Emotional	Instinctive	Reasoning	Repression

The Compliants engage with their environment through rule adherence. Their reasoning ability is least developed, and they frequently have a hard time building a solid argument for what they know.

- The Compliants are dedicated, and reliable motivated by
  - · 6 doing what is expected
  - · 1 doing what is right
  - · 2 doing good to others

6. Attachment and compliant to an external body of authority (overestimates authority)
1. Frustrated and compliant to idealistic obligations (perfectionism)
2. Rejected and compliant to always being good and loving (to be indispensable)

The Compliants have underdeveloped reasoning abilities. They have strong emotions and emotions tend to overwhelm logic and reason.
Sixes look for hidden meanings, project own fears onto others and overestimate authority approval.
Ones present themselves as pleasant while disagreeing and build pent up anger.
Twos repress personal needs and give others what they need the most themselves.

Type Six: *I am a skeptic for a good reason*

Behavioral Pattern
Healthy: dedicated, trustworthy, engaging
Average: security seeking, committed, search for hidden meaning
Unhealthy: submissive, helpless, inferiority, irrational

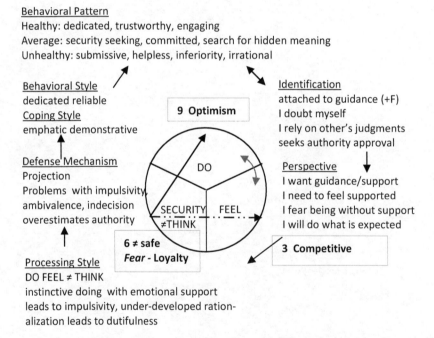

Behavioral Style
dedicated reliable
Coping Style
emphatic demonstrative

Defense Mechanism
Projection
Problems with impulsivity
ambivalence, indecision
overestimates authority

Processing Style
DO FEEL ≠ THINK
instinctive doing with emotional support
leads to impulsivity, under-developed rationalization leads to dutifulness

9 Optimism

DO

SECURITY   FEEL
≠THINK

6 ≠ safe
Fear - Loyalty

Identification
attached to guidance (+F)
I doubt myself
I rely on other's judgments
seeks authority approval

Perspective
I want guidance/support
I need to feel supported
I fear being without support
I will do what is expected

3 Competitive

Figure 67: Behavioral Pathway Type Six

Look!

Childhood experience: a child grows up in an environment they felt was un-predictable and inconsistent. They develop self-doubt and feel unsafe. They get anxious without guidance and support of an authority figure and learn to do what is expected of them.

- Counter-phobic Six:
    - deals with fear by fighting it: authority defiant
    - assertive, provocative, challenges authority
- Phobic Six:
    - deals with fear by giving in: authority abiding
    - withdrawn, observant, modest
- self-doubt, over-thinks, procrastinates
- lacks inner-guidance, finds answers outside themselves
- anxious, skeptical, questions everything
- suspicious, distrustful, looks for hidden meanings
- favors policies and procedures

Listen!

A Type Six typically makes statements involving obedience.
- I could always rely on my father
- My father is my best friend
- I am careful to be responsible
- I want to know the rules and find the boundaries
- I am skeptical and ask many questions
- I am cautious for a reason
- I don't really trust people

Type Six sees themselves as reliable, dedicated, dependable, and trustwor-thy. The underlying theme is finding security by doing what is expected from them. Others see healthy Sixes the same but see average and unhealthy Sixes as defensive, approval dependent, anxiously doubting self while blam-ing others and lashing out.

Sixes have a positive identification with the Father (+F) and felt secure trusting his guidance. They have self-doubt and rely on guidance provided by an authority figure. Their reasoning is underdeveloped and can lead to authority dependencies or worse, blind obedience. They are inclined to over-estimate the value of authority figures.

They link self-esteem to rule adherence and approval of others. Disapproval leads to anxiety and fear for negative consequences. Their self-doubt develops into a never-ending search for hidden meanings, creating their confusion, anxieties, and fears. They then resort to doing what they believe is expected from them. And that makes them feel good about themselves. They make excellent employees, work hard and rely on policies and procedures. They are security seeking and typically have problems with self-doubt, impulsivity, anxiety, and fear. Their biggest fear is loss of guidance and support, and therefore partners are under constant scrutiny while being tested for support. They grow by finding security within themselves and trusting their personal guidance.

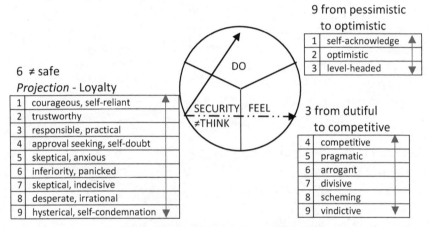

9 from pessimistic to optimistic

1	self-acknowledge
2	optimistic
3	level-headed

6 ≠ safe

Projection - Loyalty

1	courageous, self-reliant
2	trustworthy
3	responsible, practical
4	approval seeking, self-doubt
5	skeptical, anxious
6	inferiority, panicked
7	skeptical, indecisive
8	desperate, irrational
9	hysterical, self-condemnation

3 from dutiful to competitive

4	competitive
5	pragmatic
6	arrogant
7	divisive
8	scheming
9	vindictive

Figure 68: Type 6 integration - disintegration

Sixes process information emotionally and are action oriented. Their reasoning is under-developed and they rely more on authority approval. Many Sixes are reactive and emotionally demonstrative. Their favored defense mechanism is *Projection* and in their anxiety, they apply their shortcomings and drama to others as they want others to feel the way they do.
Sixes are dedicated, reliable, loyal, and emotionally demonstrative.
At healthy levels, they are self-reliant, inner-directed, loyal, and committed. They found their inner strength by relying on their personal perspectives and solutions and shed their need for authority approval. They are self-reliant and come to their own conclusions.
At average levels, they are dedicated, loyal, defensive, and dutiful. They project their fears and anxiety onto others sharing their drama liberally. They tend to test others for their support.
At unhealthy levels, they are guidance and support-dependent, submissive, paranoid, and self-destructive.

154

Sixes deteriorate from self-reliance to dependence on authority approval, and even blind obedience.

Type Six summarized

Type 6	Vice: Fear	
Childhood perception	"I don't trust my own judgment."	
Key fear	I fear being abandoned and alone	
Key need	I want security through guidance and reassurance of support	
Key perspective	I must do what others expect of me (Safety seeking)	
Willfully ignores	Authority fallibility	
Behavioral Pathway:	*From security seeking to overestimation of authority (blind obedience)*	
Styles	Dedicated Reliable	Emphatic Demonstrative
Defense mechanism: Projection	Applying own attributes to others (personal rejection avoidance) *Presenting image of loyalty by doing what is expected while feeling personal rejection. Typical problems: self-doubt impulsivity*	
Healthy	"I replaced self-doubt with optimism, trusting my judgment." Self-reliant, vigilant, reliable, disciplined, courageous, committed, loyal, responsible, trustworthy	
Average	"I want your reassurance and guidance to feel secure." Obedience to authority figure, dutiful, traditional, ambivalent, cautious, over-compensating for anxieties and fears	
Unhealthy	"I must have your support and guidance because I just don't know." Self-doubt, defensive, worry wart, pessimistic, indecisive, over-reactive, clings to authority, decision dependent	
Disintegration *Creating my own fears*	"My actions hurt my own security." From insecure and dutiful to exploitative and vindictive *My insecurity, anxiety, and inner conflict drives others away, and now I am without guidance, support, and I am alone*	

M

Overestimation of authority is part of the perspective of a Six. Her sisters claim her dad abused them as children, but M could not believe it since it never happened to her. Her dad, her hero, her confidant is an abuser? That was a pill too hard to swallow. At age thirty-five, she recognized her dad's behavioral pattern through her Enneagram studies. She then realized his behavioral pattern was befitting a Three with many unusual and immature choices. She then acknowledged her sisters' claims.

Type One: *Let me tell you ...*

Behavioral Pattern
Healthy: wise, realistic, objective, realizes "good enough" is perfect
Average: reality-ideal conflicts, critical, judgmental, impatient
Unhealthy: enforces personal standards, self-righteous, intolerant

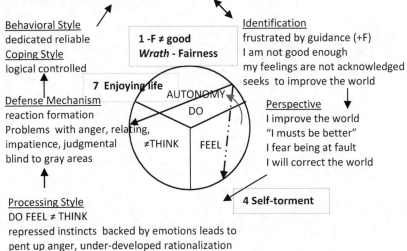

Behavioral Style
dedicated reliable
Coping Style
logical controlled

1 -F ≠ good
Wrath - Fairness

7 Enjoying life
AUTONOMY
DO

≠THINK   FEEL

Defense Mechanism
reaction formation
Problems with anger, relating,
impatience, judgmental
blind to gray areas

Identification
frustrated by guidance (+F)
I am not good enough
my feelings are not acknowledged
seeks to improve the world

Perspective
I improve the world
"I musts be better"
I fear being at fault
I will correct the world

4 Self-torment

Processing Style
DO FEEL ≠ THINK
repressed instincts backed by emotions leads to
pent up anger, under-developed rationalization
leads to emphatic certainty

Figure 69: Behavioral Pathway Type One

Look!

Childhood experience: a child who felt guidance provided was flawed and compensates by creating personal standards. They were often heavily criticized and learn to be perfect to avoid condemnation. They focus on improving the world by sharing their standards.

- self-critical thoughts ("inner critic") and perfectionistic
- critical, judgmental, enforces personal standards
- feels flawed and uses criticism to balance self-esteem
  - "you are just as bad, corrupt, flawed as I am"
- compares self to others, corrects others, needs to be right
- self-righteous, presents self with moral superiority
- resentful of those deviating from they believe is correct
- impulse suppression leading to pent-up anger
- built up anger leads to explosive expression of anger

Listen!

A Type One typically makes statements involving perfectionism.

- My father expected me to be better all the time
- My father blamed me for everything
- I constantly walked on eggshells
- I know right from wrong
- Things can always be better and improve
- My father always had the last word
- I have higher standards than anybody else
- I am prudent and reasonable
- That is not how I taught you

Type One sees themselves as objective, reasonable, prudent, principled, and in the know. The underlying theme is to improve the world with integrity. Others see healthy Ones the same but see average and unhealthy Ones as self-righteousness, inflexible, angered, critical, and judgmental.

Ones grow up frustrated with the guidance provided by the Father (-F). During a critical phase in their young lives, they figured the guidance received was inadequate or faulty. They create their own rules and standards essentially guiding themselves. Their inclination is to feel "not good enough" and learn to strive for being better and chase perfectionism. For fear of being criticized and condemned, they repress their emotions and impulses leading to pent up anger. This will eventually come out in an explosive, confrontational and angry manner.

Their self-esteem is linked to improving the world and doing the right thing. They seek to have moral integrity. They find their independence by adhering to their self-guiding principles. They provide others with their rules which is what they need the most themselves. They grow by letting go of their perspective they are the ones to judge right from wrong and open up regarding alternative ideas and solutions.

Type One is Autonomy seeking and action oriented. They are fueled by emotions and least in touch with reasoning. They typically have problems with impatience, anger and relating to others. They fear condemnation, repress their emotions and impulses. Being "not good enough" is counteracted by chasing perfectionism and leaves no room for gray areas. Emphatic certainty reinforces their black and white perspective. Their need to better the world can range from principled and realistic views to intolerance and

and punitive conduct. Their Vice is "Wrath" and repression with long term self-denial can only lead to an explosive release of pent-up anger.

The favored defense mechanism of a One is *Reaction Formation* or doing the opposite of what is deemed unacceptable. For instance, being extra nice to a person you dislike while suppressing built up anger reactions and the need to correct others.

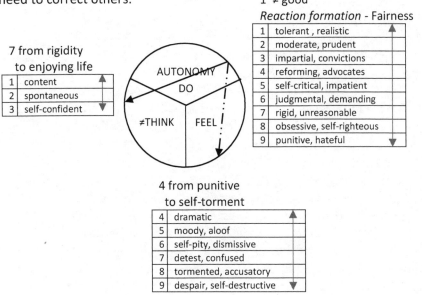

1 ≠ good

Reaction formation - Fairness

1	tolerant , realistic
2	moderate, prudent
3	impartial, convictions
4	reforming, advocates
5	self-critical, impatient
6	judgmental, demanding
7	rigid, unreasonable
8	obsessive, self-righteous
9	punitive, hateful

7 from rigidity
to enjoying life

1	content
2	spontaneous
3	self-confident

4 from punitive
to self-torment

4	dramatic
5	moody, aloof
6	self-pity, dismissive
7	detest, confused
8	tormented, accusatory
9	despair, self-destructive

Figure 70: Type One integration - disintegration

Ones present themselves as logical and methodical. They are dedicated and reliable with a strong conviction adherence.
At healthy levels, they are principled, have integrity, and conscientious.
They are inclusive of others, fair and impartial. They learned to not to judge and accept gray areas.
At average levels, idealism replaces realism with a focus on what could be. They become critical of others and self and chase their personal ideal. They see things in extremes and lose track of gray areas. They repress their instinctive doing and emotions leading to pent up anger.
At unhealthy levels, they are narrow-minded, self-righteous, and focus on pointing out the faults in others while rationalizing their mistakes (hypocrisy). They enforce their standards and are emotionally demonstrative. They are prone to using absolute words like never, always, nothing, completely, none, right, wrong, etc.

Type One summarized

Type 1	Vice: Wrath	
Childhood perception	"I am not good enough."	
Key fear	I fear not being good enough and being condemned	
Key need	I want to improve the world and make it perfect	
Key perspective	I must be better, even perfect (Criticism)	
Styles	Dedicated Reliable	Logical Methodical
Willfully ignores	Gray areas	
Behavioral Pathway:	*From morally astute to critical perfectionism*	
Defense mechanism: Reaction Formation	Undesirable response is replaced by the opposite (condemnation avoidance) *Presenting amicable image repressing inner anger.* *Typical problems: Anger and impatience*	
Healthy	"I replace perfectionism with being good enough within context." Wise, conscientious, rational, and ethical.	
Average	"I want others to try as hard as I do to be perfect." Idealism strives for perfection, critical, and judgmental	
Unhealthy	"I tell others how to be perfect." Intolerant, self-righteous, rigid, and enforces own standards	
Disintegration *Creating my own fears*	"My ideals are wrong, and I must consider the perspectives of others." From intolerant and punitive to withdrawal and emotionally tormented *My conviction to be the moral compass gives me condemnation instead.*	

Pee

Enforcing personal standards is part of the One's perspective. Two acquaintances just laid their brother, a fireman, to rest. With tears in their eyes, they said it was a wonderful ceremony, worthy of hero. Pee corrected them, "Just because he is a fireman doesn't make him a hero." He emphatically argued his point for twenty minutes. The demoralized couple left but not as fast as Pee's credibility did. He was asked what was going on with the couple leaving, and he, once again, argued his point for some fifteen minutes with his friends. Type Ones are emphatically certain and notoriously resistant to change.

Type Two: *let me take care of you*

<u>Behavioral Pattern</u>
Healthy: altruistic, takes care of own needs, genuine, generous
Average: good intentions, overly involved, self-sacrificing
Unhealthy: creating dependencies , self-deceptive about intentions, coercive

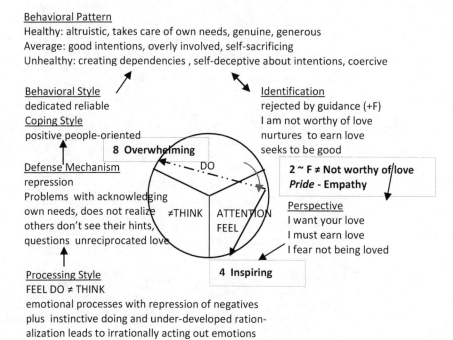

<u>Behavioral Style</u>
dedicated reliable
<u>Coping Style</u>
positive people-oriented

<u>Defense Mechanism</u>
repression
Problems with acknowledging
own needs, does not realize
others don't see their hints,
questions unreciprocated love

<u>Identification</u>
rejected by guidance (+F)
I am not worthy of love
nurtures to earn love
seeks to be good

8 Overwhelming

2 ~ F ≠ Not worthy of love
Pride - Empathy

≠THINK   ATTENTION
FEEL

DO

<u>Perspective</u>
I want your love
I must earn love
I fear not being loved

4 Inspiring

<u>Processing Style</u>
FEEL DO ≠ THINK
emotional processes with repression of negatives
plus instinctive doing and under-developed rationalization leads to irrationally acting out emotions

Figure 71: Behavioral Pathway Type Two

Look!

Childhood experience: a child felt unloved and underappreciated and compensates by earning love and appreciation. They learn they will only be
loved if they give to others first. The primary focal point is to decipher the
needs of others and then attend to those needs.

- links self-esteem to how good they are to others
- social, gregarious, hosts parties
- focus on other's needs and forgets their own needs
- adapts to others to be good to them
  - others control boundaries
  - feels controlled by others
- seeks approval by becoming needed and indispensable
- over gives, overly involved, overly good
- unaware they give to get back
- retaliates when their time and effort is not reciprocated
- feels selfish when own needs gain importance

- · inhibits own needs and favors needs of others
  - · only hints at own needs
- overextends themselves by meeting needs of too many
- prone to martyrdom and hypochondria
  - · may create physical illnesses to be taken care off

Listen!
A Type Two typically makes statements involving love.
- I love my dad but he didn't notice
- I know I am good
- I give, give, give
- I am a people pleaser
- I love others more than I love myself
- I go out of my way to be nice
- I like to help
- It feels good to be needed
- Love solves all problems
- I am the best friend you can wish for

Type Two sees themselves as loving, caring, giving, and selfless. The underlying theme is always being good. Others see healthy Twos the same, but view average and unhealthy Twos as demonstrative, overbearing, needy, clingy, overly involved, and playing a victim role.

Type Twos grow up feeling rejected by their Father (~F), feel unloved, unwanted, and not appreciated. Their perspective is "I am not worthy of love". They learn to mimic the mother by always being good to the father. As an adult, they project being good on everyone else. Twos must be good and earn love and appreciation. The Two's vice is *Pride* in being needed. Twos seek to take care of others to feel good about themselves and maintain their self-esteem. They are more prone than other Types to start second families. This way, they can take care of the young and vulnerable and fulfill their ego needs to be needed.
Their self-esteem is linked to being good to others. They get the attention they need by attending to the needs of others. Preoccupation with the needs of others leads to self-forgetting and not acknowledging their own needs. In doing so, Twos give others what they need the most themselves. They grow by accepting personal needs realizing this is not selfish rather a necessity.

Type Two is attention seeking and processes information emotionally. They can act out their emotions through immediate instinctive action. Their reasoning ability is under-developed. Twos have limited ability to express their needs logically and directly. They resort to hinting and expect others to recognize such hints as they can themselves. The Two's favored defense mechanism is *Repression*. They don't acknowledge their needs and store negative feelings away to prevent feeling anxious about not being loved. They feel they will not be loved unless it is earned and are forced to present themselves as good. They believe others will like their false persona better than the way they really are. By always being good, others are in charge of boundaries, which they don't discover until it is too late. They expect a return on their efforts, but when under-appreciated, their long-term repressed anger can be explosively expressed with ruthless violence. The Two, unworthy of love, now tells others, "you are not worthy of my love." Ruthless violence is a natural consequence of rejection, and so, the Two created their own biggest fear: "Now I am truly unloved".

Side note: Violence by a Two tends to be directed at those they have relationships with like family members and other intimates.

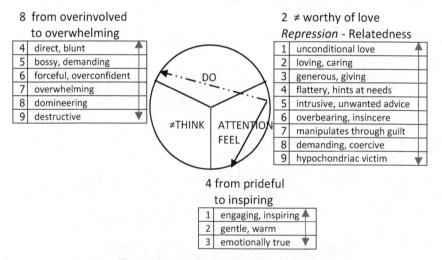

Figure 72: Type Two integration - disintegration

Twos are dedicated to their rule of always being good to others. They are reliable, positive-minded, and people-oriented.

At healthy levels, they are generous, engaging, positive, and love uncondi-tionally. They see good in others, are encouraging and want nothing but the best for them. Their love is the epitome of altruism.

At average levels, unconditional love becomes people pleasing, and good intentions now require a return. They are emotionally unfulfilled, get over-involved, intrusive, clingy, and make themselves indispensable. They may even discourage love interests as their perspective is "I am not worthy of unconditional love". They resist what they want the most and becomes a self-fulfilling prophecy.

At unhealthy levels, they feel unwanted and unloved. They are bitter and resentful for not getting a return on their time and efforts. They become self-serving, manipulative, coercive, and demanding but still believe in their good intentions. They might feel and act like victims.

Type Two summarized

Type 2	Vice: Pride	
Childhood perception	"I am not worthy of love."	
Key fear	I fear not being loved	
Key need	I want to be loved and appreciated	
Key perspective	I must earn your love and appreciation (Flattery)	
Styles	Dedicated Reliable	Positive-minded People-oriented
Willfully ignores	Their own needs	
Behavioral Pathway:	*From being good and loving to creating dependencies de-manding attention*	
Defense mechanism: Repression	Providing others what they need the most (own needs avoid-ance)	
	Presenting image of selflessness masking own neediness. Typical problems: Clinginess over-involvement	
Healthy	"I am loved; I love myself."	
	Altruistic, loving, generous, genuine	
Average	"I want to be loved, and must earn your love."	
	Friendly, good intentions, self-sacrificing, over-involved, and with intent of getting love and appreciation in return	
Unhealthy	"I need to be loved, and force myself on you."	
	Self-serving, manipulative, self-deceptive about true motives, victim role, resentful for lack of return on investment	
Disintegration	"My actions drive others away instead of appreciating me."	
	From overly involved and needy to overwhelming and	
Creating my own fears	domineering	
	My good deeds drive others away, and now I am not loved	

9.3 The Withdrawns (9,4,5)

The Withdrawns identify with the emotional nurturer and the guide, protector, and provider in their lives. They either feel attached (9), frustrated (4) or rejected (5) by both role models. They feel more secure when alone in their imaginary world. Although social, they maintain emotional distance from others. They seek outside approval which puts everybody in the position of judge.

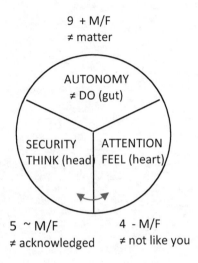

Figure 73: The Withdrawns

Type	Primary	Secondary	Least developed	Defense Mechanism
9	Reasoning Emotional	Instinctive	Instinctive Doing	Narcotization
4	Emotional	Reasoning	Instinctive Doing	Introjection
5	Reasoning	Emotional	Instinctive Doing	Isolation

The Withdrawns process information through reasoning and emotions, and instinctive doing is least developed. They are the procrastinators of the world.

- Withdrawn and imaginative motivated by
  - 9 independence through self-containment
  - 4 attention by being emotionally unavailable
  - 5 security by keeping others at a distance

9. Attachment to others and dissociate from reality through intense identification (merges)
4. Frustrated by others and dissociates from reality through imagination (introspection)
5. Rejected by others and dissociates from reality through encompassing thought processes (isolation)

The Withdrawns have under-developed instinctive action and is expressed as procrastination.
Nines withdraw into their inner sanctum negating negatives and emphasizing positives.
Fours apply negative environmental inlfluences to themselves and don't see what they have.
Fives distance themselves from others and their emotions and don't see what's right in front of them.

Type Nine: *"Whatever..."*

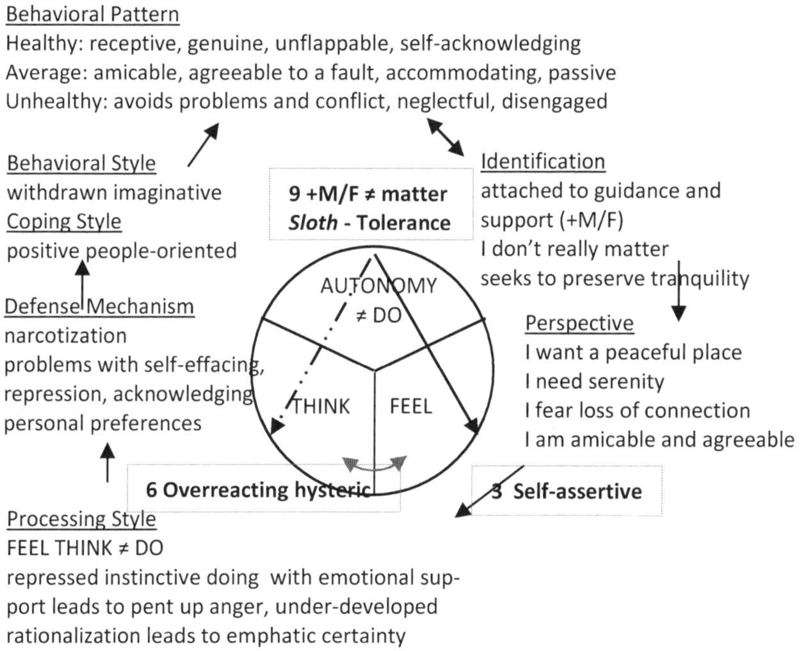

Behavioral Pattern
Healthy: receptive, genuine, unflappable, self-acknowledging
Average: amicable, agreeable to a fault, accommodating, passive
Unhealthy: avoids problems and conflict, neglectful, disengaged

Behavioral Style
withdrawn imaginative
Coping Style
positive people-oriented

Defense Mechanism
narcotization
problems with self-effacing, repression, acknowledging personal preferences

9 +M/F ≠ matter
Sloth - Tolerance

AUTONOMY
/ ≠ DO

THINK | FEEL

6 Overreacting hysteric

3 Self-assertive

Identification
attached to guidance and support (+M/F)
I don't really matter
seeks to preserve tranquility

Perspective
I want a peaceful place
I need serenity
I fear loss of connection
I am amicable and agreeable

Processing Style
FEEL THINK ≠ DO
repressed instinctive doing with emotional support leads to pent up anger, under-developed rationalization leads to emphatic certainty

Figure 74: Behavioral Pathway Type Nine

Look!

Childhood experience: a child growing up identifying with both role models and accommodating both. They are self-forgetting and feel like they were ignored and not important enough. They keep their opinions to themselves and seemingly agree with others to avoid conflict.

They never felt the need to differentiate themselves and are the most passive Type.

- avoids conflict at all cost out of fear of abandonment
- agreeable, amicable, self-forgetting
  - merges perspective with others
  - does not express personal preferences
- assesses all sides of issues
  - difficulty prioritizing
  - difficulty to take a side
  - lengthy thought wanderers
- presents self as relaxed and peaceful
- prioritizes comfort and self-indulgence
  - repetitive mind-numbing tasks like reading, watching TV, hobbies, cleaning, gardening

Listen!

A Type Nine typically makes statements involving indecision and passivity.

- My parents are nice
- I am not that important
- I don't get upset easily
- It's a waste of time to try to change things
- Let them be
- It's easier to go with the flow
- Too many choices are confusing
- I can't make up my mind
- I am easy-going
- Everyone has the right to their opinion
- I do whatever they want to do

Nines see themselves as relaxed, stable, kind, gentle, easy-going, amicable, and peaceful. The underlying theme is conflict avoidance and keeping the peace. Others see healthy Nines the same but see average and unhealthy Nines as complacent, appeasing, disengaged, and passive-aggressive.

The Nine grew up with a positive identification with both parents (+M/F). They feel connected to both role models and during conflict don't want to take sides out of fear of losing support of one of them. They learn to become agreeable and instead of taking a side, they will negotiate between both role models. In doing so, they are self-forgetting and feel not important enough to express their opinion. Their sense of self, their personal ID, is through identification with others. Unlike the other Types, they never felt the need to differentiate themselves.

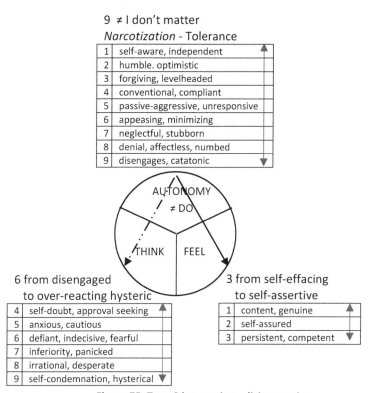

9 ≠ I don't matter
Narcotization - Tolerance

1	self-aware, independent
2	humble. optimistic
3	forgiving, levelheaded
4	conventional, compliant
5	passive-aggressive, unresponsive
6	appeasing, minimizing
7	neglectful, stubborn
8	denial, affectless, numbed
9	disengages, catatonic

AUTONOMY
≠ DO
THINK   FEEL

6 from disengaged
to over-reacting hysteric

4	self-doubt, approval seeking
5	anxious, cautious
6	defiant, indecisive, fearful
7	inferiority, panicked
8	irrational, desperate
9	self-condemnation, hysterical

3 from self-effacing
to self-assertive

1	content, genuine
2	self-assured
3	persistent, competent

Figure 75: Type 9 integration - disintegration

As amicable and agreeable as Nines are, they repress personal preferences and anger which eventually must be expressed. They want to avoid conflict and fear loss of support. They use withdrawal and mind-numbing repetitive tasks to avoid thinking about the real issues. Their desire for inner peace initially outweighs expression of their personal preferences, but nothing lasts forever. Ignoring unpleasant issues, self-neglect, and not expressing personal opinions leads to lack of self-awareness and loss of individuality.

Eventually, Nines feel they were not heard, and when pent up anger built sufficiently, they will assert themselves aggressively and explosively.

Nines seek autonomy by disappearing into their private and safe inner sanctum. They process information rationally and emotionally. There is often conflict between objectivity and subjectivity and they mix like oil and water. To find resolve takes time with procrastination as the end result. Instinctive doing is, therefore, the least developed. Their amicable attitude can develop into passivity and apathy. And thus, their Vice is "Sloth" or keeping themselves busy with unimportant tasks to avoid conflict. They grow by finding themselves important enough to be heard. They need to replace an appeasing role with self-assertion.

The Nine's favored defense mechanism is *Narcotization,* or dissociation through repetitive, habitual, and mind numbing activities. They withdraw mentally using distractions like books, internet, movies, quilting, gardening or just spacing out.

Nines are withdrawn, imaginative, positive-minded, and people-oriented. Their conflict within themselves is attempting to match objectivity with subjectivity.
At healthy levels, they are self-possessed, acknowledge their personal preferences, and feel worthy of being heard. They are positive, optimistic and balance their needs with those of others.
At average levels, they are self-effacing, easy-going, passive, and avoid conflict. They appear agreeable but hold their opinions back.

Others see them as pleasant, yet, they are passive-aggressive. Their unexpressed opinions, combined with adaptation, leads to pent-up anger.
At unhealthy levels, they are self-forgetting. After years of accommodating others, they no longer know who they are. They stubbornly avoid conflicts; dissociate themselves from situations and others, and eventually from themselves as well.

Type Nine summarized

Type 9	Vice: Sloth	
Childhood perception	"I don't matter."	
Key fear	I fear loss and separation	
Key need	I want harmony and peace	
Key perspective	I must be amicable, agreeable (Indolence)	
Styles	Withdrawn Imaginative	Positive-minded People-oriented
Willfully ignores	Personal preferences	
Behavioral Pathway:	*From keeping the peace to stubbornly neglectful*	
Defense mechanism: Narcotization	Mind numbing activities through habitual, repetitive tasks (conflict avoidance) *Presenting an image of harmony and peace while feeling conflict* *Typical problems: neglectful stubbornness*	
Healthy	"I express myself and acknowledge myself." Self-assured, patient, agreeable, positive, perceptive, acknowledges self as equal to others	
Average	"I need to keep the peace." Maintains support by being amicable, agreeable, without expressing own views, fears loss of support	
Unhealthy	"I must keep the peace." Emotionally unavailable, passive-aggressive, disengaged, complacent, self-forgetting, building pent-up anger, withdrawn into safety of an imaginary world	
Disintegration *Creating my own fears*	"You are not worthy of my support." From disengaged to overreacting hysteric *My hysterics drive others away, and I lost support*	

W

Conflict avoidance and passivity are part of the perspective of a Nine. W wants to buy his friend's wife a drink. He asks his permission first. His friend assures him this is okay, and he can do that anytime. A few weeks later, just to make sure, he asks for permission again. Nines fear loss of support and W just has to make sure he is not misunderstood and avoids conflict at all cost.

K

During a discussion regarding personality types, K said she always loved her parents and had a great relationship with them. She admitted she avoids conflict to keep her own peace of mind. She is the "glass is half full" kind of woman and said, "I don't want to deal with conflict. Her Nine perspective was shining through when she said, "yeah, I will tell them they are right even though I know they are not. I just walk away and think "whatever and let them be". During difficult times, she will work on projects by herself, like art and quilting. This conflict avoidance technique is Narcotization, or a mind-

numbing repetitive task to stay preoccupied with anything other but confronting conflict.

H

My dear friend H is a Nine and he explained his parents were always fighting. As a child, he learned to keep his mouth shut and walk away. Even as an adult he has great difficulty with confrontation and feels his opinion, just like in his childhood, does not really matter. He developed a Nine's perspective and has not expressed his point of view very often.

Type Four: *I am the only one who feels this way*

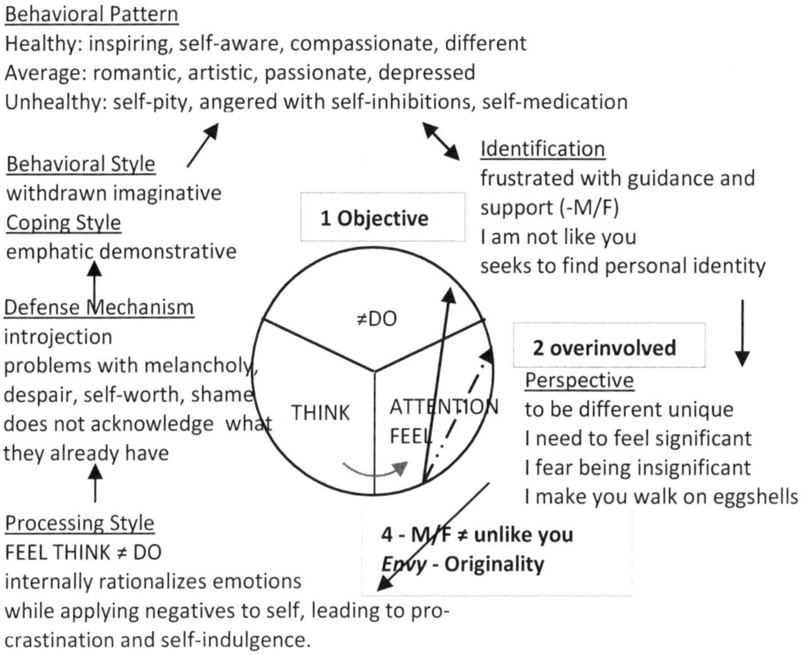

Behavioral Pattern
Healthy: inspiring, self-aware, compassionate, different
Average: romantic, artistic, passionate, depressed
Unhealthy: self-pity, angered with self-inhibitions, self-medication

Behavioral Style
withdrawn imaginative
Coping Style
emphatic demonstrative

Defense Mechanism
introjection
problems with melancholy,
despair, self-worth, shame
does not acknowledge what
they already have

Processing Style
FEEL THINK ≠ DO
internally rationalizes emotions
while applying negatives to self, leading to procrastination and self-indulgence.

1 Objective

≠DO

THINK   ATTENTION
        FEEL

Identification
frustrated with guidance and
support (-M/F)
I am not like you
seeks to find personal identity

2 overinvolved

Perspective
to be different unique
I need to feel significant
I fear being insignificant
I make you walk on eggshells

4 - M/F ≠ unlike you
Envy - Originality

Figure 76: Behavioral Pathway Type Four

Look!

Childhood experience: A child felt abandoned, alone and not noticed. He did
not understand why and felt there must be something wrong with them.
They compensate by internally assessing situations to find an answer to why
they are so different.

- intensely emotional, dramatic, moody
  - melancholy, depression, despair
- self-conscious and feels misunderstood
  - tugs on emotional strings of others
  - withdraws to be noticed and rescued
  - affinity for super-heroes
- focus on what's missing and wants what others have
- dichotomy is to fit in by being different
  - dress code from unique to bizarre
  - excess accessories
- clings on to problems

- makes others walk on eggshells
- idealizes fantasies and artistic expression

Listen!
A Type Four typically makes statements involving suffering and sadness.
- My parents weren't really interested in me
- The more I looked at myself, the less I liked me
- I am a bit of a loner
- I feel alone
- I feel unloved
- I feel misunderstood
- I feel others should help me
- I think about death at times
- My childhood wasn't a happy one
- I don't feel good

Type Four sees themselves as different, unique, self-aware, sensitive, and inspiring. The underlying theme is to differentiate themselves. Others see healthy Fours the same but view average and unhealthy Fours as temperamental, individualistic, moody, irrational, and self-indulgent.

Type Four grew up frustrated with both role models (- M/F) and did not identify with either of them. They don't feel acknowledged for who they are and feel insignificant. They conclude something must be wrong with them because the parents don't like me. They disconnected from both parents telling themselves "I am not like them" and learn to focus on being different. They have the need to fit in by being different, and that is a dichotomy in itself. As they need to create their identity, they end up in a long quest for finding themselves, putting bits and pieces of likes and dislikes of others together like a puzzle. They will express opinions that go against the mainstream with a melancholy undertone.

Fours are attention seeking which they accomplish through withdrawal and by being emotionally unavailable. They hope someone will notice how sad they really are and then pats them on the back. They look for a "rescuer" and are often drawn to Superheroes. They process information emotionally supported by rationalization. They apply negative twists to themselves and typically have problems with self-worth, shame, and despair. The Four compares themselves to emphasizing a "You have, and I don't" point of view. That attitude leads them to losing track of what is right in front of them.

Their Vice is *Envy* or longing for what others have through these comparisons. It seems a substitute ideation for the lack of parental connection.

Typical defense mechanism is *Introjection* or internalization of negative above positive information, while unable to distinguish which is actually true. "But his game is nicer than mine."

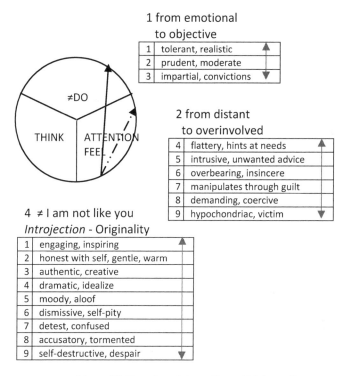

1 from emotional
to objective

1	tolerant, realistic
2	prudent, moderate
3	impartial, convictions

2 from distant
to overinvolved

4	flattery, hints at needs
5	intrusive, unwanted advice
6	overbearing, insincere
7	manipulates through guilt
8	demanding, coercive
9	hypochondriac, victim

4 ≠ I am not like you
Introjection - Originality

1	engaging, inspiring
2	honest with self, gentle, warm
3	authentic, creative
4	dramatic, idealize
5	moody, aloof
6	dismissive, self-pity
7	detest, confused
8	accusatory, tormented
9	self-destructive, despair

Figure 77: Type Four integration - disintegration

Fours are withdrawn, imaginative, emotional, and demonstrative through withdrawal.
Healthy Fours embrace themselves and life. They are introspective, inspiring, and creative.
Average Fours are individualistic, self-absorbed, and excessively self-indulgent.
Unhealthy Fours are alienated, resentful, depressed, and live in despair.

Type Four summarized

Type 4	Vice: Envy	
Childhood perception	"I am not like you" (there must be something wrong with me)	
Key fear	I fear being insignificant	
Key need	I want to be different and unique	
Key perspective	I must distinguish and be myself (Melancholy)	
Styles	Withdrawn Imaginative	Emphatic Demonstrative
Willfully ignores	Satisfaction with what they already have	
Behavioral Pathway:	*From self-awareness to self-consciousness*	
Defense mechanism: Introjection	Internalization of environmental aspects to self (to find own ID) *Presenting image of being unique and different while feeling insignificant* *Typical problems: moodiness irrationality*	
Healthy	"I am different, and I have my own identification." Self-aware, creative, inspiring, personal insight, emotional understanding	
Average	"I don't relate and express myself as different and unique." Wants to be different and fit in the mainstream Finds outlet in expressive mediums like the arts	
Unhealthy	"I am different but want to fit in. I am insignificant. Will you rescue me?" Others see them as different and at times bizarre, makes others walk on egg-shells Moody, irritable, emotionally demanding, dramatic, self-pity, self-indulgent	
Disintegration *Creating my own fears*	"I am wasting good opportunities, ruining my own life." From aloof to overly involved and demanding *By being different, I will never fit in and become insignificant*	

X

Being emotionally unavailable, and self-pity is part of the Four's perspective. He is single, sits alone at the bar, and drinks too much. Fours tend to lighten up from melancholy when others show interest in them. He admitted to having superheroes or imaginary rescuers. He gave his Type away with the Batman tattoo on his arm.

Type Five: *Knowledge is power*

Behavioral Pattern
Healthy: extraordinary perceptive, inquisitive, insightful, aware
Average: intellectual pursuits, studious pre-occupied
Unhealthy: reclusive, nihilistic, social detachment, eccentric

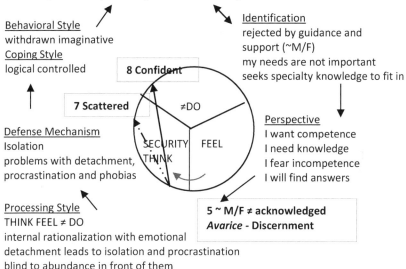

Behavioral Style
withdrawn imaginative
Coping Style
logical controlled

Identification
rejected by guidance and
support (~M/F)
my needs are not important
seeks specialty knowledge to fit in

8 Confident

7 Scattered   ≠DO

Perspective
I want competence
I need knowledge
I fear incompetence
I will find answers

Defense Mechanism
Isolation
problems with detachment,
procrastination and phobias

SECURITY   FEEL
THINK

Processing Style
THINK FEEL ≠ DO
internal rationalization with emotional
detachment leads to isolation and procrastination
blind to abundance in front of them

5 ~ M/F ≠ acknowledged
Avarice - Discernment

Figure 78: Behavioral Pathway Type Five

Look!

Childhood experience: role models provided mixed messages and the child concluded the world is unpredictable. They felt unacknowledged, unloved, and intruded upon. They compensate by maintaining emotional distance, observe, and gain knowledge to cope with unpredictably.

- private, quiet, emotionally distant
- easily overwhelmed with too much stimulation
- withdraws to avoid commitment and intrusions
- compartmentalizes to detach emotions and be objective
- thinks before they speak favoring measured responses
- information gatherers
  - researchers
- minimalist, nihilistic
  - my needs are not important to you
  - I will cling on to what I already have or know
- may isolate self and become a loner

Listen!

A Type Five typically makes statements involving knowledge.

- My parents are okay but cold and distant
- I think for myself
- I am inquisitive and observant
- I keep my distance to avoid obligations
- Knowledge is power
- I am a loner
- I don't like small talk
- I prepare before I do
- That's stupid
- I don't want to intrude
- I love spending time alone and think
- I love to share what I have learned
- I like to stay out of the limelight
- I don't like crowds that much
- I like predictability

Type Five sees themselves as smart, intelligent, observant, perceptive, and inquisitive. The underlying theme is to develop a unique knowledge base. They try to be acknowledged and fit in by offering a skill others do not have. Others see healthy Fives the same, but view average and unhealthy Fives as preoccupied, detached, conceptual, eccentric, and at times as single-minded and over-specialized.

Fives grow up with ambivalence toward both role models (~M/F). They felt their needs were not important, felt rejected, unloved, and unacknowl-edged. They searched for something unique to contribute to gain security and nurturance, but never felt they fit in. They resolve their ambivalence by not identifying with either role model and withdraw in thought. In doing so, they learn thoughts are safe, and the outside world is unsafe and unpredict-able. From their perspective, the world is unreliable, and they learn to ob-serve and focus on their immediate environment.

Patrick Jane, the Mentalist (Type Five), says, "There are no such things as psychics. I just pay attention."

Type Five is Security-seeking and uses reasoning to process information supported by emotions. They detach emotions to preserve objectivity and Instinctive doing is least developed. They typically have problems with anxiety, isolation, paralysis analysis, and nihilism. They received mixed signals from their role models, presenting them with a confusing, unreliable, and unpredictable environment, forcing them to be observant and learn to anticipate. Fearing not being able to respond adequately to the world, they withdraw, gather and process information, setting them up for a lifelong quest for knowledge and meaning within context. Naturally withdrawn and imaginative, they rationalize situations and favor delayed and measured responses. Problems arise when excess theorizing develops into useless over-specialization. A tell-tale stress reaction is "intellectual arrogance".

Dr. Phil sitting back and crossing his arms:
"Do you think I <u>know</u> what I am doing?"
"If you are so <u>smart</u>, how come this isn't working?"
"I <u>have been doing this for thirty years</u>, so don't you tell me how to do my job."

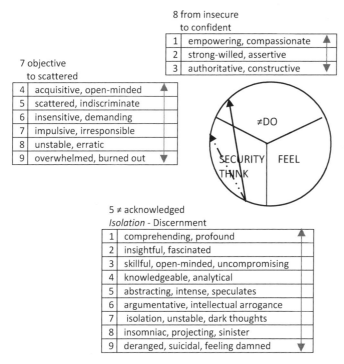

	8 from insecure to confident
1	empowering, compassionate
2	strong-willed, assertive
3	authoritative, constructive

7 objective
to scattered

4	acquisitive, open-minded
5	scattered, indiscriminate
6	insensitive, demanding
7	impulsive, irresponsible
8	unstable, erratic
9	overwhelmed, burned out

≠DO

SECURITY THINK FEEL

5 ≠ acknowledged
Isolation - Discernment

1	comprehending, profound
2	insightful, fascinated
3	skillful, open-minded, uncompromising
4	knowledgeable, analytical
5	abstracting, intense, speculates
6	argumentative, intellectual arrogance
7	isolation, unstable, dark thoughts
8	insomniac, projecting, sinister
9	deranged, suicidal, feeling damned

Figure 79: Type Five integration - disintegration

Fives are detail-oriented researchers requiring time for themselves to figure things out. This leads to being stingy with time. Socialization can be difficult for them as they delve deeply into specialized subjects. They tend to detest small talk as it interferes their linear thinking and inner voice. Their biggest asset is time, and their Vice is "Avarice" and is best explained as retentiveness. It's the feeling the world is unreliable, there isn't enough and they cling on to what they already have.

Fives favored defense mechanism is *Isolation,* or retreating into their own minds while separating unacceptable acts or impulses from an attached emotion to prevent feeling overwhelmed.

Fives are withdrawn, imaginative, logical and methodical.
Healthy Fives found a way to be part of the world. They are observant, visionaries, and innovative.
Average Fives seek expertise, conceptualize, are preoccupied, and provocative.
Unhealthy Fives are eccentric, disappear into oblivion, nihilistic, and can be delirious.

Type Five summarized

Type 5	Vice: Avarice	
Childhood perception	I am not acknowledged, and I don't fit in	
Key fear	I fear being inadequate, incompetent	
Key need	I seek acknowledgment by offering competence (Retentiveness)	
Key perspective	I want to be knowledgeable and be competent	
Styles	Withdrawn Imaginative	Logical Methodical
Willfully ignores	Existing abundance in front of them	
Behavioral Pathway:	*From competence to useless specialization*	
Defense mechanism: Isolation	Retreating into thought and emotional detachment (emptiness avoidance) *Presenting image of being knowledgeable while feeling empty and incompetent* *Typical problems: detachment secrecy*	
Healthy	"I understand the world and feel safe in it." Profound, visionary, recognizes many points of view, from big picture to details, insightful, innovative	
Average	"I question the world and fear the unknown." Analytical, intellectual prowess, abstract thinking, and speculation overthinks, analyzes everything, farfetched ideation, and reductionism	
Unhealthy	"The world is unpredictable and I keep my distance." Lives in own mind, reclusive, isolation, nihilism, prone to distortions of reality and fantasy becomes their reality	
Disintegration	From objective reasoning to scattered thinking and hyperactivity. Reactivity without resolve.	
Creating my own fears	*By rejecting everything, my world has become meaningless*	

R

Fives provide insight and knowledge as part of their perspective. Competence feeds their egos and meeting the needs of others makes them feel fit in. R is quiet, withdrawn, and observant. He is a salesman, and pleased with his ability to read people. He goes the extra mile to serve his clients in a more than usual personal way. He proudly proclaims a lot of his business is referral based and this way his need to be part of a larger whole is met.

A

A Five firefighter friend said," *My chief and I get along very well. He helps me understand things, is experienced and knowledgeable. He is a Five and revealed his most important attribute: his need for competence.*

B

B was quietly drinking coffee during an exuberant New Year's party. He explained, he likes to observe and stay out of the limelight. He spends a lot of time researching subjects because "Knowledge is power." His wife claims he tends to be quiet and prefers to spent time alone in his computer room.

Russell Wilson

The Seahawks quarter-back is known to study the opponent at length and stated "Separation is in preparation". He is also known to share his detailed insights with his teammates. On the field, he remains calm, assesses situations and makes good choices. It comes as no surprise a t-shirt with "Russell Knows" entered the market.

"The evolution of knowledge is toward simplicity." - L. Ron Hubbard.

10. Misidentification

It is important to realize misidentification of a Type happens and most frequently because we jumped to conclusions too soon. It takes time to identify a distinct main theme in a person's perspective and consistencies in distinct known behavioral patterns. The easiest way, to recognize a Type, is through their stress reactions when they exaggerate their normal behaviors.

A friend of mine asked: *"how do you evaluate a person who has a dual personality? For example, in his work environment, this person is considered kind, helpful, competent etc., but in his personal life away from work, he is the opposite."*

Anyone going out on a first date will put their best foot forward. They dress up nice, are considerate, polite, and treat you with dignity and respect. They focus on their date with excitement and anticipation. But, after the honeymoon phase is over, they will become more themselves and fall back on their habitual patterns.

I tell young people on the dating scene to not assume the behaviors projected on them on the first few dates as necessarily being your date's norm. But do observe how your date treats others he or she has no vested interest in. How does the guy treat the waitress, the hostess, the valet, the cashier? Does he look behind him when going through a door and let others in? Is he aware of his surroundings, includes others, and treats them with dignity and respect? Observe these behaviors because that is the way you will be treated once the honeymoon is over. (*Not to mention to get a handwriting sample.*)

When meeting a person for the first time does not mean they necessarily reveal their true perspective, nor their average social and behavioral style. This also means we should not jump to conclusions too soon regarding someone's type. We might have a good idea and think in a direction of what Type someone might be but need to remain open to other Types.

We play roles in different circumstances, and this is not a dual personality. When we are at work and have a vested interest, we are professional and courteous. We are employees and work under the guidance of procedures and policies set by those in charge. We feel safe and comfortable at home, and this is where our fears and frustrations will come out. As adults, we are in charge at home and take a lead role. We play two different roles in these two different settings. And although our core fears, needs, and perspectives remain the same, we are more inhibited at work than at home. It is imperative to identify a Type within the context of circumstances. Generally speaking, the more comfortable someone is in their environment, the more likely they will be true to their nature and personal perspective.

The most noticeable observable behaviors are in the behavioral style group. The Assertives and Insistent Types (3,7,8) are self-assured, independent, assertive, and take initiative. The Withdrawn and Imaginative Types (9,4,5) are introverted, quiet, observe others, and are not as competitive. The Dedicated and Reliable Types (6,1,2) are dedicated, responsible, committed, and do what they think is the right thing to do.

Assume you meet someone at a party who is assertive and insistent, and you think in the direction of Type Three, Seven, or Eight. Is he generally a more withdrawn Type but displays confident behaviors because he is in a comfortable environment (9,4,5)? Or does he not know anybody and asserts himself with confidence not caring about the emotional impact he has on others (3,7,8)? Is he mentally healthy or unhealthy and are his behaviors adjusted accordingly? Context is everything.

To identify someone's Type takes time, experience, and a strong foundation in the Enneagram. Over time, our accuracy and proficiency will become adequate. And still, misidentification remains a possibility. There are various reasons for misidentification. Two different types can behave similarly at certain mental health levels. Or our exposure to a person is limited to work only, and we don't know how they behave in more comfortable settings. No person will always fit exactly according to our expectations of the model.

Healthy people are often harder to identify since they blend many healthy and socially acceptable traits. They don't exaggerate as much as a stressed individual. Our core perspective never changes, and our key fear and need will remain the same. One of the easiest ways to identify a Type is to observe their stress reactions. Remember, at average and unhealthy levels, we tend to exaggerate our normal behaviors.

Personally, I have a harder time to recognize Type Six and Type Nine quickly. I think the reason behind this is, for me at least, these Types do not reveal their perspectives readily. Sixes do what is expected from them and Nines tend to agree with others. It generally takes me longer to identify these types and is so consistent, that when I can't figure a Type fairly easily, I start thinking in the direction of Six or Nine.

A Type Two who is naturally loving, caring and giving will at average and unhealthy levels exaggerate these behaviors by being extra loving, extra caring and extra giving. We interpret this as overly involved, needy, and clingy. When we see a person's stress reaction, it will become clear what Type a person is.

Such exaggeration of normal behavior is also helpful when in doubt about Type and wing. The stress response of a 1w2 might be enforcing personal standards with emphatic certainty, whereas the 2w1 tend to become overly involved and clingy.

Type One vs. Type Six
Type One grows up frustrated with the guidance received and set their own rules and standards. Since they set the rules, only they know right from wrong. They are Autonomy seeking and attempt to create an ideal world according to their standards. They learn to strive to be better and might even chase perfectionism. They will tell others the right thing to do, enforce personal standards, and can do so with emphatic certainty. From all appearances, a One is purposeful, self-reliant, and principled.

A Six grows up with self-doubt and learn to rely on guidance received. Without guidance and support, they feel anxious and not safe. They learn to abide by the rules provided by an authority figure, usually the father, and they need frequent reassurance. They do what is expected of them to feel secure. A Six is typically responsible, dutiful, and trustworthy.

183

The One and Six are often misidentified although there are significant differences in their perspectives. Their behavioral styles have a noteworthy overlap making identification all the more difficult. The core difference between a One and a Six is *emphatic certainty (1)* and *self-doubt (6)*. Give it time, and their perspectives and stress reactions will shine through.

Both One and Six have strong similarities in their behaviors but for very different reasons:
- strict rule adherence
 Ones are compliant to the demands of their own ideals ("inner critic").
 Sixes are compliant to the demands of other people ('inner committee").
- Guilt feelings about doing something not in line with their rules.
 One has guilt over doing things not in line with their own standards.
 Six has guilt over doing things not in line with expectations of others.
- They emphasize intuition and emotion and are furthest removed from deductive reasoning.
 A One knows without knowing why, and their emotions fuel their intuitive opinions.
 A Six operates in two distinct modes. Intuitive and emotional or reasoning by itself.
- You can't tell either of them what to do. Both have strong opinions and adhere strictly to their rules.
 Ones adhere to their strict personal standards.
 Sixes adopt rules others created.
- They present themselves as good.
 Ones present themselves as good to better the world.
 Sixes present themselves as good to gain support.

They are relatively easy to distinguish by their emotional makeup. Ones are *emphatically certain* and convince others of their rules. An average One enforces personal standards onto others. They are extremely decisive as only they know right from wrong. They think in black and white terms and are blind to gray areas. Sixes have self-doubt, are *uncertain* and rely on reassurance, back-tested rules and known procedures. An average Six is anxious, indecisive, ambivalent and reactive. They find it difficult to relate to others with confidence. They become either dutiful and dependent or rebellious and defiant. These indecisive traits are entirely absent in a One.

184

Since a Five is logical and controlled like a Three, a Five wing adds control and deductive reasoning to the Six. For that reason, the 6w5 and One are one of the more common misidentifications.

D

D is a mature female, strong-willed, and opinionated. We discussed whether she was a One or a Six at length. We never reached consensus which is irrelevant. We are who we are without a Type attached to us.

Remember, Sixes have attachment to the patriarchal role model (+F). They like to do what is expected from them as they adhere to guidance provided to feel safe and find support. Ones have a negative identification with the Father (-F). This is generally the patriarchal role model and most often the father. Type One abides by their self-created rules and standards. In our exchanges, D comes over as a strong-willed, self-assured, and with strong opinions. She also stated she ended a bad relationship in her younger years and vowed to "never be dominated again." Her perspective, word selection, and handwriting behavior are in line with a Type One presenting herself with certainty (1) instead of self-doubt (6). Her view, to be never dominated again, is not like a Six who is more authority abiding and does what is expected. Yet, it is entirely possible she is a counter-phobic Six and rebelled against authority.

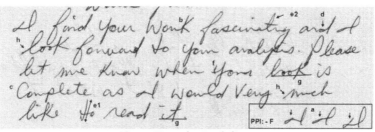

Figure 80: authority defiant

Handwriting traits supporting Type One are:
- Handwriting is with minimal hesitation and intense pressure implying certitude (1)
- a: The PPI implies frustration with the Father figure (1)
- b: The enlarged K's imply authority defiant (1 or counter-phobic 6)
- c: Unexpected capitals imply authority defiant (1 or 6)
- d: Distortions in the "d" imply non-conformist (1)
- e1: The "t" height implies pride in accomplishments (1 or 6)

- e2: The unexpected looped t-stem implies sensitivity to the word "fascinating" and implies she is not convinced regarding handwriting analysis (6 or 1)
- f: The repaired stroke implies fixing things and tend to be done by perfectionists (1)
- g: Strokes violating an established baseline imply hidden intentions and poor urge control (1 or 6)
- h: Straight lead-in strokes imply resentment and in line with the anger Triad (1)

"Every relationship is mutually defined" - Dr. Phil

11. Relationship dynamics

Trust

Every relationship is influenced by the push of needs and the pull of wants. The quality of a relationship is determined by how much the needs of the parties involved are met.

We say relationships are built on trust and this requires us to define trust. Most people define trust by stating someone else behaves in a consistent manner. In other words, I trust you because I know what to expect from you and my expectation of you is in line with my own core beliefs.

In gist, this is how dictionaries define trust:
- certainty based on past experience
- believing in the honesty of others
- complete confidence in a plan or person
- belief someone is reliable
- firm belief in truth, ability, integrity of someone
- when actions mirrors values in a consistent manner
- reliance on strength, integrity, ability of a person

As we can see, trust is labeled as an interpretation of other people's behavioral choices. But, that is only half the equation. We play a far more important role in the definition of trust. Have a look in the mirror.

Someone who acts outside our belief system and oversteps our personal boundaries tends to create anxiety. It generates pain, fear, and frustration within us. We tend to react by exaggerating our normal behaviors in order to protect our beliefs and ego boundaries. We feel uncomfortable with the views and behaviors of others and say "I don't trust him". We don't trust because he did not behave within our boundaries or within an established expectation pattern. We now keep a close and mistrusting eye on him because he might repeat the same behavior in the future and *"we don't know how to deal with him"*.

The second part of the trust equation is therefore you. It is you *"who feels uncomfortable with someone else, not because of what he did, but because you don't know how to deal with it"*. Trust is, without a doubt, a function of how well you handle any curve-ball thrown at you. And so, healthy individuals who work from a solid and steadfast foundation will trust themselves to manage the same misdeed in the future. They don't go on the offensive by exaggerating their normal behaviors to protect their egos, rather, they tend to dismiss or redirect such infractions. They tend to not blame the other person rather, they look within themselves and point out the responsibilities others have in the equation.

Birds of a Feather

"Birds of a feather flock together" is an idiom freely translated as people with the same tastes and interests tend to stick together. It makes sense the Types who process information in a similar fashion tend to understand each other better. Despite differing motivations, they do have similar tendencies in broad terms. This suggests they also know what to expect and they relate to each other better.

Style	Information process	Motivated by
Assertive and Insistent I am forceful and insist on my needs being met	Rational and Intuitive	I need to excel I need a new experience I need to be in control
Dedicated and Reliable I abide by a core rule	Intuitive and Emotional	I need to follow rules I need to improve the world I need to earn love
Withdrawn and Imaginative I step back and think	Rational and Emotional	I need to have serenity I need to be unique I need to be competent

The Assertives (3,7,8) process information combining intuition and rationalization. Emotional attachment is under-developed. They justify their behavior after the act. They are assertive, insistent, and can overstep boundaries with relative ease. Their motivations are entirely different as Threes don't feel worthy and seek to be acknowledged for what they do. Sevens don't feel nurtured and become acquisitive and hyperactive. Eights don't feel protected and take control to protect themselves. They take charge and self-promote being blind to failure (3), are demanding and intrusive while blind to personal limitations (7), and are forceful and overwhelming while blind to the emotional impact they have on others (8). Threes, Sevens, and Eights *trust themselves* to deal with others and have no qualms about moving forward. Their strong qualities are perseverance (3), spontaneity (7) and candor (8). They can be confrontational and tend to violate the rights of others.

The Compliants (6,1,2) process information combining intuition and emotions. They have strict rule adherences and are notoriously resistant to change. Rationalization is under-developed. Again, motivation behind their rule adherences is entirely different. Sixes have self-doubt and do what is expected to gain support. Ones don't feel good enough and abide by their own rules to gain independence. Twos don't feel loved and abide by their self-set rule to always be good in order to be loved and appreciated. They have rule adherence in common. They seek guidance to gain support and overestimate authority (6). They need to improve the world and are blind to gray areas (1), and they need to be good to others and are blind to their personal needs (2). Their strong suits are loyalty (6), fairness (1), and empathy (2). They *trust rules* and enforce their rules on themselves and others. They can violate themselves and others.

The Withdrawns (9,4,5) process information combining rationalization and emotions. They have to match objectivity and subjectivity before they move forward leading to procrastination. They are the most withdrawn and cautious Types. Their instinctive doing is under-developed. The motivation behind each Type is distinct and different. Nines don't feel their voice matters and they are amicable and agreeable out of fear for loss of support. Fours don't feel significant and they withdraw in self-pity to be noticed. Fives don't feel acknowledged and they seek to bring specialty knowledge in order to be acknowledged. They have withdrawal and caution in common and are the more timid types. They need to maintain tranquility and don't acknowledge personal preferences (9). They need to distinguish themselves by being different and unique while they don't see what they already have (4). They seek knowledge and competence in order to anticipate the world but are blind to what is readily available (5). Their strengths are tolerance (9), originality (4) and discernment (5). They *don't trust themselves* and shy away from the world resolving conflict within their imagination. They are more likely to violate themselves than others.

Relationship dynamics within the same group and Types outside a group can of course create conflict. The Assertives might battle with other Assertives through aggressive insistence; the Withdrawns might not come to a conclusion with another withdrawn; the Compliants might never agree on a rule adherence. The Assertives might overwhelm the Withdrawns who tend to sit back and observe or they might disagree with the rule adherence of a Compliant Type, etc. As we can see, relationship dynamics is based on our perspective, how we process information and how much we trust ourselves (healthy-average-unhealthy) to manage adversity.

"Behaviors in isolation do not reveal a Type; Type recognition comes with a significant number of observations befitting a known behavioral pattern."

12. Look and Listen!

We need to recognize patterns to identify types. Healthy individuals are harder to pinpoint since they integrate many healthy qualities. The average and unhealthy Types are easier identified as fears and needs are exaggerated. Pattern recognition is possible because the patterns are distinct and consistent. You know the patterns and now you need to "Look and Listen":

- what perspective is frequently expressed
      1. I am not good enough
      2. I am not worthy of love
      3. I am not worthy
      4. I am insignificant
      5. I don't feel acknowledged
      6. I am not safe
      7. I don't feel nurtured
      8. I am not protected
      9. I don't really matter
- what main theme shines through
      1. I am critical and judgmental
      2. I am loving and caring
      3. I am better than you
      4. I am sensitive and unique
      5. I am inquisitive and knowledgeable
      6. I do what is expected of me
      7. I am experience-oriented and busy
      8. I am strong and bossy
      9. I am relaxed and keep the peace

- what core need is emphasized
    1. autonomy seeking
    2. attention seeking
    3. security seeking
- what seems to be a problem
    1. anger / relating to others
    2. self-worth / shame
    3. fear / anxiety
- what social style is favored
    1. logical / methodical
    2. emphatic / demonstrative
    3. positive-minded / people-oriented
- what behavioral style is favored
    1. assertive / insistent
    2. dedicated / reliable
    3. withdrawn / imaginative
- how do they process information
    1. intuitively (response immediacy)
    2. emotionally (heartfelt)
    3. rationally (logical reasoning)
- what are the main role model influences
    1. attachment
    2. rejection
    3. frustration
- what defense mechanism is favored
    1. reaction formation
    2. repression
    3. identification
    4. introjection
    5. isolation
    6. projection
    7. rationalization
    8. denial
    9. narcotization
- what key words resonate
    1. objective, reasonable, prudent
    2. loving, caring, selfless
    3. admirable, desirable, driven
    4. sensitive, different, unique
    5. inquisitive, perceptive, intelligent

6. dependable, reliable, trustworthy

7. free-spirited, enthusiastic, adventurous

8. strong, assertive, direct

9. relaxed, peaceful, easy-going

- what are the main stress reactions

1. anger outbursts

2. overly involved, clingy

3. arrogance, condescending

4. withdrawn, self-pity

5. withdrawn, isolation

6. dutiful, dependency

7. erratic thinking, hyper-activity

8. intimidating, overwhelming

9. passivity, complacency

- what stress reaction pattern presents itself

1. frustration anger - enforcing personal standards - withdrawal in self-pity

2. not acknowledging own needs - creating dependencies - overwhelming, domineering

3. overstating abilities - grandiosity - withdraw, disengage

4. self-absorbed - emotionally tormented - over-involvement, victim

5. intense theorizing - over-specialization - overwhelmed, scattered

6. ambivalent self-doubt - emotional over-reaction - self-punishment or rage against others

7. hyper-active - panic stricken - punitive

8. confrontational - ruthless - withdrawal, fear for retaliation

9. complacent - disengaging - over-reacting, hostility towards others

"Be ordinary, that's crazy enough." - Dutch maxim.

13. Profiling studies

The Profiling studies are of some individuals that made the headlines or people I know personally. We already have identified progressive and regressive patterns that are distinct, recognizable, and a direct consequence of a childhood perspective. In this chapter, we take a closer look at them.

Any type functioning at unhealthy levels can violate the rights of others. Certain types are prone to specific violations either against others or themselves.

The Assertives (3,7,8) are prone to violating others through direct confrontation. They assert themselves and feel entitled.
Elliot Rodger (3) violated others through self-assertion eliminating those who reminded him of his own shortcomings.

The Compliants (6,1,2) are prone to violate self or others based on a strict rule adherence.
George Zimmerman (1) violated Trayvon Martin through a black and white rule adherence assessing right from wrong: "He must be a burglar!"

The Withdrawns (9,4,5) are prone to self-destruct or violate others in secrecy and from a distance.
Ted Kaczynski (5) used his knowledge and expertise to violate others in secrecy and from a distance.

Type One: *George Zimmerman*

One: I intend to improve the world by sharing what I know to be right and wrong. But when pent up anger builds, I am judgmental, intolerant, lose control and become punitive. Then I withdraw and feel emotionally tormented.

George Zimmerman shot and killed Trayvon Martin in 2012. The not guilty verdict in 2013 shocked the nation and appears to be for a good reason. Zimmerman had previous encounters with the law. This reportedly included shoving a police officer, restraining orders filed against him, accusations of sexual molestation, and harassment of a co-worker. George Zimmerman's father worked for the US Department of Defense and later served as a Magistrate. George himself reportedly had interest in law-enforcement and wanted to become a lawyer or a judge.

The perspective of a Type One is things can "always be better" and "I must be better". They want to improve the world by sharing their right versus wrong perspective. Sharing insights can develop into enforcing personal standards onto others.

George Zimmerman noticed burglaries in his neighborhood. He organized a neighborhood watch and patrolled the streets. He noticed a black young male with a hoodie on. Type Ones see things black and white, and he immediately concluded Trayvon Martin is suspicious and therefore must be a burglar. The thought "he might live here" likely did not cross his mind, and his hoodie was hiding his identity instead of being rain protective. He called the non-emergency number and he hesitated describing his suspect's skin color. This suggested there was no racial undertone. Although race might have contributed to his preconceived conclusion, the primary motive for his suspicion was more likely burglary.

George followed Trayvon Martin in his truck, which caused Martin to become suspicious of Zimmerman. Martin tried to de-escalate the situation by moving away from the scene. George told the non-emergency operator *"Shit, he's running"* and revealed his perspective: The *"hooded burglar will not get away, not on my watch!"*

As soon as George said, "he's running," we heard the door chimes in his truck. He climbed out to confront, what he assumed was a burglar, while he knew Sanford PD was on their way. George claimed he was suddenly attacked by Trayvon and his broken nose and minor head wound attest to that. According to Zimmerman's own words, the suspect was running away, and the real question is, *"Why did Trayvon suddenly change his mind from de-escalation to full blown attack? And what triggered his change of mind?"*

The answer is relatively simple[35]: Trayvon Martin was suspicious of George and saw him coming out of his truck *with a gun in his hand*. Trayvon could not outrun a bullet, and George initiated confrontation by pursuing Trayvon. Martin, now in fear for his life, sucker-punched him. Personally, I don't think George Zimmerman intended to shoot Trayvon Martin, rather stop him from fleeing to set a perceived wrong right. However, the balance of power shifted when George was hit square in the face. George had multiple alternatives, but with a gun in hand and now fearing to get badly hurt, George chose to shoot the young man.

George Zimmerman's story did not add up. He seemed to tell the truth but certainly left critical details out. He claimed Trayvon reached for his gun while punching him a dozen times or so and bashing his head against the concrete walkway multiple times. This cannot be an accurate recollection of events. George would have been dead or at minimum unconscious with far more head wounds, facial lacerations, and hemorrhaging. In an interview with a detective, George mindlessly re-enacted taking his gun from its holster and reached behind his back. This means Trayvon would not have been able to see, nor feel the gun while sitting on top of Zimmerman. It would have been hiding behind his back and pinned in between his body and the ground[36].
Through *Reaction Formation*, he presented himself as a law-abiding citizen patrolling the neighborhood, but in the end, overstepped his boundaries. George demonstrably lied in the Hannity interview about not knowing the "stand your ground law". Professor Alex Carter testified he taught George the law himself.

Zimmerman had several brushes with the law since his 2013 acquittal. He has been charged with aggravated assault, battery and criminal mischief. He pointed a gun at his girlfriend's face, smashed a coffee table and physically removed her from the premises. He reportedly threw a wine bottle at

[35] Elfers, Marcel D.: "Case Study: George Zimmerman". *The Graphologist, the journal of the British institute of Graphologists.* (Winter 2012, vol. 30, no. 4. P. 73-81)
[36] Bloom, Lisa: "Suspicion nation" (2014)

another girlfriend and was charged once again with aggravated assault in early 2015. The girl later recanted her accusation. He has been pulled over a few times for traffic violations. He smashed the iPad of his ex-wife days after she filed divorce papers. The man has limited impulse control and functions as a low level Type One.

We all create our own worst fear:
A Type One, who moved from being wise and critically astute with good moral judgment to angrily enforcing personal standards onto others in poor judgment, creates their own biggest fear: "Now I act against my own moral guiding principles and the world is condemning me."

Handwriting George Zimmerman

Sanford Police Department released the Zimmerman police narrative to the public. His handwriting is obviously shaken and anxious, but that is to be expected. It was written about three hours after he shot and killed Trayvon Martin. There are some very interesting features in his handwriting behavior and word selection.

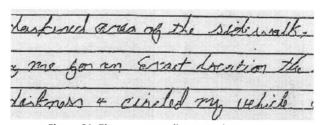
Figure 81: Zimmerman police narrative excerpt

Zimmerman's handwriting is slower and deliberate which is consistent with a One's logical and methodical attributes.

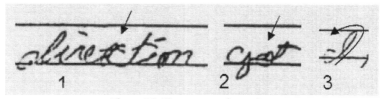
Figure 82: Zimmerman deception

1. making corrections or the repair in the word "direction" is linked to perfectionism. Generally speaking, the author was not satisfied with the end result and felt compelled to improve what was done already.

2. the double loop in "got" is known as the liar's loop. They deceive others as well as themselves. Generally speaking, when Mid-Zone structures are muddled or unclear, the author confuses the situation by making it unclear. The process of muddying structures is based on distractions by intrusive thought patterns. In other words, they think one thing but write another competing thought.

3. the Personal Pronoun I is reversed and suggests the author follows his own rules away from the norm.

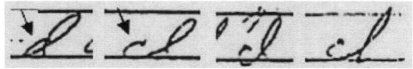

Figure 83: Zimmerman fluctuating self-image

Zimmerman's Personal Pronouns (PPIs) are inconsistent in size, slant, and initial loop and suggests a fluctuating self-image.

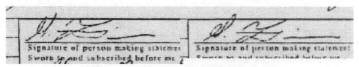

Figure 84: Zimmerman self-negating

This fluctuation in self-image feature returns in his signature. First, he signs with G only for George and then Zimmerman, albeit illegible. Signing with the first letter only while last name is in full de-emphasizes personal value. Note how both Gs are distorted, and the left G is not even finished.

The last name is illegible, and the Z is crossed with a right to left line through it. The combination suggests he is self-negating.

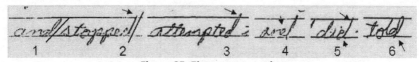

Figure 85: Zimmerman vanity

The letter "d" is linked to our moral code, our personal value system. The tall "d" stem implies vanity based on personal lifestyle and beliefs. It may also be indicative of arrogance and entitlement. Note how the letter "d" varies in body size, body shape, length and slant of the stem. A varying and distorted belief system is suspected.

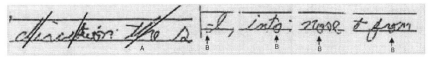

Figure 86: losing control

We write from left to right and in doing so, we move forward towards the right. A sudden change in forward slant implies a person who mentally *"suddenly lunged forward"* (A). This suggests impulsivity, poor impulse control and sudden emotional outbursts. Letters that drop below the baseline (B) can be indicative of unpleasant and unconscious urges. These impulses may not be acknowledged, and actions linked to these urges are likely *hidden and subversive*[37].

Statements George Zimmerman

40. and nose and stopped my breathing. At this point I felt the
41. the suspect reach for my <u>now exposed </u>firearm and say "
42. "Your[sic] gonna die tonight Mother Fucker! I
43. <u>unholstered</u> my firearm in fear for my
44. life as he assured he was going to kill

Generally speaking, when we speak from memory, events are recalled sequentially as we relive them one step after the other. A statement seemingly out of order is probably not recollection from memory and increases the likelihood of deception or embellishments.

9-11. I saw a male approximately 5'11" to 6'2" casually walking in the rain looking into homes.
Zimmerman called the non-emergency line because he felt Martin was suspicious and a potential burglar. That implies that seeing him hooded and looking into windows are the most important subjects. To mention "casually walking" and "rain" before "looking into homes" is probably fabrication to justify his act.

- Line 40-41: *"At this point, I felt the suspect reach for my <u>now exposed</u> firearm"* is out of order. A firearm must be exposed before you can know about it and reach for it. Whether Martin felt it, saw it or heard it is irrelevant, but he must have awareness before he will reach. Zimmerman clearly placed reaching for the firearm before awareness of it. This out-of-order sequence

---

[37] Kimon Iannetta: "Danger between the Lines" (2008) p. 157-158

implies deception. This collaborates with the police interview video, where Zimmerman mindlessly pointed at the position of *his gun on his back*. And, therefore, with Zimmerman on his back and Martin on top, the gun must have been underneath him. How could Martin have seen or felt it? How could Martin even have reached for it? Zimmerman's story does not add up.

- Line 41: *"and say"* is also interesting. After all, when we speak from memory, something happened in the past. Zimmerman's verb tense is generally correct, yet, he used "say," instead of, "said" which implies he did not recall this from memory. He used "say," instead of "said" because it was not said but he imagined he would. There is a good likelihood Martin never said "You're gonna die tonight."

- Line 43: *"unholstered"*: Generally speaking, exaggeration is a sign of the opposite. The exaggeration lies in the word "unholstered" and is twofold. First, Zimmerman claimed his head was bashed against a concrete walkway around a dozen times. He should be dead or at minimum unconscious with far more head wounds. Despite the severity of attack and Martin reaching for Zimmerman's gun, he "calmly unholstered" instead of "grabbing my gun in a panic". The word "reaching" implies nobody had the gun yet, but there is no mention of Zimmerman trying to prevent it nor is there any mention of a struggle for the gun. This suggests there was no struggle for the gun. The second exaggeration is Zimmerman making the unnecessary point *"when"* he unholstered his gun. The need to mention at what point he unholstered his gun was apparently important to him. Exaggeration is a sign of the opposite. Zimmerman used "unholstered" because that is probably how he remembered the action. I suspect he did not grab his gun during the struggle but he unholstered when he got out of his truck. He had his gun in his hand and that is why Trayvon Martin saw it and reached for it. The word "unholstered" seems a dead giveaway. And now we have a conceivable motive why Martin changed his mind from de-escalation to a full-blown attack. Martin saw Zimmerman coming with a gun in his hand and he could not outrun a bullet. It was Martin who was in fear for his life.

39. to yell "Help". As I slid the suspect covered my mouth
40. and nose and stopped my breathing. At this point I felt the
41. the suspect reach for my now exposed firearm and say "
42. "Your[sic] gonna die tonight Mother Fucker![sic] I
43. unholstered my firearm in fear for my
44. life as he had assured he was going to kill

45. Me and <u>fired one shot</u> into his torso. The suspect
46. sat back allowing me to sit up and said "you got me"!
47. At this point <u>I</u> slid out from underneath him and

Zimmerman used the Personal Pronoun I (PPI) twenty-four times before and ten times after line 45.

- Line 45: *"and fired one shot"* instead of his usual "and I fired one shot". A suddenly missing PPI suggests the author does not want to own the statement, and is generally based on guilt, shame, or fear. Zimmerman distanced himself from this statement for a reason and implies deception.

He used the word "me" fourteen times in the following lines:
- "asking me" (16); "asked me" (19); "asked me" (22); "told me" (25); "punched me" (30-31); "on top of me" (32); "told me" (33); "kill me" (44-45); "allowing me" (46); "asked me" (49); "help me" (52); "handcuffed me" (56); "disarmed me" (56); "place me" (57) and in line 44, the word *"me"* is missing.

- Line 44: *"as he has assured he was going to kill"*. There are two suspicious issues with this sentence. First, he normally used "me" but not in this sentence which implies Zimmerman wasn't assured to be killed. He was not even in fear for his life. If I was told I was going to be killed, it would have for sure grabbed my attention and the habitual use of the word "me" would not have been forgotten. Secondly, the verb's present tense implies Zimmerman did not recall this event from an experience in his past. This line is probably fabricated and deceptive.

In summary, we see deceptive tendencies in critical stages of the narrative:
- "now exposed" out of sequence
- "say," instead of, "said"
- the lack of PPI in "and fired"
- the missing "me" in "he has assured"
- the use of "has assured" instead of "had assured"

George Zimmerman told the truth, just not the whole truth. He left critical details out and used misdirection in his story line. He was most likely deceptive in his police narrative. Over time, Zimmerman demonstratively lied during televised interviews regarding his knowledge regarding the "stand your ground law".

George Zimmerman was acquitted of the charges, but the world seems to think he was a vigilante and recklessly indifferent to life.

Type One: *One pissed off mother*

One: I have my own standards and strong personal convictions. I tend to enforce my beliefs on others. I can be impatient and intolerant.

In 2013, "one pissed off mother" wrote an anonymous letter to a neighborhood mother with an autistic teenager. The letter is the epitome of a Type One functioning at low levels of mental health. Mentally stressed out Ones, functioning temporarily or permanently at low levels, believe they are the moral gatekeepers in the world. They make comparisons between themselves and others. They have a compulsive need to correct what they perceive as wrong and enforce personal standards and present their facts with puritanical certainty. They lost the ability to consider alternatives since they see things black and white. Alas, Type Ones, who fear being condemned, are now condemning others. They moved from being healthy, critically astute and reasonable to unhealthy judgmental, being utterly unreasonable, and lose credibility.

Transcript letter:
0. To the lady living at this address
1. I also live in this neighborhood and have a problem!!! You have a kid that is
2. mentally handicapped and you consciously decided that it would be a good idea to
3. live in a close proximity neighborhood like this??? You selfishly put your kid
4. outside every day and let him be a nothing but a nuisance and a problem to
5. everyone else with that noise polluting whaling he constantly makes!!! That noise
6. he makes when he is outside is *DREADFUL!!!!!!!!!!* It scares the hell out my
7. normal children!!!!!!! When you feel your idiot kid needs fresh air, take him to our
8. park you dope!!! Crying babies, music and even barking dogs are normal sounds in
9. a residential neighborhood!!!!! He is NOT!!!!!!!!!!!!!!!!!

10. He is a hindrance to everyone and will always be that way!!!!! Who the hell is
11. going to care for him?????? No employer will hire him, no normal girl is going to
12. marry/love him and you are not going to live forever!! Personally, they should take
13. whatever non-retarded body parts he possesses and donate it to science. What the
14. hell else good is he to anyone!!! You had a retarded kid, deal with
15. it... properly!!!!! What right do you have to do this to hard working people!!!!!!! I
16. HATE people like you who believe, just because you have a special needs kid you
17. are entitled to special treatment!!! GOD!!!!!!
18. Do everyone in our community huge a favor and MOVE!!! VAMOSE!!!
19. SCRAM!!!! Move away and get out of this type of neighborhood setting!!! Go live
20. in a trailer in the wood or something with your wild animal kid!!! Nobody wants
21. you living here, and they don't have the guts to tell you!!!!!
22. Do the right thing and move or euthanize him!!! Either way, we are ALL better
23. off!!!
24. Sincerely,
25. One pissed off mother!!!!!

Perspective analysis:
In her misplaced zest to improve the world, the author used many words with a black and white perspective. The use of words like *nobody, everyone, every day, constantly, nothing but, no employer, no normal girl* are selections with absolute terminology. It cannot be true he constantly whales as he won't whale while eating or sleeping. Of course, it is not true nobody wants him living here as the mother and father have already proven.

Type Ones compare themselves to others and this is reflected in her word selection. Compare *my normal kids* to *your idiot kid*. Compare including myself in *hard working people* to your *entitlement*. They also become judgmental and assign characteristics to others through name calling like *you dope, idiot kid, retard, and wild animal kid*, which are all comparisons away from the expected and accepted norm.

Even the sentence, *"You selfishly put your kid outside"* is a comparison. After all, the addressed lady is selfish, while the author is doing the neighborhood a favor by placing herself in the position of community spokesperson and presents herself as "unselfish". This is the One's *"I need to improve the world"* perspective.

On a side note, we see parallels with George Zimmerman, who took it upon himself to set up and run a neighborhood watch and, like the "one pissed off mother", failed to see gray areas. He never realized Trayvon Martin might be somebody living in the complex. Once again, we see two Type Ones with the same perspective, but the details differ.

Type Ones see themselves as prudent, objective, and reasonable. This perspective is the driver behind the author's ability to come into action. She did not foresee others will interpret her actions as severely misguided, tyrannical, extremely critical, judgmental, and self-righteous.
Of course, once she vented her anger and calmed down, she may have asked herself the question "what have I done?" She may think twice the next time, and reconsider the quality of her actions, tone, and opinion. But the damage to her reputation has been done and she lost credibilty. Hindsight is 20/20 and the internet is an everlasting memory.

Type One processes information primarily instinctively fueled by strong emotions with deductive reasoning least developed. This letter is a prime example of a Type One, who became emotionally reactive, impatient, and released pent up anger without forethought. This processing style provides the One, especially the 1w2, with emphatic certainty. They just know right from wrong and jump to conclusions without anticipating the consequences of their strong opinions. The letter contains one hundred and ten (110) exclamation marks with the sentence *He is NOT [normal]* receiving sixteen and *DREADFUL* thirteen exclamation marks. Ones tend to be obsessive and compulsive at lower levels of functioning which comes with uncontrollable emotion fueled and explosive anger.

Type Ones believe only they know right from wrong and will not only point out the faults in others, but they will also tell them what they should do in order to be a better person. This perspective shines through loud and clear in her word selection as she orders the reader to *do the right thing, euthanize him, donate his body parts to science, move away,* and *go live in a trail-*

er in the woods. Once again, this reflects on a black and white perspective, emphatic certainty and aggressively enforcing her personal standards.

This author, at the time of the writing, was functioning at unhealthy mental levels and might have been neurotic. Words like judgmental, demanding, rigid, self-righteous, cruel, and hateful come to mind.

In the meantime, the author will, hopefully, realize over time her idealistic views are extreme and wrong. Let me correct this: dead wrong. She will eventually realize she must consider the perspectives of others or be condemned herself. She will realize instead of being astute and prudent she was intolerant, obsessive, and inflexible. Once she realizes what she has done, she will withdraw in self-pity and emotionally torment herself. If this author expressed her opinion on the Dr. Phil show, he would have said to her "look, you can be right, or you can be happy".

Type One: *Cyril Wecht*

Cyril Harrison Wecht, M.D., is a forensic pathologist and author. In 2010, he expressed regret and guilt feelings for not pursuing a career in music. He played the violin and performed on large stages. His parents, first-generation immigrants, had other ideas and told him from a young age to become a doctor. He concluded his interview answer with *"So, that was it"*. Apparently, Dr. Wecht did not have much choice in careers and implied a strict upbringing.

Dr. Wecht is well informed and opinionated. He doesn't shy away from presenting his convictions with vigor and oppose other pathologists when needed. In his book "*Who killed JonBenét Ramsey*", he explained there was no intruder and points toward the Ramsey's involvement.

In televised interviews, he comes over as robust, opinionated, with a true versus not true perspective. He concluded his investigation of the John F. Kennedy assassination with *"The single bullet theory is a joke"* and dismissed the Warren commission report.

After reading his childhood experience of being "pushed" into medical school, somewhat regretting a musical career, and then finding a handwriting sample in a second-hand bookstore, it became clear he is a Type One. They have strong opinions, are known to resist change, and tend to be perfectionistic.

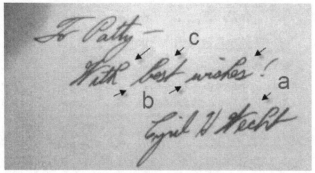

Figure 87: Type One traits

The long Lower-Zone and long crossbar structures imply a strong drive. In life, he is a doctor, an attorney, a coroner, and author. The Mid-Zone is the social zone and the tight W's (a) imply anxiety and closed mindedness. The straight lead-in strokes (b) suggest subconscious resentment indicating deep seeded hurts from the past. Such hurts could be coming from a strict up-bringing and not being allowed to do what he wanted to do. Type Ones distanced themselves from the guidance they received and set their own standards and rules. In doing so, they know right from wrong and can become perfectionistic enforcing those standards. The repaired strokes (c) in the Upper-Zone improve what was already done and suggests perfectionism. In a professional setting, such authors do not leave one stone unturned to find the truth.

Type Two: *Patsy Ramsey*

Two: I want to earn love and appreciation by being good to others. When my hard work, time, and efforts are not reciprocated, I become overwhelming and demanding.

The body of six-year-old JonBenét Ramsey was discovered in the basement of her home. She was in full rigor mortis. A peculiar two-and-a-half page ransom note was found at the bottom of the stairs leading to the living room. The note is the most important clue to solving that night's events. Many books have come and gone, but the ransom note never left us. The case continues to haunt us because motivation of the little girl's demise has eluded us. The explanations provided by John and Patsy Ramsey have been, are, and will remain unconvincing and improbable.

When we look at known facts, list them, and put all the misdirection's, innuendos, and interpretations aside, there can only be one conclusion: There was no intruder.

Known facts:
- December 26, 1996, Patsy called 911, and 7 minutes later, she opened the door for officer French. He noticed she was fully dressed, hair and make-up intact. It turned out, she wore the same attire on Christmas day.
- John Ramsey and police confirmed all doors were locked.
- They claimed an intruder came in through a broken window, but an undisturbed spider web told us otherwise. Spiders are not active in the winter, and a new web would not have been made after an intruder entered through that window.
- The window sill was undisturbed and an intruder would have made marks in the debris.
- John Ramsey found her body in a small room in the basement. His friend Fleet White, who looked in the same room much earlier with ambient light, did not see her. She was, however, wrapped in a light colored blanket. If she was in that room when he looked, he should have seen her. John was missing during the day, and possibly moved the body.
- The Ransom note was written on a notepad, with a Sharpie, belonging to the home. Patsy's fingerprints were on the note alongside those of investigators. The Sharpie was placed back in the container where it belonged. An intruder would have prepared a note in advance.
- The garrote was made from materials belonging in the home, including the handle of a broken paintbrush.

There were no disturbances suggesting an intruder or intruders came and went. The cold facts were straightforward and told us there could not have been an intruder. And that left us with three suspects; those who were in the home: John, Patsy, and Burke.

The Ramseys behaved suspiciously from the very first words Patsy uttered in her 911 call with law-enforcement:
1. *Patsy Ramsey (PR): (inaudible) police*
2. *911: (inaudible)*
3. *PR: 755 Fifteenth Street*

4. 911: What's going on ma'am?

5. PR: <u>We</u> have a kidnapping ... Hurry Please

6. 911: Explain to me what is going on, ok?

7. PR: <u>We</u> have a <u>...</u> There is <u>a note</u> left and <u>our</u> daughter is <u>gone</u>

8.911: A note was left and your daughter is gone?

9. PR: Yes

10. 911: How old is your daughter?

11. PR: She is six years old; she is blond ... six years old

12. 911: How long ago was this?

13. PR: I don't know. <u>Just</u> found a note ... a note and <u>my</u> daughter is <u>missing</u>

14. 911: Does it say who took her?

15. PR: <u>What</u>?

16.911: Does it say who took her?

17. PR: No I don't know it's there ... there's a ransom note

18. 911: It's a ransom note?

19. PR: It says S.B.T.C Victory .... <u>please</u>

3. We talk about what we deem most important first. Patsy started by providing her address instead telling police her daughter was kidnapped. Her priority was apparently where the police should be going and makes the address the starting point of her story line. The home is more important to her than the kidnapped child. The home is where it all starts and where it is happening.

5. Patsy then said "We have <u>a</u> kidnapping", and again does not tell police who is missing. The word selection "*a*" is non-descript. This could be the kidnapping of a neighbor's child or an adult staying with them over Christmas time. This suggests she emotionally distanced herself from the kidnapping of her child. A more believable sentence would be, *"My daughter has been kidnapped!"*

The first statements are suspicious and telling. Patsy was distancing herself from the kidnapping and left out critical information while we expect she would be emotionally involved and motivated to assure urgent assistance. I have heard many emergency calls and I expect Patsy to not introduce herself and yell at the operator *"My daughter has been kidnapped, I found a ransom note! Find her!!!"*

7. *We have a* ....is an unfinished sentence. This is likely a repeat of line 5. This suggests lack of spontaneity and an attempt to follow a rehearsed script.

7. ... *There is a note left and our daughter is gone*. The use of *We* and *our* means involving more than one person. Most people who feel guilt dilute responsibility by including others.

7. Her daughter is Patsy's third priority after address and the note.

7. The word *gone* is much stronger than *missing*. According to the ransom note, the daughter was taken and guarded. That is not *gone* rather *missing*. Subconsciously, Patsy might have accidentally made a reference to her already knowing JonBenét being dead with the use of *gone*.

13. So far, Patsy used pronouns properly. The Personal Pronoun I (PPI) is missing in the answer *Just found a note*. The lack of a PPI suggests the speaker does not want to own the statement and is a marker for deception.

13. *Our daughter (7)* changed to *my daughter*. My daughter is more realistic given the situation yet, it is also a change in her reality.

13. *Gone (7)* changed to *missing*... My interpretation is the word *gone* was used under higher stress levels and reflects on what she already knew. JonBenét was *gone forever*. After the conversation was initiated, Patsy calmed down a little and fell back on her rehearsed story line. Now the child was just *missing* implying "misplaced" and to be found. This is a correction in her fabricated perspective to maintain the illusion of a kidnapping. She moved from reality with "gone forever" to fabrication or "to be found".

15. To answer a question with a question is stalling for time so you have more time to think about what to say. Reduction in spontaneity is a sign of deception.

19. We are well into the conversation and Patsy explained the last sentence of the ransom note. Again, we talk about what is most important to us and S.B.T.C [sic], as I will explain, is the most important conclusion of the storyline. So far, she has not asked for help, although *Please* pointed in that direction. As a rule, callers who don't ask for assistance for the victim or ask for assistance for themselves, are guilty or involved.

JonBenét was found the same day of the emergency call. The Ramseys were reportedly minimally cooperative and would not interview with Boulder Police. On January 1st, 1997, they allowed a nationwide televised CNN interview with Brian Cabell.

Cabell : *Why did you decide you wanted to talk now?*
John Ramsey: *Well we have been pretty isolated -- totally isolated -- for the last five days, but we've sensed from our friends that this tragedy has touched not just ourselves and our friends but many people. And we know that there's many people that are praying for us, that are grieving with us.*

And we want to thank them, to let them know that we are healing, and that we know in our hearts that JonBenét is safe and with God and that the grieving that we all have to do is for ourselves and for our loss, but we want to thank those people that care about us.

A theme is emerging. Finding the killer of their daughter is not a priority. The word *"Well"* stalls for time to think. John Ramsey is reflecting on everyone else, their prayers, the healing we need to do, and thanked them all. Although he said they were *isolated*, they were in contact with *friends*, and that is not isolated.

The word *tragedy* is very interesting. John thought of the murder of his child as a *tragedy*. A car accident is tragic, but to use the word *tragedy* for the murder of your six-year-old daughter is not just downplaying the facts. A tragedy suggests lack of intent and intruders would have intent.

I would expect something like this: *We are here to make clear to you, the murderer of my JonBenét, we will be moving heaven and earth to find you. If the public knows anything, hears anything, please help us bring justice for my daughter, JonBenét.*

After Patsy made a comment how overwhelmed they were, John continued with: *But the other -- the other reason is that -- for our grief to resolve itself we now have to find out why this happened. This -- we cannot go on until we know why. There's no answer as to why our daughter died.*

And the word *why* is telling us his perspective. John and Patsy were not interested in *what* happened or *how* it happened. The "what and how" could lead to finding the intruder and suggested they were not interested in finding the murderer of his six-year-old daughter. That makes sense and is in line with their behavior before the body was found.

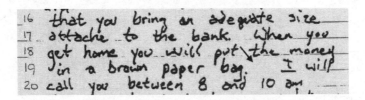

Figure 88: Intrusive thought

The note stated to expect a call, but the handwriting told us otherwise. We write from left to right and during an intrusive thought (a "distraction") we stop writing but our hand still moves forward. This creates a larger than usual space in between words. The abnormally large space before the line "I will call" suggests fabrication. There was not going to be a call and the author knew it. The Ramseys were reportedly[38] not paying attention to the deadline. Ten o'clock "came and went" which is in line with the hesitation in the handwriting. One reasonable conclusion is: there was no intruder and they already knew what happened.

Patsy's interest in "why" it happened also suggests disbelief. As we will see, why fits the scenario both parents were involved and it was an accident. The phrasing, There is no answer implied they knew all along no intruder would be found. They knew what happened, but didn't understand why it all happened. The subconscious use of the word why is very significant. This implies there was no intent because with intent, he would have known why she died. And now the use of the word tragedy and its perspective is clear. Likewise, the word tragedy[39] suggests lack of intent and points in the direction of an accident. They just didn't know why. Why did it happen? Why did she have to die? Why us?

The District Attorney exonerated the Ramseys in 2008 and wrote, "Significant new evidence has recently been discovered through the application of relatively new methods of DNA analysis".

Investigator Kolar[40] wrote the District Attorney in 2006 and stated, "If I am correct in my assessment, there may be a plausible explanation for the presence of the DNA in the underwear and it may have nothing to do with the death of JonBenét."

Both statements are references to touch DNA found on JonBenét's clothing. It is called touch DNA because we all leave traces of cells behind on anything we touch. By artificially developing minuscule DNA findings into strands of DNA, we can use them for identification purposes. The touch DNA found on her clothing is not necessarily from the murderer. It could easily be from a factory worker where the clothing was manufactured and packaged.

There are many reasons why the Ramseys were likely involved in the death of their own daughter. Foremost, the ransom note points in their direction, as it was written on a notepad found in the home. The handwriting is widely

---

[38] "JonBenét, inside the murder investigation", Steve Thomas p. 26

[39] The synonyms: calamity, disaster, catastrophe, misfortune lack intent.

[40] A. James Kolar "Foreign faction" page 296

believed to match Patsy's and according to document examiner, "24 of 26 letters match Patsy's characteristics"[41]. Her fingerprints were found on the note, along with those of investigators. Although Patsy told investigators John picked up the note, his finger prints were not found on the note. This excludes him from writing the note as he would have left his prints on the paper.

The ransom contains many highly questionable statements and unexpected changes in perspective. The author changed from a group perspective to singular and back to group perspective. This is a significant change in reality and suggests the author did not experience the events. There was no group.

2.	We are a group	7.	our posession [sic]
19.	I will call you	10.	our instructions
25.	We might call you	29.	my instructions
		53.	our instructions

Another hint a woman wrote the note is women relate better to cats. The author used a derogatory term for the dog while the cat received a compliment.

40-41. If we catch you talking to a stray dog
59 -60. You are not the only fat cat around

The wording *constant scrutiny* implies every breath you take is observed, recorded, and analyzed. This perspective does not match the two *if* statements. If the author was truly scrutinizing and monitoring the Ramseys, then they would be certain and expect to catch them.

55-57. You and your family are under constant scrutiny
23-24. if we monitor you getting
40. if we catch you talking

Patsy opened the door for officer French, and he noticed she was fully dressed, with hair and makeup intact. It is hard to believe a mother, who reported finding a ransom note and her daughter kidnapped, calmly dressed herself and did her make-up before calling police. Later, it was discovered,

---

[41] "JonBenét, inside the murder investigation" Steve Thomas p. 74

she was wearing the same outfit she wore the day before. A reasonable conclusion is: She never went to bed.

I am in the camp of those who believe the Ramseys were involved. We know nothing happens in a vacuum. The known facts, their behaviors, word selection and handwriting evidence overwhelmingly point in their direction. No intruder would attempt to kidnap a six-year-old girl, murders her, hides her in the basement, and then take their time to write a two-and-a-half page ransom note. He just lost his leverage. The author had to think about what to say and how to say it. Other trial notes were found and the note was likely written with the non-dominant hand. The note would have taken at least thirty minutes if not an hour and a half and was apparently not concerned about being caught. This suggests the author belonged in the home. The intruder theory is utterly illogical, not probable, nor plausible.

Many handwriting experts compared Patsy's handwriting with the handwriting of the ransom note and concluded Patsy likely wrote the note. The content was clearly written by an inept criminal. The note made no sense and a sentence like *"We are a group of individuals that represent a small foreign faction"* was likely written by someone under high stress levels and not thinking with clarity.
Many other references were indicative of Patsy being the author, but enough has been written about that already. The author was someone who was tormented, distraught, and emotionally attached to the victim. Line 9 is an example of high levels of anxiety, and within context implies emotional attachment to the victim.

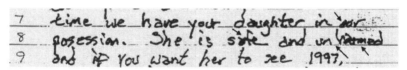

Figure 89: emotional involvement

The note was written with a Sharpie and in line 9 the author became very worried. The portion *"if you want her to see 1997"* shows an increase in anxiety traits. The pressure lightened up as the ink deposits became much thinner than the line above and below. This suggests the author lost initiative and suggests emotional attachment to the victim. The author was likely a parent in denial and shock. The word "un harmed" has "un" separated from "harmed", and the latter is cramped up in anxiety as well. This suggests the word had a negative emotional impact on the author and implies the author knew the child was harmed already and would not see 1997.

It's reasonable to conclude Patsy wrote the note and the Ramseys were involved. The real questions are "what happened, why did it happen, what was their motivation, and why cover it up?" And why did they not call 911 and try to save the child? Why would they cover for each other? And most importantly, what does the acronym S.B.T.C [sic] mean?

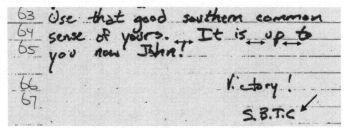

Figure 90: S.B.T.C [no period behind C]

During my research of this case in 2007, I was bothered most by lack of motive. Why and how could the Ramseys have been involved? Why would well-meaning parents end up being involved in the death of their own child? Or was it an accident?

While re-reading *JonBenét, inside the Ramsey murder investigation,* I was struck by what lead investigator Steve Thomas wrote[42]: *"When we checked the photos from a big manila envelope marked as evidence item #85KKY, I almost fell out of my chair. A picture shows Webster's New Collegiate Dictionary on a coffee table in the first-floor study, the corner of the lower left-hand page sharply creased and pointing like an arrow to the word incest. Somebody had apparently been looking for a definition of sexual contact between family members."*

The photograph opened the door to a logical theory of what could have happened that night. It could explain the motivation behind writing the ransom note, as well as a compelling explanation for the acronym S.B.T.C [sic]. What if Patsy saw John in a compromising position with JonBenét, and enraged, she swung with the force to hit an adult, but accidentally struck the little girl as John turned around and away? Whether incest occurred or not, and there is no reported history there was, is entirely irrelevant.

---

[42] "JonBenét, inside the murder investigation" Steve Thomas. Page 263.

But one thing is very, very clear. Somebody found it necessary to look up the definition of incest, and somebody believed an encounter sexual in nature between family members occurred. This matches the conclusion of a panel of pediatric experts, who determined JonBenét suffered vaginal trauma[43] prior to the day she was killed. They concluded the trauma was consistent with *chronic* physical abuse. Chronic is a loaded word, as such abuse can only be accomplished by someone with easy access while not being suspected of abuse.

And now a possible motive to cover up the events of that night has arisen. John and Patsy were both involved and both had something to hide. Patsy accidentally struck and killed her daughter. She was a cancer survivor, did not want to go to prison, and run the risk of dying during incarceration. Patsy had control over John through the threat of incest accusations. He might face prison time himself, not to mention long term public scrutiny[44]. With both parents in prison, their son Burke would be left to fend for himself. Although this theory is speculative in nature, it is a viable and reasonable one. From this perspective, motivation would be explained, and the content of the note suddenly makes a whole lot more sense. There was an equilibrium between the two main players and they held each other in check.

9. and if you want her to see 1997,	58. Don't try to grow a brain
10. you must follow our instructions to	59. John. You are not the only
11. the letter.	60. fat cat around so don't think
12. You will withdraw $118,000	61. that killing will be difficult.
13. from your account. $100,000 will be	62. Don't underestimate us John.
14. in $100 bills and the remaining	63. Use that good southern common
15. $18,000 in $20 bills. Make sure	64. sense of yours. It is up to
16. that you bring an adequate size	65. you now John!
17. attache to the bank. When you	66. Victory!
18. get hoe you will put the money	67. S.B.T.C

And that very equilibrium was questioned in the note with a definite shift in the balance of power. The shift is written in the last paragraph. The letter started with "Mr. Ramsey, Listen carefully!" which means John specifically had to pay close attention to the message. Patsy, the author, took initiative and John is the recipient. The word "Listen" suggests he had to listen, not read, and implies Patsy was trying to convince John verbally before she

---

[43] "JonBenét, inside the murder investigation" Steve Thomas. Page 227.
[44] It is entirely possible public scrutiny was discussed and the reason why the word appeared in the ransom note.

wrote the note. "Listen" was followed by demands like *must, will, will, will, make sure,* and *will.*

Remember the three stages of influence: manipulation, domination, and control. Patsy was in control and John had no choice. She was past the manipulation phase. She convinced John to participate in the fabricated intruder story line prior to writing the note. John likely disagreed and is why the note is addressed to him. It took effort to gain his cooperation as the tone of the letter implies "I need to convince".

But the balance of power moved toward John as the note came to a close. The author felt no longer sure who would have control as the kidnapping story would unfold over time. The formal "Mr. Ramsey" changed to the more intimate "John", and not only softened the stand-off but also suggests familiarity. The line *"use that good southern common sense of yours"* is not a command, rather an appeal to not change his mind over what was agreed upon. The intimacy theme reared its head again as the author apparently knew John was from "the South" and feared his common sense. The fear lies in the word *"that"* which shows distancing from "common sense". It is clear, the author perceived common sense as a threat. If John came to his senses, there would be negative repercussions for the author. This supports the idea Patsy killed JonBenét and, at the time of the writing, knew the child was dead and in the home.

58. *Don't try to grow a brain* suggests the author feared John might take control and tell what happened that night.
63. *Use that good southern common sense of yours* implies John had alternatives like exposing the author.
64. *It is up to you now John!* indicates in the end, it was John who was in charge of the only and most important decision. To tell or not tell. That is the question.

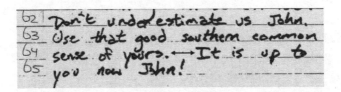

Figure 91: Intrusive thought

And so, Patsy had another hesitation in the very last line. The increased spacing before "It" as well as mild increases in the rest of the sentences suggests she was releasing her control. She knew it was up to John, and not her what would happen next.

For the author to reveal John was in charge has one valid conclusion: *There was no intruder. End of story. Period.* An intruder would have maintained control. An intruder would have left his mark in the home. An intruder, who took his time writing the ransom note, would also carry the dead body away from the house to keep his leverage. The intruder theory is utter nonsense.

For the author to admit, she might no longer be in charge of future out-comes, matches the speculative story line and explains the shift in balance of power. When all was said and done, Patsy could not possibly be sure whether John would talk with authorities. That is why she demanded him to "*Listen carefully!*" and ended the ransom note with a word of hope: *Victory!* Then Patsy, known to use acronyms frequently, signed with S.B.T.C [sic]. She knew who was now in charge and ended the note with an acronym reflect-ing on "whatever happens, happens." She signed the note with S.B.T.C [sic], meaning:

"So Be The Case"

S.B.T.C [sic] as the natural conclusion of the ransom note is compelling, and explains the unexpected shift in control presented in the note. Patsy ad-dressed John directly, and "So Be The Case" explains he needed convincing, both were fully aware of the events, and so, both were involved.

Interestingly, the acronym's last letter, the "C", did not receive a period. A sentence typically ends with a period as the task at hand has been final-ized. At the time of the writing, in shock, pain, in denial and distracted by thoughts about what the future would bring, the period was forgotten. The distracting thoughts were her assessments of how the story line could unfold and S.B.T.C [sic] without the period was a story without an end. Subconsciously, she told us there was much more to tell.

From all accounts, Patsy was a loving and caring mother, who lived vicari-ously through her daughter. Patsy was a beauty queen herself and did eve-rything Texas style. She loved to entertain and was busy with many social functions. She did have a tendency to overdo things, which is consistent with the length of the ransom note. Patsy was a 2w3 based on her known handwriting, and reported social and behavioral style. A Two under stress will act like an average to low level Eight. The length and demanding tone of the note reflect on such traits. Her Type also matches the ransom note's bizarre story line. Type Twos process information emotionally, and under stress act out their emotions and become irrational. A Type Two, who sees wrong being done, which is in conflict with their core perspective of always being good, can become explosively violent and ruthless like an Eight. This matches the idea of Patsy instinctively and impulsively striking out with a heavy object in the direction of a wrongdoer. It also matches the Twos becoming specifically violent toward loved ones. Doing things for others with a lack of return is their anger trigger; "after all the things I have done for you, you do this to me?"

Type Two's main theme is "to be good to others", and there is evidence of this in the note as well. The author took the reader's perspective into consideration through statements of concern and a show of kindness. The brutal murder and abduction scenario doesn't match the concern and kindness for John Ramsey:

15. *Make sure that you bring an adequate size attache to the bank.*
22. *The delivery will be exhausting so I advise you to be rested.*
33. *The two gentlemen watching over your daughter*

To tell the father of a kidnapped child to rest is irrational. To refer to hard core criminals as gentlemen is not very threatening. This is more in line with a kind person who sees males as gentlemen, and is the opposite of intimidating hard core criminals.

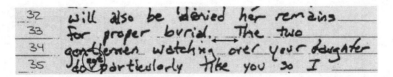

Figure 92: Intrusive thought

Again, the sudden increase in space before "The two gentlemen" suggests deception. The author fabricated this sentence because there were no intruders and she did not know what to call the kidnappers.

We are inclined to talk about what is most important to us because that is foremost on our minds. It is very hard to lie, because fabrication requires imagination. Without the actual experience we also lack emotional impact which reduces imprinting a memory. It is very hard to remain consistent and outward expression of internal dialogue slips in like we see in lines 27 and 35:

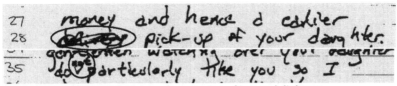

Figure 93: Outward expression of internal dialogue

The intruder's point of view was to deliver your daughter to you, and then changed her mind towards you picking her up. Such mistakes strongly suggest the note was fabricated instead of based on existing experiences. This is not a hardcore criminal who experienced the presented scenario of kidnapping and murdering a child.

34. gentlemen watching over your daughter
35. do \not/ particularly like you so I
36. advise you not to provoke them.

In line 35 the word "not" was initially forgotten. That is likely because the author "does particularly like" John and then changed this to "not like." A slip of the tongue is an outward expression of your inner perspective.
The "So Be The Case" and shift in the balance of power could also fit a speculation regarding Burke. That would mean Burke was the one who chronically sexually experimented with JonBenét at a very young age. He then somehow became violent while preoccupied with Christmas gifts.
He hit her on the head with a heavy object, and the parents decided to cover it up. This story line has been suggested by some, but in my experience, a 9-year-old would have cracked under pressure of the investigation. Moreover, Burke went to school without supervision right after the Christmas holidays were over. This suggests he did not know what happened, and the parents were sure he could not talk about it either. John and Patsy went to great lengths to cover events up and if Burke had known anything, they would have spent time and energy in preventing him to accidentally give details away. Burke, by the very nature of the actions and decisions of his parents, was not a risk factor. He was, is, and never will be a suspect.

We might never know what happened that night. It's a compelling conclusion for the Ramseys to be involved. If the story line is correct, and Jon-Benét's untimely death was an accident, then the Ramseys have punished themselves more than enough. They lost their child and lived a life under public scrutiny. John moved on, reportedly remarried, and made some public appearances where body language and word selection show deceptive tendencies.

John Ramsey was interviewed by Anderson Cooper and John was engaging, attentive and leaned forward. There were many long pauses and he weighed his words carefully. He consistently faced Cooper but looked down to his knees when he said, *"This person came into our home"*. The inability to face the interviewer and veering away from his norm means an increase in anxiety and is likely deceptive. Later, he looked down for a full second, shaking his head "no" during the sentence, *"uhm, John Douglas, who is a well-known fine profiler, said he believes someone that was either angry at me or jealous of me."* Many people shake no for "not true" when telling a fib. The unnecessary compliment toward John Douglas is an exaggeration to emphasize credibility in support of his intruder theory.

He also had a sudden and very strong change in body language when asked, *"Was Patsy in any way involved?"* John could not help but reactively stutter a lengthy "nooooo" and anxiously turned completely away from Anderson. Some sixteen years after the child's death, that question continued to make him anxious, and unable to face the interviewer. That question hit home.

Oprah interviewed John after receiving the exoneration letter in 2008, and he interpreted the letter as *"a step in the right direction"*. He literally told everyone there was no finality to the case for a simple reason: There was no intruder and the theory is not believable. According to documents released in 2013, a Grand Jury agreed to indict them in 1997 as they believed they were responsible for her death. But the D.A. did not move forward on the recommendation.

Early in the investigation, it was believed Patsy "abused, tortured, and murdered" her daughter. This theory requires Patsy to be the only one involved. She would have murdered her daughter for an unspecified reason, put her in the basement, and wrote the ransom note. John would not have been aware of his wife not coming to bed. That theory does not make sense as the ransom note reflects on John's involvement with the shift in power, *"It's up to you now, John!"*

The sentence received one of three exclamation marks in the note for emphasis reflecting on its significance and importance.

The author told us John had a choice to make. If John was not involved and didn't know about what happened, then he would have no choice but to follow instructions. There would not have been the need to tell John, *"It's all up to you now"* if John had no clue he even had a choice. Patsy was not the only one involved and with the last line she implicated John. He knew what happened prior to writing the note. Second, a husband who discovers his wife abused and brutally murdered his daughter while he had nothing to do with it, would not have incentive to elaborately cover it up and chose to live with public scrutiny for the rest of his life. He would first be thinking about how to protect his son Burke from his wife.

Patsy made a very interesting remark in line 59 when she wrote, *"You are not the only fat cat around"*. Initially, this seems to come out of left field and odd. But it suggests John is replaceable by another fat cat.

59. John. You are not the only
60. fat cat around so don't think
61. that killing will be difficult.

She continued by staying on track with the story line and warns him about killing his daughter which seems to be a substitute for retaliation. A logical interpretation of the last paragraph is *"John is involved, and if you tell, I will retaliate and replace you."*

And that is in line with the speculation John did something that angered Patsy so much, she instantly attempted to hit him with a heavy object, missed, and hit JonBenét instead.

Patsy lost her struggle with cancer in 2006. May she rest in peace.

Type Two: *Steven Powell*

Two: I am a people pleaser and need to be needed and live for appreciation. I can make others feel dependent on me and become intrusive in their lives. I am prone to repress negatives and don't recognize nor admit to them.

Steven Powell is the father of Josh Powell, who is widely believed to have been involved in the disappearance of his wife Susan Cox Powell in December 2009. In 2012, Josh killed his two sons and himself after custody of his children was granted to Susan's parents.

Steven Powell was caught by Susan watching her getting dressed. In 2012, Steven Powell was indicted with child pornography and the charge was later dismissed. He was convicted of voyeurism instead.

Steven Powell produced a four-page handwritten "motion for writ of mandamus" to the Superior Court in Pierce County, WA. Mr. Powell put in a request to the court for the department of corrections to pay for his sex offender treatment program.

Perspective Analysis:
page 2 line 13-14 .. *in complete disregard of his <u>exemplary behavior</u>*
page 2 line 24-25 .. *in disregard of his <u>good behavior</u>*
page 3 line 2 .. *with no <u>good-behavior</u> time honored*

Mr. Powell made the argument three times despite his good behavior he did not receive a sentence reduction. Type Twos present themselves as being good and want a return on that investment.

Handwriting Analysis:

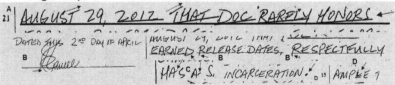

Figure 94: optimism and poor urge control

A) Words move upward from the baseline, and the crossbars for the T, H, and A are also moving upward. These are traits linked to optimism. Types 7,9 and 2 are positive-minded and put positive twists even to negatives.

B) Letters dropping below the baseline imply subconscious urges which are poorly controlled. This is especially significant in PPIs, signatures, and the letter "d". Interestingly, the signature is our personal shingle or how we present ourselves to the outside world. Notice how different the signature is from the body of the text, and implies that you will not get what you see.
C) The crossbars of the A move too far and implies the author does not know when to stop and is akin to poor urge control.
D) The heavy period and the triple stroke for the L imply obsessive compulsive thinking patterns.

Type Twos grow up feeling unloved and learn to present themselves as good and selfless in order to earn love and appreciation. Problems arise when they become self-deceptive in the sense they believe they are being good but can no longer distinguish acceptable from unacceptable behaviors or downright evil ones.

Type Three: *Elliot Rodger*

Three: I want to earn admiration and work hard to be a success. I pretend to be better than I really am and then fail to live up to self-created expectations. When rejected and made to feel unworthy, I become competitive, exploitative, and violently vindictive. Then I disengage.

In June 2014, Elliot Rodger went on a murderous rampage in Santa Barbara, CA. Rodger was attention-seeking, image-oriented, and overstated his self-importance. He was still a virgin at age 22 and enraged with girls rejecting him. His anger built over time and outbursts like throwing coffee on a kissing couple and at two girls at a bus stop was a precursor for things to escalate. In his retribution video, Elliot was *calm, collected, articulate, and spoke with deliberate intent.* He reached the unhealthy development levels of the Type Three Behavioral Pathway. He became arrogant and condescending. The last step in his deterioration pattern is *violence without remorse.*

Retribution video transcript:
Well, this is my last video; it has all had to come to this. You girls have never been attracted to me. I don't know why you girls aren't attracted to me, but I will <u>punish</u> you all for it. You will finally see that I am in truth the <u>superior</u> one. Well, now I will be a <u>god</u> compared to you. I've wanted a girlfriend; I've wanted sex, I've wanted love, affection, <u>adoration</u>. You think I'm <u>unworthy</u> of it.

Type Three's biggest fear is being unworthy, and he repeats this in his 141-page Manifesto:

p. 32 cruel treatment from women is ten times worse than from men. It made me feel an insignificant, <u>unworthy</u> little mouse.
p. 53 I bet that lucky bastard took great satisfaction from my envy. There I was, watching a boy four years younger than me experience everything I've longed for ... to kiss a girl... to be <u>worthy</u> of a girl's attraction
p. 71 I will never have sex. I will never have love. Girls deem me <u>unworthy</u> of it
p. 91 To remind me that girls think I am <u>unworthy</u> compared to others boys.
p. 107 once I become wealthy, I would finally be <u>worthy</u> enough to all the beautiful girls
p. 112 girls have always deemed me <u>unworthy</u> of their love and sex
p. 117 women deemed me <u>unworthy</u> of having them, and so they deprived me

Type Three, not able to win, will become condescending
p. 48 And they didn't seem to mind that he was such an evil <u>bastard</u>
p. 65 He truly was disgusting and a treacherous little <u>bastard</u>
p. 71 I never understood what that pretty girl saw in her <u>brute</u> of a boyfriend

Type Three's focus is on admiration and self-esteem is linked to "success."
p. 53 I bet I was the first kid at that school who has done such <u>prestigious</u> things.
p. 107 once I become <u>wealthy</u>, I would finally be worthy enough to all the beautiful girls
p. 113 I have always had a penchant for <u>luxury, opulence, and prestige</u>

Type Three is image-oriented (shirt comment), at low levels vindictive (coffee), and emotionally detached (satisfaction without considering the emotional impact on others).

p. 100 As I made my way back from school one day during the first week, I was stopped at a stoplight in Isla Vista when I saw two hot blonde girls waiting at the bus stop. <u>I was dressed in one of my nice shirts, so I looked</u> at them and smiled. They looked at me, but they didn't even deign to smile back. They just looked away as if I was a fool. As I drove away, I became very infuriated. It was such an insult. This was the way <u>all girls treated me</u>, and I was sick and tired of it. In a rage, I made a U-turn, pulled up to their bus stop and _splashed my Starbucks latte all over them_. _I felt a feeling a spiteful satisfaction as I saw it stain their jeans._

These sentences taken together form a perspective with consequent escalating behavioral choices. You think I am unworthy, but I am better than you. I will punish you; I will be god. And so, slowly but surely, Elliot could not cope with his inner conflict, and became "the vindictive psychopath" [45].

When law-enforcement was alerted by his parents, they visited him at his apartment. They left after a few minutes because he was _"articulate, polite, and timid"_. If the officers had known the Behavioral Pathway of a Type Three and recognized his pattern in his videos, they would expect him to be logical and controlled. The combination of rage, entitlement, arrogance, and condescension, with his _"polite, articulate, and timid"_ behavior was _the red flag_. His Behavioral Pathway ends with vindictive violence, and they could have or should have entered his apartment only to find his guns and notebooks. Through _Identification,_ he managed to create a false image of cooperation and formed a brief alliance with law-enforcement. And so, they left because he was _articulate, polite, and timid._

We create our own biggest fear:
The biggest fear of a Three is being worthless or being rejected for not performing better than others. Ironically, when they move from being authentic and ambitious to shameless self-promotion and exploitation of others, _they are abandoned because of their arrogance, condescension and exploitation. They are now truly worthless in the eyes of others, and worse, in their own eyes._

Type Three: _Aaron Ybarra_

On July 5th, 2014, Aaron Ybarra killed a student and wounded another at the Seattle Pacific University. He too left a Manifesto in the form of a diary which was made public later. Ybarra had mental difficulties and was reportedly diagnosed with psychosis and obsessive-compulsive disorder[46].

This one was close to home for me. Aaron, also a Type 3w4, was a regular at my favorite pool hall. He was like Elliot Rodger withdrawn, quiet, sociable,

---

[45] Don Riso/ Russ Hudson "Personality Types" Type Three, Level 9 "the vindictive psychopath"
[46] Seattle Times July 19, 2014

and a little odd. His sister was shocked that an otherwise so normal person could do a school shooting like this. *"His friends described him as sociable, well-adjusted, and able to make them laugh."* But then again, he also called 911 in 2010 stating he was suicidal and enraged while others described him as having violent outbursts[47]. In 2012, Ybarra was laying drunk on the street in front of his home, and yelled at the SWAT team to shoot him and make him famous.[48]

Ybarra and Rodger planned their events long in advance and wrote about it. They managed to remain social, calm, collected, and deceptive. All they wanted was to be admired and acknowledged. Rodger wanted to be god, a show of superiority, and Ybarra wanted to be famous like his idol Eric Harris (Columbine 1999).

Ybarra diary:
"no matter how cute the girl is and no matter how cool the guy is, I just want people to die! And, I'm gonna die with them" (suicide by cop ideation).
"I'm doing some people a favor by sending them to heaven. But those who are sinners like me, I'll see you in hell." (3 arrogance by placing himself in a position of judge and jury and 4 self-negating).

Ybarra was more troubled and had less control than Rodger, but their behavioral style and perspectives are one and the same. Both could not reconcile their need for admiration with the rejection they received. Their dichotomy is a particular difficult one. On the one hand they feel they should be admired (entitlement tall "d" stems) and use identification to get what they want; on the other hand, they feel insignificant and are self-loathing. Rejected by others and thrown off their self-created superiority pedestal, the only way out for an unhealthy Type 3 is to put others down using arrogance, condescension, and remove those who remind them of their own shortcomings. Vindictive violence was the end result in both cases.

Rodger: "I will be god (3)" – self-destruction (4)"
Ybarra: "I will be famous like Eric Harris (3) – self-destruction (4)"

and so, "They are the same; it's the details that differ."

---

[47] Personal conversations with those who knew him
[48] Associated Press June 6, 2014

Aaron Ybarra and Elliot Rodger are the same Type. Rodger appeared far more controlled and deliberate.

Seattle Police Department released a portion of Ybarra's diary to the public which showed his handwriting behavior as erratic, confused, and unstable.

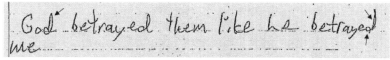
Figure 95: Ybarra entitlement

Like Zimmerman, Ybarra felt entitled as the tall "d" stems imply. The distorted "d" formations denote a distorted personal value system. Clearly, Ybarra's handwriting is unstable with variations in size, slant, structures, speed, and spacing. This infers emotional and mental instability. Compare the size, placement, and shape of the marked t-bars for instance. This suggests shallowness of purpose, resignation, and discouragement.

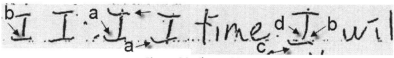
Figure 96: Ybarra PPIs

The marked Personal Pronoun I (PPI) has particular significance. Kimon Iannetta[49] says the following about the three key features of his PPI:

a. The concave base indicates shallowness of purpose and unreliability. The author appears independent and strong, yet, is emotionally unstable.

b. The disconnection between the bottom horizontal and the stem is called segmentation. This suggests weak boundaries between conscious thought processes and subconscious drives and urges. Segmentation in PPI or signatures implies serious disturbances in self-concept.

c. Letter structures dropping below the baseline imply unpleasant unconscious urges affecting the author's value and belief system. Such urges are not expressed, hidden, and subversive. A PPI that drops below the baseline is especially significant.

d. Backward pointed stroke final and implies self-castigation and self-blame. Iannetta, *"May place himself in a situation that result in some form of punishment."*

---

[49] Kimon Iannetta: "Danger between the Lines" (2008) p 92-94 (a), 95-97 (b) , 157-158 (c), 260-261 (d)

NBC news reported on June 13, 2014, Ybarra was being held without bail and attorneys are planning to use the insanity defense. This is in line with mental instability in his handwriting.

Type Three: *Conman*

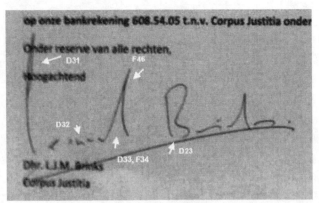

Figure 97: Conman

A scam letter circulated in the Netherlands in 2013. The letter originated from Corpus Justitia and claimed the recipient must pay a € 129,30 (~$110) debt or face property seizures. It was hand signed likely with a false name to avoid identification and prosecution. The signature fits the conman's letter like a tailored glove. The distorted Mid-Zone (D32[50]) imply unrealistic thinking and evasiveness. The tight "e" body shows ability to violate the rights of others and combined suggest amorality. The first letter intrudes in the typed area and combined with the very tall Upper-Zone implies distorted and irrational thinking. The tall (F46) and distorted "d" (D33) suggest gross overestimation of self-worth and distorted personal value system. Amorality and grandiosity come to mind. The "d" also formed a tent-like structure (F34) which is linked to stub-bornness, and this goes hand in hand with being unreasonable and antagonism. The open bottom in the B means hypocrisy and lack of moral judgment. Traits like grandiosity and entitlement combined with the exploitative nature of the letter suggests we are dealing with an unhealthy exploitative Three.

---

[50] the references are from "Danger between the Lines" by Kimon Iannetta

228

Type Three: *Flip Flop Romney*

Three: I am ambitious and a workaholic. I link my self-esteem and self-worth to a job well done. I need admiration and be applauded. I have the need to win or at minimum be better than others. When I lose control, I become competitive, arrogant and condescending.

Mitt Romney is a successful businessman and was a Presidential Candidate in 2012. Type Threes are ambitious, competitive, and link their self-esteem to an image of success.

Type Three grew up with unconditional approval and mother's admiration. They have self-worth issues in the sense they did not feel worthy of the accolades received. Their perspective is "I have to earn praise and admiration" with a basic need to feel worthy and valuable. With self-worth linked to performance, they become ambitious and competitive. They believe an image of success is more acceptable than being appreciated for who they are. They feel pushed to do better and better. After all, repeating the same task receives less praise and thus, they seek to improve the same task to find admiration for better performance.

The typical Type Three processes information rationally and intuitively. Generally speaking, their emotional connectedness to themselves and others is under-developed. They favor *Identification* as an ego defense mechanism and are inclined to act as if they are like you without stating their perspectives or intentions. They deceive others through misrepresentation. They are blind to failure and overstate their abilities.

Mr. Romney earned his nickname "Flip Flop Romney" as his gaffes and emotionally disconnected comments made painfully clear. There were many bloopers in his campaign. Although remarks were intended to be humorous in an attempt to connect with others, candidate Romney could have realized some were not appropriate within the context of running for President. In the end, he lost the campaign because he shifted opinions frequently, had too many slip-ups, was not believable and lost credibility.

Romney, on British soil and in front of the press, interpreted Britain's Olympics as a potential failure. He cited the potential for not enough security personnel and the strikes by immigration departments. Not to mention calling Labour Leader Ed Milliband "Mr. Leader". Such "gaffes" show a lack of commitment to your cause. To be this poorly prepared as a Presidential candidate does not bode well for your leadership abilities.

Romney made very clear how successful he really is. He consistently distanced himself from the general public with unusual commentary. He claimed 47% of the population will vote for President Obama because they are government dependent. He offered Rick Perry a $10,000 bet as if it was pocket change. The ordinary citizen has to work three months for that kind of money.

Fact checking was not his strong suit either. His instinctive nature allowed him to move forward without forethought. "Syria is Iran's route to the sea" made clear he did not realize the two countries are not connected. He accused President Obama saying he apologized for America and showing sympathy for the attackers of the 2012 Benghazi attack. Mr. Romney called President Obama out as a liar for not labeling the Benghazi attack as an act of terror. President Obama handed the then Governor his shovel by saying "Please proceed, Governor." America noticed and voted accordingly.

Type Four: *Janis Joplin*

Four: I need to find myself, fit in, and be unique and different. I tend to withdraw in self-pity and hope to be discovered. I might feel and act like a victim and become self-destructive.

Janis Joplin was a singer-songwriter who gained fame at the Monterey Pop Festival (1967). Janis always was "unhappy and unsatisfied without attention". Janis described herself as "a misfit" in high school. She was different and unique, and had several rants about her failed love life. She passed away in 1970 due to a heroin overdose. Through *introjection*, Janis saw herself in a negative light. She self-medicated with drugs.

We create our own biggest fear:
The Four's fear is insignificance and being without an identity. The self-pitying and emotionally tormented Four can drain energy and push others away. *They are now alone and insignificant.*

Side note: Type Four is probably least likely to violate the rights of others. They blame themselves, try to find answers from within, and are prone to self-loathing and self-destruction.

Type Four: *Stressed*

A Type Four stood accused of child molestation. This emotional and mature male gained single custody of his child. The justice system and Child Protective Services determined the case was without merit, and it was determined the accuser coached the child.

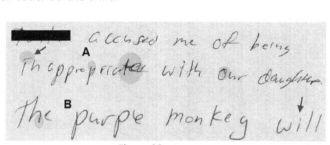

Figure 98: stressors

The author was asked to write down what happened during the accusations (A) and to write down a nonsense sentence (B). Sample A was highly upsetting to the emotional Four, who would rather hurt himself than anybody else, let alone his child. Note the Mid-Zone distortions, corrections, and the overall irritability in the slashes and tics. Sample B is more stable with better control than sample A. As we can see, stress and anxiety has an immediate influence on our handwriting. Fours process emotionally, and this whole situation was very taxing on this gentleman.

Type Five: *Yours truly*

Five: I believe I must provide a niche in order to fit into the world. I will re-search a subject extensively and then offer insights to others. When stressed, I withdraw and isolate myself to figure out a measured response.

I grew up with an ambivalent identification with both parents and developed into a typical Type Five. I heard about the Enneagram and read the Type Five chapter in a second-hand bookstore. I was shocked and intrigued at the same time. I realized this chapter might as well have been written about me. And like a typical Five, I had to study this, research it, compare notes, continue to observe people, and in the end, it all made perfect sense.

Fives are generally withdrawn, imaginative, logical, and controlled. They can be socially awkward, do not like small talk, mentally isolate themselves, and see the world as unsafe and unpredictable. They can lose objectivity and become scattered in their thinking. When they acquired sufficient knowledge, they need to present the world with what they learned like for instance this book.

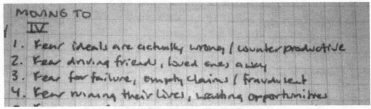

Figure 99: Yours truly studying

My handwriting is vertical and fairly consistent reflecting on the logical and controlled traits. When I study, my handwriting gets smaller reflecting on my ability to concentrate for hours on end.

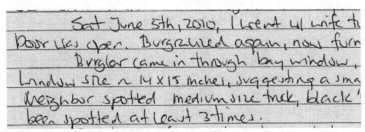

Figure 100: Yours truly police narrative

In 2012, my home was burglarized twice, and this handwriting sample shows the police narrative reporting the second burglary. This example shows my response to being emotionally upset. The size increased, and an increase in spontaneity is visible. Fives process information rationally and detach their strong emotions to preserve objectivity.

Type Five: *Ted Kaczynski*

Fives: I felt ignored, unacknowledged, and did not fit into the family unit. I try to be acknowledgment and find support by offering insight and knowledge. When my ideation is heavy on theory and no longer realistic, I become hyperactive and scattered in my thinking. Schizophrenia and brilliance are therefore close cousins.

Ted Kaczynski, the Unabomber, lived in a 10x12 foot cabin in the woods, with no electricity and no running water. He was isolated and expressed his ideology in his Manifesto. He carried out his crimes from a distance, logically, methodically, and in secrecy. His first bombing was in 1978 and his last in

1995. He was arrested in 1996 after his brother recognized his word selection and sentence construction in his published Manifesto. Fives need to share what they know and Kaczynski was caught when his brother recognized the subject matter.

Kaczynksi was socially isolated and used violence from a distance. The withdrawn Fives habitually use knowledge and secrecy as their weapons and are more prone to be driven by ideological causes than personal vengeance. Through *Isolation* or retreating into his mind and emotional detachment, he was able to execute his bombings and justify the mayhem he caused.

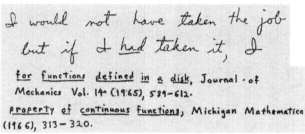

Figure 101: Ted "Unabomber" Kaczynski

We create our own biggest fear:
Fives find the world unpredictable and threatening. Their biggest fear is not being able to deal with the world and not fitting in. A withdrawn and isolated Five rejected the world and *created their personal threatening imaginary world*.

Type Six: *Fuzzie*

Six: I want to do what is expected of me to feel safe and supported. I have self-doubt and rely on those in the know to figure out what I think. Under stress, I can become dutiful or panic.

One of my dear friends is a mid-thirties wonderful woman who is a 6w5. For over a year, we went back and forth about what Type she was. She felt she was a Type One whereas I believed she was a Type 6. Misidentification of a 6w5 and a One is common; however, the perspectives of a Type One and Six are opposite. Type One has a negative identification with the Patriarchal Role Model and the Six a positive identification. To make things more confusing, her biological father divorced her mother who remarried a man Fuzzie had issues with. In essence, she had a positive identification with her biological father and a negative one with her stepfather. Yet, she is a Type

Six because her perspective, self-doubt, and behavioral style, rule adherence, match the pattern of a Type Six. She was early enamored with her father, and core perspectives establish early in life when we are most vulnerable to the impact of new experiences. This is unlike a stepfather entering later in life.

The 6w5 and the One are frequently confused since both have a strong conviction adherence. The Six are prone to do what they believe is expected from them. They adhere to rules of who they believe are authority figures and "in the know". They abide by their inner voice telling them to listen to outside guidance. This is commonly referred to as their "Inner Committee".

The Six grows up feeling secure abiding by the rules father provided. This is often the patriarchal role model or the father. They feel insecure and have self-doubt without such guidance, especially when they have to rely on themselves. Later in life, as adults, the rule adherence to fit in the family unit is projected to society as a whole. Sixes are inclined to adhere to the rules of authority figures or entities like their employer, the IRS, law-enforcement, and judicial system. The One grows up realizing the guiding principles provided are wrong, faulty, too strict, or inconsistent. They learn early in their lives to create their rules and standards. Their core perspective throughout their lives is, "I know right from wrong."
I set the rules and know why I set a standard. The One's rule adherence is to an inner voice or their "Inner Critic". And so, we see a major difference between the Six and the One. A Six has *self-doubt* and adheres to rules of those in the know. A One knows the rules and presents them with *emphatic certainty*. A Six is critical of themselves rather than critical of others. The Ones are critical of themselves when they feel they are not living up to their own set of expectations. A One is judgmental of others when they do not try as hard to better the world. It's the "you need to live up to my standards" attitude.

Both want to do the right thing but have differing motivations. The One and Six can easily be distinguished during stress reactions when behaviors become exaggerated. Sixes have enormous self-doubt and become anxious, indecisive, and impulsive. The One presents themselves with anger filled emphatic certainty even when they are demonstratively wrong. Sixes and Ones will tell others what to do and clearly with very different motivations. Sixes order others around because they feel their security and stability are at risk when they see others as irresponsible, disruptive, irrational or erratic.

234

Ones enforce personal standards in the name of their particular idealistic perspective. As we see, both the 6w5 and the One can behave similarly but have a very different view and a distinctly different stress reaction. Generally speaking, Sixes have self-doubt, and Ones are very certain of themselves.

I always wished I was my dad's favorite

Figure 102: Fuzzie Type Six or Type One?

Her perspective shows she wanted to be daddy's favorite but felt her sister took first place. This was established during a critical phase in her childhood unlike the negative identification with the stepfather, which came later in life and after the identification with the biological father already had taken shape.

"I always wished I was my dad's favorite because I loved him so much + wanted to be just like him but I always sensed that my sister was his favorite which made me jealous + feel rejected …. Unworthy maybe.
So in order to get his love + win his favor I worked extra hard to be "better" than my sister which still didn't work even though I was a close 2nd place."

A Type One is frustrated with the Patriarchal Role Model and typically doesn't want to be like him. Ironically, the One sets their rules and standards often even more rigidly than their father did. Then, at average and unhealthy levels of development, enforce those standards on others. I once said to a typical One, *"I am so glad you are not like your father"* and he beamed with pride. Another One made this statement in a letter I received *"I have tried so hard not to be him* [father] *and so far have become everything he is."*

Fuzzie is the opposite of a One and worked hard to be in dad's favor. This is a Type Six perspective. She wrote *"My dad wound up becoming my confidant around this time because… he seemed to be the only one who understood + valued me."* Others also realized Fuzzie looked up to her dad. When dad left his new girlfriend, Fuzzie was confronted by her with, *"Are you happy? You finally got your dad all to yourself just like you always wanted".*

As a Six, she is concerned with security and has problems with anxiety and fear. She overestimated her father as an authority figure which is why she had a hard time letting go of him. After a conversation with her therapist, struggling about distancing herself from him, she wrote,

"My dad had always been my safety net + support system so who would catch me now? I closed my eyes + turned inward to find the answer.
I had consciously been thinking before I closed my eyes, "Oh no, who would it be now? My husband? I don't know!", but I only had to quiet down for a few seconds to get the answer from my inner knowing - Myself! Wow ..."

And with the realization she can and needs to guide herself, she shed the need to depend on authority figures and learned to provide her own guidance. She felt a weight lifted off her shoulders and is a changed woman. When we met again, she was beaming and radiated confidence I had not seen before. She used the insights of the Enneagram to her advantage.

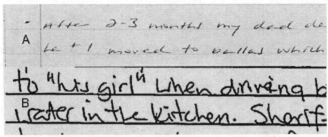

Figure 103: A 6w5 and B 5w6 (scale unknown)

Sixes process information emotionally and intuitively, and Fives rationalize things while detaching emotions to preserve objectivity. Both Types 5w6 and 6w5 have similarities yet, the core perspectives of the Type Six versus the Type Five shines through in their handwriting. Type Six is dedicated, reliable, emphatic, and demonstrative whereas the Five is logical, controlled, withdrawn, and imaginative. The more emotional Six has a stronger forward slant showing a more emotional make-up. She writes smaller and connects most letters reflecting on concentration and emotional expression. The Five writes with a vertical slant and heavy pressure showing disconnection of cognitive abilities from their emotions.

Type Six: *Rush Limbaugh*

Six: I am loyal and doubt myself. I can either be authority respectful or authority defiant. I need security and support. When I don't feel supported, I become anxious, insecure, and have a tendency to hysterically overreact. After which I become competitive and vindictive.

Rush Limbaugh was a prominent conservative radio host and known for his controversial society-opposing and misogynistic views. His commentary is instinctual and emotionally reactive, without forethought or significant insight. As a "GOP wanna be spokesperson", he promotes his extreme conservative and dogmatic views with unbridled enthusiasm.

Limbaugh quotes:
1) *What does it say about the college co-ed Sandra Fluke, who goes before a congressional committee and essentially says that she must be paid to have sex, what does that make her? It makes her a slut, right? It makes her a prostitute. She wants to be paid to have sex. She's having so much sex she can't afford the contraception.*
2) *So, Ms. Fluke and the rest of you feminazis, here's the deal: If we are going to pay for you to have sex, we want something for it, and I'll tell you what it is — we want you to post the videos online so we can all watch.*

Unhealthy Sixes are their own worst enemy as they lack inner guidance. His Fluke rhetoric is incoherent, presumptuous, and without logic. He is self-defeating as the vast majority recognizes such commentary as extreme and as nonsense.

Through *Projection*, he emphatically proclaims the perceived shortcomings in others, while not acknowledging his own. His emotionally demonstrative behavior is without a solid foundation and in line with processing information intuitively and emotionally, with reasoning under-developed.

We create our own biggest fear:
The biggest fear of the Six is to be without guidance and support. They rely on input of authority figures, yet, the deteriorating Six becomes self-defeating. They over-react, are impulsive, and irrational. In doing so, they push others away, and then they *are truly without guidance and support.*

Type Seven: *Delightful woman*

Seven: I am enthusiastic, vibrant, and gregarious. I felt not taken care off and lacked emotional nurturance. I compensate by nurturing myself through new experiences. When things get out of hand, I tend to overdo things and become involved in too many things.

This delightful young woman presented a forgery case to me as she was being victimized with false rent receipts. It was a pretty clear case of forgery, and we talked about the personality type of the forger as seen through his handwriting.

We ended up having a long talk about the Enneagram and her personality Type. Each Type is inclined to see themselves in a certain light reflecting on their perspective. One writing test, I frequently do, is ask the subject to write down five key words to describe themselves. And then I ask them to write down *"What I love about my mother* [father] *is ….."* and they chose to fill in the blank.

A Type Seven is a child growing up feeling they lacked emotional nurturance and results in frustration with the emotional nurturer which is often the Mother (-M). They end up in a constant search for nurturance through activities and new experiences. Sevens are acquisitive with an often insatiable need for new experiences or material needs. They are the busy bees in the world with full agendas. They are positive-minded, experience-oriented, assertive, and insistent. They process information rationally and intuitively, and under-develop emotional connectedness.

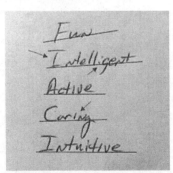

Figure 104: key words used

Perspective analysis:
When Sevens describe themselves, they prefer to use words like enthusiastic, free-spirited, on-the-go, live life to the fullest, spontaneous, and adven-

turous. This young woman used *Fun, Intelligent, Active, Caring, Intuitive.*
Notice how *Fun* slants upwards in her enthusiasm. Notice she sees herself as
Intelligent (Thinking Triad) with the last word being *Intuitive* (Doing Triad).
Of course, *Active* is a perfect description for a Seven, who is always on the
go. Her capitals and her MZi are a decent size, which combined with forceful
pen pressure, reflects on her assertive and insistent nature.

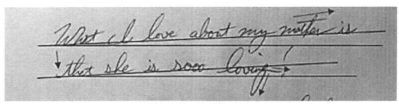

Figure 105: optimism

Handwriting analysis:
In her handwriting, we see fluidity and optimism with the rising baseline.
This author wants to move forward which is seen in forward slant, longer t-
bars, and longer final strokes. Our hand is more active in down strokes as
the muscles contract, and the longer down strokes, therefore, imply this
author is action oriented. Of course, this is in line with how she described
herself. The initial hook in "that" means being prone to acquisitiveness and
is in line with the Seven's need to seek new experiences.

Mother (-M)
The word "loving" drops off the rising baseline. The final stroke is the only
one moving down instead of up. The emotional impact linked to the word
reduced her enthusiasm. This suggests the author is not as forthcoming as
she could have been, but given the circumstances appropriately so. We also
see the word "mother" is cramped with the Upper-Zone of the "h" being
much tighter than the other Upper-Zone loops. The stem of the "h" suddenly and unexpected drops below baseline and overshoots the imaginary baseline. The emotional impact of the word reflects on increased tension and
anxiety. She explained she loves her mother, but confirmed she did not feel
nurtured. Mother was busy working hard to be able to provide her children,
and something had to give. Regardless of circumstances and mother's intentions, it is clear she did not feel nurtured. This provided her with the perspective of a Seven.
And so, her five key words as well as her handwriting revealed her outlook,
emotional impact, and behavioral character traits.

Type Seven: *7w8*

Ted Bundy was a Type 7w8, and he did the California Life Goals Evaluation. Sevens have the need to acquire new experiences to combat their feelings of deprivation and their fear of missing out. Eights need to be in control to resist feeling vulnerable. He described himself in his answers:
- to have freedom of want (7)
- to control the actions of others (8)
- to guide others with their consent (8)
- to avoid boredom (7)
- to be self-fulfilled (7)
- to live one's life one's own way (8)

Type Eight: *Chris Christie*

Eight: I have to be self-reliant and fear being at the mercy of others. When I feel vulnerable, I become domineering, bossy, and overly confident. I can be overwhelming, violent, and ruthless. Then I withdraw out of fear for retaliation.

Chris Christie is the Governor of New Jersey (2014). He has an air of over-confidence, is direct, blunt, and bossy. Like a typical Assertive, he has limited insight into the emotional impact he has on others.
Chris Christie quotes as a Governor and public figure:

1. *"You have numb nuts like Reed Gusciora who put out a statement comparing me to George Wallace and Lester Maddox. Now, come on guys, at some point, you've got to be able to call BS on those kind of press releases," Jan. 30, 2012, on a pro-gay-marriage state assemblyman.*
2. *"First off it's none of your business. I don't ask you where you send your kids to school. Don't bother me about where I send mine." – June 17, 2011*
3. *"Get the hell off the beach in Asbury Park and get out. You're done. It's 4:30; you've maximized your tan. Get off the beach." – Aug 26, 2011, encouraging people to leave as Hurricane Irene approached.*
4. *"Cry me a river." – Dec. 20, 2011, on President Barack Obama having to deal with a Republican House after two years of Democrats in power.*
5. *"What the hell are we paying you for?" — Nov. 28, 2011, on Barack Obama acting as a "bystander" in the White House after the supercommittee failed to reach an agreement on debt reduction.*

The Ebola (2014) epidemic in mostly African nations had people worried. Volunteer medical personnel from those countries could bring the virus to the United States. The Centers for Disease Control and Prevention (CDC) have known for years how Ebola spreads, and what the symptoms are. There was no reason to panic, nor for volunteer workers to quit going to African countries.

The CDC made clear an infected individual must be symptomatic before they can spread the disease. Governor Chris Christi enforced involuntary quarantine on a volunteer nurse. He defended his decision by denying known CDC facts by stating, *"I am right, and the CDC is wrong."*

The Eight's point of view is to take charge and control their environment. This theme reappears in their perspective, as we all project our views onto others.
An unarmed young black male, who just stole from a convenience store, was killed by a white police officer in Ferguson, Missouri. Christie commented that people across the country are deeply anxious. President Obama lacks leadership, and he is partly to blame. The Obama leadership theme is a mere projection of his own theme. And so, Christie's judgment tells us more about him than Obama. As a potential future presidential candidate, he might want to consider toning his overwhelming presence down since any trait in excess turns voters off.

We create our own biggest fear:
The biggest fear of the Eight is being hurt by others or being at their mercy. The Eight needs to be self-reliant and be in control. They are strong-willed, forceful, and compassionate leaders, and can become blunt, direct, and overwhelming. They can resort to violence and destruction of others. In doing so, they are forcefully rejected, and become fearful for retaliation. And now they are *at the mercy of others*.

The school bully
A child felt vulnerable at home and learned to take care of themselves. That feeling never left her and at school, she felt even more vulnerable with so many different characters. She fears others might hurt her, and she developed a quick temper. She protected herself by being assertive and confrontational. She yells at her peers, who make her feel uncomfortable, just to keep them at bay. The message is "don't mess with me". Others respond with their own defense mechanisms and become more aggressive and hos-

tile. The girl now feels even more vulnerable, and the initial yelling becomes pushing and eventually fighting. Self-protection develops into constant fighting.

The teacher tells the bully to not bully but the message does not resonate with the girl. She feels vulnerable and protects herself through assertion and initiative. Nobody can tell her to not bully because to her it means to not self-protect and cave into being vulnerable. It would be better to redirect her self-protective stance with an alternative perspective. She is aggressive out of fear being hurt by others, so she hurts them first. She needs to hear she will be supported and protected to change her mind. Her current retaliation makes others feel vulnerable, and they will eventually fight back. What comes around goes around. Eventually she will conclude that, "my aggression makes me more vulnerable instead of less".

Type Nine: *Sandra Bullock*

Nine: I am amicable and agreeable. I tend to be passive, forget about my own preferences, and under stress, I tend to disengage and manipulate passive-aggressively. At the end of my rope, I overreact and become hysterical.

Sandra Bullock was married to "bad boy" Jesse James and stated she has never been treated better in her life. After James cheated and dented the trust she had, the marriage was quickly over. Bullock never spoke badly about him, and publicly put positive spins on the negatives. Like a good Nine, she remained withdrawn, polite, and passive in interviews. She expressed a typical Nine perspective by saying *"I learned to not say yes when I don't mean it"*, a direct reflection of addressing her core fear and expressing a core need: her personal preferences.

Typically Nines deal with stress through *Narcotization* or mind-numbing habitual activities to avoid anxiety and stress. They hide in their inner sanctum where they feel safe and peaceful. Alas, lack of self-representation goes at a huge emotional cost: self-denial.

We create our own biggest fear:
The Nine's biggest fear is loss and separation. They learn to be amicable and agreeable to avoid loss of support. In doing so, they take on different roles in order to avoid being separated from others. The deteriorating Nine withdraws and not only alienates from others, they no longer recognize themselves. *They lost support from others as well as themselves.*

242

Type Nine: *Lauren Scruggs*

Lauren Scruggs, an aspiring model, walked into a spinning propeller of a small plane. She lost an eye and left arm and is commended for her amazing recovery. "It's kind of weird to say, but I wouldn't trade it. I have seen it as a miracle. I've been through a lot, but I'm living". In her NBC interview, with loving parents on her side, she is remarkably calm, reflective, and accepting of her new life. Lauren is also the first to acknowledge the support of her family and her faith.

Type Nine: *H and K*

One of my favorite questions to ask is to write down five words that describe you the best. A Nine male friend (9w8) used Positive, Happy, Easy going, Honest and Thoughtful and the words describe him to a T. He is a Nine (probably 9w8).

The five words on the right are of a mature female and describe her very well. Instead of easy going she used friendly. She is a 9w1 and we notice how she used capable and irritable.

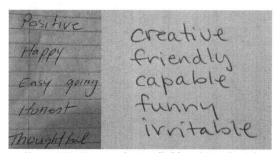

Figure 106: Five words 9w8 (left) and 9w1 (right)

Both have rounded lettering reflecting on their gentle nature. The 9w8 has a rightward slant reflecting on impulsivity. The word selections are typical for a Nine. Positive-minded, people-oriented, and easy going. Compare the wording with the addendum "Resonating Key words".

In closing

In the introduction, I asked the question *"Could the Santa Barbara spree killing have been prevented?"* The short answer is yes, and the long answer is a resounding no.

Behavioral Pathways is a natural behavioral progression model. As we have learned, we all have certain qualities and characteristics. The past provided perspective and experiences. The present gives opportunity to meet our immediate needs, whereas our long term goals and needs are within the future. Although behavioral potential does not equate to actual behavioral choice, we do know our choices are progressive in nature. This progression can be recognized in the past and present while providing predictive value to future decisions.

Logistically, we cannot prevent all crimes but there will be individual cases that could have been prevented. Anyone watching Elliot's videos could have realized he felt rejected instead of admired. He displayed many characteristics consistent with a Type Three Behavioral Pathway, flavored by Type Four:
- Entitled
- Self-promoting
- Opportunistic
- Arrogant
- Condescending
- and above all:
- Logical, controlled, and methodical

If law-enforcement had viewed the video declarations combined with basic knowledge of Behavioral Pathways, they could have recognized him as a Type Three. His number one defense mechanism would be *Identification with others* with deception at its core. They could have known Elliot Rodger would *adapt* and provide a false persona. They would have realized the videos showed grandiosity, self-promotion, and rage expressed as arrogance and condescension. Yet, he remained calm, logical, controlled, and presented himself as:

"Articulate, polite, and timid".

Nothing ever happens in a vacuum, nor did the 2014 Santa Barbara deadly massacre. Elliot Rodger was a Type Three, and his Behavioral Pathway *predicts, or at minimum includes the possibility of the natural progression toward maliciousness and vindictive violence.* Don Riso described the natural progression in detail in "Personality Types" (1996)[51]". The combination of the self-promotion, opportunistic and arrogant videos, and the well-mannered young man law-enforcement met is befitting a Type Three. Emotional detachment, and staying calm during a stressful encounter, was *the major red flag* and part of his deteriorating Behavioral Pathway. Understanding of natural progressive patterns, including existing defense mechanisms could have prompted the officers to enter his apartment, only to find his guns and Manifesto[52].

Rodger wrote in his Manifesto: *"I had the striking and devastating fear that someone had somehow discovered what I was planning to do, and reported me for it. If that was the case, the police would have searched my room, found all of my guns and weapons, along with my writing about what I plan to do with them. I would have been thrown in jail, denied of the chance to exact revenge on my enemies. I can't imagine a hell darker than that."*

This all too brief and incomplete summary of the nine distinct Behavioral Pathways is meant as a guide to learning to recognize patterns, perspectives, and consequent behavioral characteristics. We can influence with integrity when we understand their perspective. For a full description of each Type, I recommend studying *"Personality Types. Using the Enneagram for self-discovery"* by Don Riso and Russ Hudson (completely revised and updated 1996). It applies to anybody with a personality, whether at home, school or work.

---

[51] Don Riso "Personality Types" Type Three, Level 9 "the vindictive psychopath"
[52] Elliot Rodger "my twisted world" p 134

Disclaimer

All the material contained in this book is provided for informational purposes only. No responsibility can be taken for any results or outcomes from the use of this material. While every effort has been made to provide accurate information, the author does not assume any responsibility for use or misuse of the contents.

Addendum 1: Brief Biographies

Jodi Arias
Jodi Arias (1980 -) was convicted of first-degree murder of Travis Alexander in 2013. He was stabbed numerous times, had a gunshot wound to his head, and his throat slit. Arias claimed self-defense.

Ted Bundy
Ted Bundy (1946 - 1989) was an American serial kidnapper, killer, and known for necrophilia. He was executed in Florida and confessed to some thirty murders in seven different states.

Desmond Campbell
Desmond Campbell (1974 - 2014) was an American serial burglar, robber, and rapist active in Tulsa OK in 2014. He fled his last crime scene in a car that he drove into a light pole on the highway. He died later of his injuries in a local hospital.

Ariel Castro
Ariel Castro (1960 - 2013) kidnapped and imprisoned three young women in his home for a decade. He raped them repeatedly and even fathered a child. Castro was convicted and committed suicide in prison.

Lukah Chang
Lukah Chang (1990 -) was sentenced to 35 years for the murder of the motel maid where he stayed and an assault on the one-year anniversary date of this murder. He was homeless, a marine deserter, a loner, and an opportunist without a cause. He just wanted to know "what it felt like" to kill.

Jeffrey Dahmer
Jeffrey Dahmer (1960 - 1994) was an American serial killer and sex offender. He raped and murdered seventeen male victims. He was also known for cannibalism and necrophilia.

Josef Fritzl
Josef Fritzl (1935 -) is an Austrian father who imprisoned his eighteen-year-old daughter to keep her away from bad influences. He built a cellar beneath his home and maintained his double life for twenty-four years.

Patrick Jane (fictional character portrayed by actor Simon Baker)

Patrick Jane is the lead character in the series the "Mentalist". His wife and child are murdered by Red John after he mocked Red John through intellectual arrogance. Patrick Jane is a Five whereas Red John is a Three.

Randy Kraft
Randy Kraft (1945 -) is an American serial killer who raped, mutilated, and murdered young men. He was nicknamed "the Scorecard killer" and the "Freeway killer".

Eric Clinton Newman
Eric Clinton Newman (1982 -), a.k.a. Luka Rocco Magnotta is a Canadian killer convicted of the murder of Lin Jun. He dismembered and mailed body parts.

Patsy Ramsey
Patsy Ramsey (1956 - 2006) is the mother of JonBenét Ramsey, who was found dead in the cellar of her home. Patsy is widely believed to have written the ransom note.

Gary Ridgway
Gary Ridgway (1949 -) is an American serial killer better known as "the Green River killer". He targeted prostitutes and usually strangled them after the sex act. He was convicted of forty-eight murders but confessed to many more at a later stage.

Elliot Rodger
Elliot Rodger (1991 - 2014) was a British-born American spree killer who killed six and wounded thirteen before he committed suicide in Isla Vista, CA.

Addendum 2: Be a trendsetter

There are some principles to adhere to in relationship dynamics. Although the parent-child dynamics is the most important one in our lives, the rules apply to any relationship.

- present a clear and consistent foundation
- encourage natural gifts
- enjoy successes with them
- redirect with positive alternatives
- be an unwavering supporter and confidant

Thoughts become words;
words become actions;
actions become habits;
habits become values;
and values become destiny.

One mindless word or action becomes a child's inner voice and is repeated over and over again. Your word becomes their destiny. Become a positive trendsetter and incorporate the qualities of the nine Types:

- Be fair
- Relate
- Persevere
- Be original
- Be competent
- Be loyal
- Be enthusiastic
- Be forthright
- Be tolerant

Addendum 3: Types summarized

9 + M/F Anecdotalist *(Sloth)*
"my view is not important"
focus: creating serenity
amicable, agreeable
avoids conflict, unpleasantries
blind to personal preferences
problem with passivity,
stubbornness

8 ~ M Autonomist *(Denial)*
"I am vulnerable"
focus: to be self-reliant
takes charge to control environment
avoids reality
blind to impact on others
problem with dominance, bluntness

1 - F Fundamentalist *(Wrath)*
"I must be better"
focus: evaluates right vs wrong
enforces personal standards
avoids condemnation
blind to gray areas
problem with impatience, anger

7 - M Optimist *(Gluttony)*
"I am missing out"
focus: pleasure seeking
preoccupied with acquisition
avoids anxiety, pain
blind to personal limitations
problem with impulsivity,
superficiality

2 ~ F Devotist *(Pride)*
"I am not worthy of love"
focus: meet needs of others
selflessly ingratiates
avoids personal needs
blind to personal needs
problem with acknowledging
personal needs

AUTONOMY
relating, anger
DO (gut)

SECURITY
fear, anxiety
THINK (head)

ATTENTION
self-worth, shame
FEEL (heart)

6 + F Loyalist *(Fear)*
"I don't trust my judgment"
focus: search for hidden meanings
do what is expected of me
avoids personal rejection
blind to overestimation of authority
problem with self-doubt, impulsivity

3 + M Opportunist *(Deceit)*
"I am not worthy"
focus: performance acknowledgment
perseverance leads to success
avoids failure
blind to personal failure
problem with competitiveness

5 ~ M/F Realist *(Avarice)*
"I need to be acknowledged"
focus: developing competence
seeks abstract understanding
avoids feelings of emptiness
blind to existing abundance
problem with isolation, nihilism

4 - M/F Pessimist *(Envy)*
"I am unlike you"
focus: identity search
integrates environmental influences
avoids ordinary
blind to what they already have
problem with self-pity, self-indulgence

Addendum 4: Look and Listen!

Observe what they do and listen to what they say. A Type is recognized over time by paying attention to the following traits:

1. main theme
2. key needs and key fears
3. potential problems
4. social style
5. behavioral style
6. information processing
7. role model influences
8. defense mechanism
9. resonating key words
10. stress reactions
11. stress reaction pattern

Main Theme
1. I judge right from wrong and act nice to repress my anger
2. I relate and I am good to others repressing my own needs
3. I either win or lose and act successful to avoid feeling worthless
4. I compare common versus originality and I fantasize being unique to avoid insignificance
5. I assess true or not true and I develop a niche to avoid incompetence
6. I need to be supported and I do what is expected to avoid loss of support
7. I am preoccupied with finding the next thrill and to avoid inner anxiety
8. I assess safe versus not safe and I am bossy to avoid feeling vulnerable
9. I either accept or don't accept but act in agreement to avoid conflict

Addendum 5: Behavioral Pathway progression

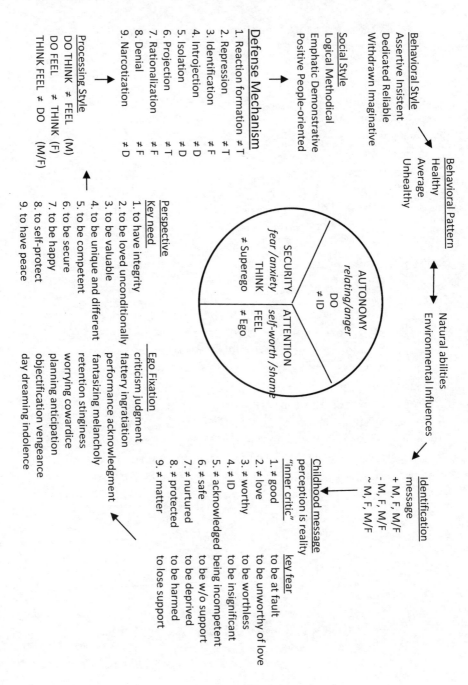

Behavioral Style
Assertive Insistent
Dedicated Reliable
Withdrawn Imaginative

Social Style
Logical Methodical
Emphatic Demonstrative
Positive People-oriented

<u>Defense Mechanism</u>
1. Reaction formation ≠ T
2. Repression ≠ T
3. Identification ≠ F
4. Introjection ≠ D
5. Isolation ≠ D
6. Projection ≠ T
7. Rationalization ≠ F
8. Denial ≠ F
9. Narcotization ≠ D

<u>Processing Style</u>
DO THINK ≠ FEEL (M)
DO FEEL ≠ THINK (F)
THINK FEEL ≠ DO (M/F)

<u>Behavioral Pattern</u>
Healthy
Average
Unhealthy

Natural abilities
Environmental Influences

<u>Identification</u>
message
+ M, F, M/F
- M, F, M/F
~ M, F, M/F

<u>Childhood message</u>
perception is reality
"inner critic"

AUTONOMY
relating/anger
DO
≠ ID

SECURITY
fear/anxiety
THINK
≠ Superego

ATTENTION
self-worth/shame
FEEL
≠ Ego

	key fear
1. ≠ good	to be at fault
2. ≠ love	to be unworthy of love
3. ≠ worthy	to be worthless
4. ≠ ID	to be insignificant
5. ≠ acknowledged	being incompetent
6. ≠ safe	to be w/o support
7. ≠ nurtured	to be deprived
8. ≠ protected	to be harmed
9. ≠ matter	to lose support

<u>Ego Fixation</u>
1. criticism judgment
2. flattery ingratiation
3. performance acknowledgment
4. fantasizing melancholy
5. retention stinginess
6. worrying cowardice
7. planning anticipation
8. objectification vengeance
9. day dreaming indolence

<u>Perspective</u>
Key need
1. to have integrity
2. to be loved unconditionally
3. to be valuable
4. to be unique and different
5. to be competent
6. to be secure
7. to be happy
8. to self-protect
9. to have peace

Addendum 6: Core fear and typical stress reaction

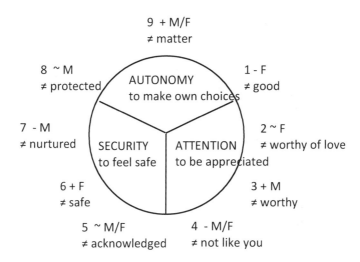

Type One feels not good enough and seeks to be better. Stress reactions are expressed with impatience and anger.

Type Two feels unworthy of love and seeks to be loved. Stress reactions include becoming overly involved and being needed.

Type Three feels not worthy and seeks to be worthy. Stress reactions include competitiveness, contempt and exploitation.

Type Four feels insignificant and must find personal significance. Stress reactions include withdrawal, moodiness and self-pity.

Type Five feels unacknowledged and seeks competence. Stress reactions include impractical preoccupation and intellectual arrogance.

Type Six does not feel safe and seeks security. Stress reactions include impulsivity and becoming dutiful.

Type Seven does not feel nurtured and seeks nurturance. Stress reactions include hyper-activity and scattered thinking.

Type Eight feels vulnerable and self-protects through confrontation. Stress reactions include over-confidence and overwhelming behaviors.

Type Nine feels they do not matter and seeks peace and quiet. Stress reactions include passivity, complacency and they disengage.

Addendum 7: *Behavioral Pathway One*

Behavioral Pattern
Healthy: wise, realistic, objective, realizes "good enough" is perfect
Average: reality-ideal conflicts, critical, judgmental, impatient
Unhealthy: enforces personal standards, self-righteous, intolerant

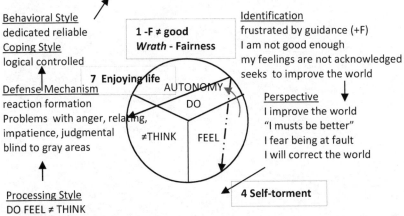

Behavioral Style
dedicated reliable
Coping Style
logical controlled

1 -F ≠ good
***Wrath* - Fairness**

Identification
frustrated by guidance (+F)
I am not good enough
my feelings are not acknowledged
seeks to improve the world

Defense Mechanism
reaction formation
Problems with anger, relating,
impatience, judgmental
blind to gray areas

7 Enjoying life
AUTONOMY
DO

≠THINK   FEEL

Perspective
I improve the world
"I musts be better"
I fear being at fault
I will correct the world

Processing Style
DO FEEL ≠ THINK
repressed instincts backed by emotions leads to
pent up anger, under-developed rationalization
leads to emphatic certainty

4 Self-torment

One sees self	others may see
objective	striving
prudent	orderly
reasonable	critical
	inflexible
	contradictory
	punitive

Addendum 8: *Behavioral Pathway Two*

Behavioral Pattern
Healthy: altruistic, takes care of own needs, genuine, generous
Average: good intentions, overly involved, self-sacrificing
Unhealthy: creating dependencies , self-deceptive about intentions, coercive

Behavioral Style
dedicated reliable
Coping Style
positive people-oriented
Defense Mechanism
repression
Problems with acknowledging
own needs, does not realize
others don't see their hints,
questions unreciprocated love

Identification
rejected by guidance (+F)
I am not worthy of love
nurtures to earn love
seeks to be good

2 ~ F ≠ Not worthy of love
Pride - Empathy

Perspective
I want your love
I must earn love
I fear not being loved

8 Overwhelming

≠THINK   ATTENTION
          FEEL

DO

4 Inspiring

Processing Style
FEEL DO ≠ THINK
emotional processes with repression of negatives
plus instinctive doing and under-developed rationalization leads to irrationally acting out emotions

Two sees self	Others may see
loving	demonstrative
caring	intrusive
selfless	overbearing
	manipulative
	coercive
	parasitic

Addendum 9: *Behavioral Pathway Three*

<u>Behavioral Pattern</u>
Healthy: authentic, self-accepting, well-adjusted, ambitious and modest
Average: image oriented, meets expectations of others, competitive, self-promoting
Unhealthy: exploitative, arrogant and condescending.

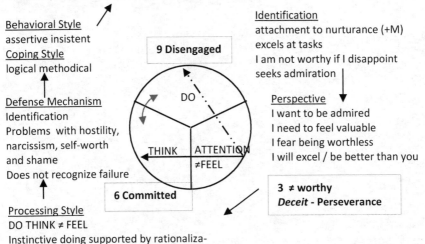

<u>Behavioral Style</u>
assertive insistent
<u>Coping Style</u>
logical methodical

<u>Defense Mechanism</u>
Identification
Problems with hostility,
narcissism, self-worth
and shame
Does not recognize failure

<u>Processing Style</u>
DO THINK ≠ FEEL
Instinctive doing supported by rationalization, with under-developed feelings allows
for overstepping social boundaries

9 Disengaged

DO

THINK | ATTENTION
≠FEEL

6 Committed

<u>Identification</u>
attachment to nurturance (+M)
excels at tasks
I am not worthy if I disappoint
seeks admiration

<u>Perspective</u>
I want to be admired
I need to feel valuable
I fear being worthless
I will excel / be better than you

3 ≠ worthy
Deceit - Perseverance

Three sees self	Others may see
desirable	career-oriented
admirable	expedient
charming	self-promoting
	deceptive
	opportunistic
	relentless

Addendum 10: *Behavioral Pathway Four*

Behavioral Pattern
Healthy: inspiring, self-aware, compassionate, different
Average: romantic, artistic, passionate, depressed
Unhealthy: self-pity, angered with self-inhibitions, self-medication

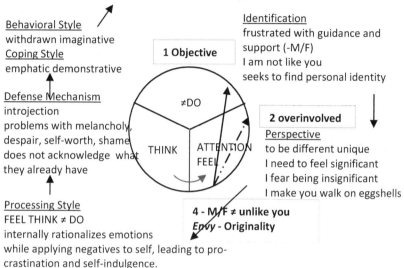

Behavioral Style
withdrawn imaginative
Coping Style
emphatic demonstrative

Defense Mechanism
introjection
problems with melancholy,
despair, self-worth, shame
does not acknowledge what
they already have

Processing Style
FEEL THINK ≠ DO
internally rationalizes emotions
while applying negatives to self, leading to procrastination and self-indulgence.

Identification
frustrated with guidance and
support (-M/F)
I am not like you
seeks to find personal identity

1 Objective

≠DO

THINK   ATTENTION
FEEL

2 overinvolved
Perspective
to be different unique
I need to feel significant
I fear being insignificant
I make you walk on eggshells

4 - M/F ≠ unlike you
Envy - Originality

Four sees self	Others may see
sensitive	individualistic
different	temperamental
unique	decadent
gentle	self-inhibiting
	clinically depressed
	self-destructive

Addendum 11: *Behavioral Pathway Five*

Behavioral Pattern
Healthy: extraordinary perceptive, inquisitive, insightful, aware
Average: intellectual pursuits, studious pre-occupied
Unhealthy: reclusive, nihilistic, social detachment, eccentric

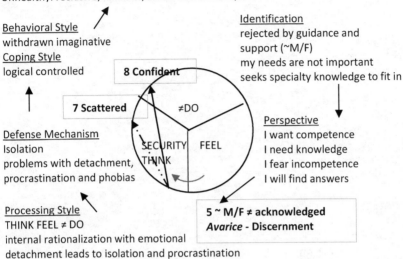

Behavioral Style
withdrawn imaginative
Coping Style
logical controlled

Identification
rejected by guidance and
support (~M/F)
my needs are not important
seeks specialty knowledge to fit in

8 Confident

7 Scattered   ≠DO

SECURITY   FEEL
THINK

Defense Mechanism
Isolation
problems with detachment,
procrastination and phobias

Perspective
I want competence
I need knowledge
I fear incompetence
I will find answers

Processing Style
THINK FEEL ≠ DO
internal rationalization with emotional
detachment leads to isolation and procrastination
blind to abundance in front of them

5 ~ M/F ≠ acknowledged
Avarice - Discernment

Five sees self	Others may see
perceptive	knowledgeable
inquisitive	preoccupied
insightful	provocative
smart	eccentric
	delirious
	psychotic

Addendum 12: *Behavioral Pathway Six*

Behavioral Pattern
Healthy: dedicated, trustworthy, engaging
Average: security seeking, committed, search for hidden meaning
Unhealthy: submissive, helpless, inferiority, irrational

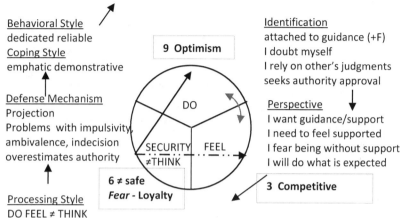

Behavioral Style
dedicated reliable
Coping Style
emphatic demonstrative

Defense Mechanism
Projection
Problems with impulsivity
ambivalence, indecision
overestimates authority

Processing Style
DO FEEL ≠ THINK
instinctive doing with emotional support
leads to impulsivity, under-developed rationalization leads to dutifulness

9 Optimism

DO

SECURITY   FEEL
≠THINK

6 ≠ safe
Fear - **Loyalty**

3 Competitive

Identification
attached to guidance (+F)
I doubt myself
I rely on other's judgments
seeks authority approval

Perspective
I want guidance/support
I need to feel supported
I fear being without support
I will do what is expected

Six sees self	Others may see
dependable	loyal
reliable	defensiveness
trustworthy	blaming
	clingingly dependent
	lashing out
	self-destructive

Addendum 13: *Behavioral Pathway Seven*

Behavioral Pattern
Healthy: spontaneous, appreciative, well-rounded, grateful
Average: materialistic, variety seeking, acquisitive
Unhealthy: impulsive, narcissistic, addictive, erratic

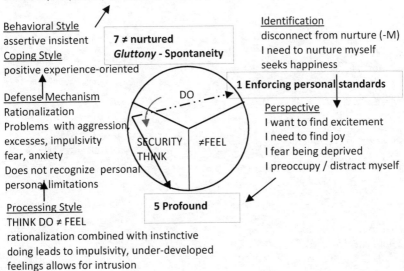

Behavioral Style
assertive insistent
Coping Style
positive experience-oriented

7 ≠ nurtured
Gluttony - Spontaneity

Identification
disconnect from nurture (-M)
I need to nurture myself
seeks happiness

1 Enforcing personal standards

Defense Mechanism
Rationalization
Problems with aggression,
excesses, impulsivity
fear, anxiety
Does not recognize personal
personal limitations

DO

SECURITY
THINK   ≠FEEL

Perspective
I want to find excitement
I need to find joy
I fear being deprived
I preoccupy / distract myself

5 Profound

Processing Style
THINK DO ≠ FEEL
rationalization combined with instinctive
doing leads to impulsivity, under-developed
feelings allows for intrusion

Seven sees self	Others may see
enthusiastic	variety seeking
free-spirited	hyperactive
adventurous	excessive
spontaneous	escapist
fun	reckless
	burned out

Addendum 14: *Behavioral Pathway Eight*

Behavioral Pattern
Healthy: authoritative, protective, resourceful
Average: self-reliant, domineering, untrusting
Unhealthy: overwhelming, hard-headed, reckless, overly confident

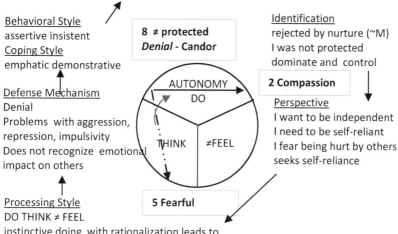

Behavioral Style
assertive insistent
Coping Style
emphatic demonstrative

8 ≠ protected
Denial - **Candor**

AUTONOMY
DO
THINK   ≠FEEL

Identification
rejected by nurture (~M)
I was not protected
dominate and control

2 Compassion

Perspective
I want to be independent
I need to be self-reliant
I fear being hurt by others
seeks self-reliance

Defense Mechanism
Denial
Problems with aggression,
repression, impulsivity
Does not recognize emotional
impact on others

5 Fearful

Processing Style
DO THINK ≠ FEEL
instinctive doing with rationalization leads to
candor and bluntness, under-developed feelings allows for confrontation

Eight sees self	Others may see
strong	enterprising
assertive	dominating
action oriented	intimidating
direct	dictatorial
	terrorizing
	destructive

Addendum 15: *Behavioral Pathway Nine*

<u>Behavioral Pattern</u>
Healthy: receptive, genuine, unflappable, self-acknowledging
Average: amicable, agreeable to a fault, accommodating, passive
Unhealthy: avoids problems and conflict, neglectful, disengaged

<u>Behavioral Style</u>
withdrawn imaginative
<u>Coping Style</u>
positive people-oriented

<u>Defense Mechanism</u>
narcotization
problems with self-effacing,
repression, acknowledging
personal preferences

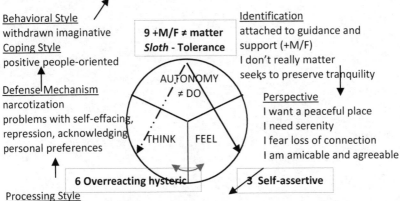

9 +M/F ≠ matter
Sloth - Tolerance

AUTONOMY
/ ≠ DO
THINK   FEEL

6 Overreacting hysteric

3 Self-assertive

<u>Identification</u>
attached to guidance and
support (+M/F)
I don't really matter
seeks to preserve tranquility

<u>Perspective</u>
I want a peaceful place
I need serenity
I fear loss of connection
I am amicable and agreeable

<u>Processing Style</u>
FEEL THINK ≠ DO
repressed instinctive doing with emotional support leads to pent up anger, under-developed
rationalization leads to emphatic certainty

Nine sees self	Others may see
peaceful	agreeable
relaxed	complacent
easy-going	appeasing
	neglectful
	disoriented
	disappearing

Addendum 16: Key fear, need, focus, pay off

	childhood perception: key fear	Perspective: key need	Focus	Pay off
1	I am not good enough	I must be better, even perfect	I want to improve the world and make it perfect	When I am perfect, you won't criticize me
2	I am unloved and not appreciated	I must earn your love and appreciation	I want to be loved and appreciated	When I am good to you, you will love me
3	I am not worthy	I must excel to feel worthy	I want to earn admiration	When I perform well, you will admire me
4	I am insignificant, do not identify	I must distinguish myself	I want to be different and unique	When I am different, you will notice me
5	I am inadequate nor acknowledged	I must provide special knowledge to be acknowledged	I want to be knowledgeable and adequate	When I am knowledgeable, you will acknowledge me
6	I am not safe and have self-doubt	I must do what is expected of me	I want security through guidance and reassurance of support	When I do what is expected of me, I feel safe and secure
7	I am not taken care off and am deprived	I must seek pleasant and exciting experiences	I want to have freedom and happiness	When I acquire new experiences, I feel less anxious
8	I am vulnerable	I must be in control	I want to be self-reliant	When I am self-reliant, I don't depend on you
9	I do not really matter	I must be amicable, agreeable	I want harmony, peace and quiet	When I am agreeable, I avoid confrontation

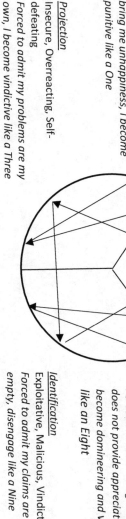

Narcotization
Neglectful, Dissociating, Self-abandoning
Forced to face own problems, I become over-reactive and hysterical like a Six

Denial
Ruthless, Omnipotent, Violent
Forced to admit, I am vulnerable and fear retaliation, I withdraw and emotionally detach like a Five

Rationalization
Impulsive, Compulsive, Hysteric
Forced to admit my activities bring me unhappiness, I become punitive like a One

Projection
Insecure, Overreacting, Self-defeating
Forced to admit my problems are my own, I become vindictive like a Three

Isolation
Isolated, Delusional, Schizoidal
Forded to admit my emotions are real, I become overwhelmed, hyperactive and scattered like a Seven

Introjection
Alienated, Tormented, Self-destructive
Forced to admit I ruin my own life with negativity, I become coercive and play victim role like a Two

Identification
Exploitative, Malicious, Vindictive
Forced to admit my claims are empty, disengage like a Nine

Repression
Self-deceptive, Coercive, victim
Forced to admit their generosity does not provide appreciation, I become domineering and violent like an Eight

Reaction formation
Intolerant, hypocritical, Punitive
Forced to admit my ideals are wrong and counter-productive, I become emotionally tormented and withdraw in self-pity

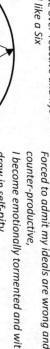

---

[53] The Behavioral Pathways is written from personal experience, assembled and summarized from "Personality Types" Riso / Hudson (1996) and other sources.

Addendum 18: George Zimmerman police narrative

1. In August of 2011 my neighbors house was broken into while
2. she was home with her infant son. The intruders attempted to attack
3. her and her child; however, SPD reported to the scene of the crime
4. and the robbers fled, My wife saw the intruders running from the
5. home and became scared of the rising crime within our neighborhood
6. I, and my neighbors formed a "Neighborhood Watch Program". We
7. were instructed by SPD to call the non-emergency line if we
8. saw anything suspicious + 911 if we saw a crime in progress.
9. tonight I was on my way to the grocery store when I saw
10. a male approximately 5'11" to 6'2" casually walking in the
11. rain looking into homes. I pulled my vehicle over and called
12. SPD non-emergency phone number. I told the dispatcher took
13. what I had witnessed, the dispatcher took
14. note of my location + the suspect fled

15. To a darkened area of the sidewalk, as the dispatcher was
16. asking me for an Exact location the suspect emerged from
17. the darkness + circled my vehicle, I could not hear if he
18. said anything. The suspect once again disappeared between the
19. back of some houses. The dispatcher once again asked me for
20. my exact location I could not remember the name of the street
21. so I got out of my car to look for a street sign. The dispatcher
22. asked me for a description and the direction the suspect went
23. I told the dispatcher I did not know but I was out of my
24. vehicle looking for a street sign + the direction the suspect went
25. The dispatcher told me not to follow the suspect + that an officer
26. was in route. As I headed back to my vehicle the
27. suspect [sic] emerged from the darkness and
28. said "you got a problem" I said "No"
29. The suspect said "you do now". As I looked

30. And tried to find my phone to dial 911 the suspect punched
31. me in the face. I fell backwards onto my back. The
32. suspect got on top of me. I yelled "Help" several times
33. The suspet [sic] told me "Shut the Fuck up" as I tried to sit up
34. right, The suspect grabbed my head and slammed it into
35. the concrete sidewalk several times. I continued to yell "Help"
36. each time I attempted to sit up, the suspect slammed my head
37. into the side walk. My head felt like it was going to explode.
38. I tried to slide out from under the suspect and continue [sic]
39. to yell "Help". As I slid the suspect covered my mouth
40. and nose and stopped my breathing. At this point I felt the
41. the suspect reach for my now exposed firearm and say"
42. "Your[sic] gonna die tonight Mother Fucker![sic] I
43. unholstered my firearm in fear for my
44. life as he has assured he was going to kill

45. Me and fired one shot into his torso. The suspect
46. sat back allowing me to sit up and said "you got me"!
47. At this point I slid out from underneath him and
48. got ontop of the suspect holding his hands away from
49. his body. An onlooker appeared[sic] and asked me if I was ok
50. I said "no" he said "I am calling 911" I said "I don't
51. need you to call 911 I'd already called them I need you to
52. help me restrain this guy". At this point a SPD officer
53. arrived and Asked "who shot him" I said "I did" and
54. I placed my hands ontop of my head and told the officer
55. where on my persona my firearm was holstered. The
56. officer handcuffed me and disarmed me. The officer
57. then place me in the back of his
58. vehicle.

265

Addendum 19: Ramsey Ransom note page 1

1 Mr. Ramsey,

2   Listen carefully! We are a
3 group of individuals that represent
4 a small foreign faction. We do
5 respect your bussiness but not the
6 country that it serves. At this
7 time we have your daughter in our
8 posession. She is safe and unharmed
9 and if you want her to see 1997,
10 you must follow our instructions to
11 the letter.

12   You will withdraw $118,000.00
13 from your account. $100,000 will be
14 in $100 bills and the remaining
15 $18,000 in $20 bills. Make sure
16 that you bring an adequate size
17 attache to the bank. When you
18 get home you will put the money
19 in a brown paper bag. I will
20 call you between 8 and 10 am
21 tomorrow to instruct you on delivery.
22 The delivery will be exhausting so
23 I advise you to be rested. If
24 we monitor you getting the money
25 early, we might call you early to
26 arrange an earlier delivery of the

Addendum 20: Ramsey Ransom note page 2

```
27  money and hence a earlier
28  delivery pick-up of your daughter.
29       Any deviation of my instructions
30  will result in the immediate
31  execution of your daughter. You
32  will also be denied her remains
33  for proper burial. The two
34  gentlemen watching over your daughter
35  do particularly like you so I
36  advise you not to provoke them.
37  Speaking to anyone about your
38  situation, such as Police, F.B.I., etc.,
39  will result in your daughter being
40  beheaded. If we catch you talking
41  to a stray dog, she dies. If you
42  alert bank authorities, she dies.
43  If the money is in any way
44  marked or tampered with, she
45  dies. You will be scanned for
46  electronic devices and if any are
47  found, she dies. You can try to
48  deceive us but be warned that
49  we are familiar with Law enforcement
50  countermeasures and tactics. You
51  stand a 99% chance of killing
52  your daughter if you try to out
53  smart us. Follow our instructions
```

Addendum 21: Ramsey Ransom note page 3

```
54  and you stand a 100% chance
55  of getting her back. You and
56  your family are under constant
57  scrutiny as well as the authorities.
58  Don't try to grow a brain
59  John. You are not the only
60  fat cat around so don't think
61  that killing will be difficult
62  Don't underestimate us John.
63  Use that good southern common
64  sense of yours. It is up to
65  you now John!

66
67
                        Victory!

                        S.B.T.C
```

time we have your daughter in our
posession. She is safe and un harmed
and if you want her to see 1997,
you must follow our instructions to
the letter.

Addendum 24: JonBenét Ransom Note transcript

1. Mr. Ramsey.
2. Listen carefully! We are a
3. group of individuals that represent
4. a small foreign faction. We ~~xx~~
5. respect your business but not the
6. country that it serves. At this
7. time we have your daughter in our
8. posession. She is safe and un harmed
9. and if you want her to see 1997,
10. you must follow our instructions to
11. the letter.
12. You will withdraw $118,000.00
13. from your account. $100,000 will be
14. in $100 bills and the remaining
15. $18,000 in $20 bills. Make
16. that you bring an adequate size
17. attache to the bank. When you
18. get home you will put the money
19. in a brown paper bag. I will
20. call you between 8 and 10 am
21. tomorrow to instruct you on delivery.
22. The delivery will be exhausting so
23. I advise you to be rested. If
24. we monitor you getting the money
25. early, we might call you early to
26. arrange an earlier delivery of the
Page 2:
27. money and hence a earlier
28. ~~delivery~~ pickup of your daughter.
29. Any deviation of my instructions
30. will result in the immediate
31. execution of your daughter. You
32. will also be denied her remains
33. for proper burial. The two
34. gentlemen watching over your daughter
35. do \not/ particularly like you so I
36. advise you not to provoke them.
37. Speaking to anyone about your
38. situation, such as Police, F.B.I.,etc.

39. will result in your daughter being
40. beheaded. If we catch you talking
41. to a stray dog, she dies.
42. If you alert bank authorities, she dies.
43. If the money is in any way
44. marked or tampered with, she
45. dies. You will be scanned for
46. electronic devices and if any are
47. found, she dies. You can try to
48. deceive us but be warned that
49. we are familiar with Law enforcement
51. stand a 99% chance of killing
52. your daughter if you try to out
53. smart us. Follow our instructions
Page 3:
54. and you stand a 100% chance
55. of getting her back. You and your
family
56. are under constant
57. scrutiny as well as the authorities.
58. Don't try to grow a brain
59. John. You are not the only
60. fat cat around so don't think
61. that killing will be difficult.
62. Don't underestimate us John.
63. Use that good southern common
64. sense of yours. It is up to
65. you now John!
66.   Victory!
67.   S.B.T.C

References

Douglas, John, and Olshaker, Mark: *The anatomy of motive* (1999)

Elfers, Marcel D.: *"Case Study: George Zimmerman"*. The Graphologist, the journal of the British institute of Graphologists. (Winter 2012, vol. 30, no. 4. P. 73-81)

Hare, Robert D, Ph.D.: *Without conscience: the disturbing world of the psychopaths among us* (1995)

Iannetta, Kimon S., and Craine, James F, Ph.D.: *Danger between the lines, reference manual for the profiling of violent behavior* (2008)

IGAS instruction department: *Fears and defenses* (1994)

Leyton, Elliot, Ph.D.: *Hunting humans, the rise of the modern multiple murder* (2003)

McClish, Mark: *I know you are lying* (2012)

Poinzer, Annette, Ed.D., RSW: *"Clinical Graphology: an interpretative manual for mental health practitioners"* (2012)

Riso, Don Richard, and Hudson, Russ: *Personality Types: Using the Enneagram for Self-Discovery* (1996)

Riso, Don Richard, and Hudson, Russ: *Understanding the Enneagram, the practical guide to personality types* (revised edition 2000)

Riso, Don Richard, and Hudson, Russ: *The wisdom of the Enneagram, the complete guide to psychological and spiritual growth for the nine personality types* (1999)

Stout, Martha: *"the sociopath next door"* (2006)

Thomas, Steve, and Davis, Donald A.: *JonBénet, inside the murder investigation* (2000)

Vronsky, Peter: *Serial killers, the method and madness of monsters* (2004)

Wecht, Cyril, M.D.: *Who killed JonBenét Ramsey?* (1998)

Recommended

Bloom, Lisa: *Suspicion nation: The inside story of the Trayvon Martin injustice and why we continue to repeat it* (2014)

Bunker, M.N.: *Handwriting analysis, the science of determining personality by graphoanalysis* (1972)

Ekman, Paul: *Telling lies, clues to deceit in the marketplace, politics, and marriage* (2001)

Foster, Don W.: *Author unknown* (2000)

Givens, David, Ph.D.: *Crime signals. How to spot a criminal before you become a victim* (2008)

Hodges, Andrew G., M.D.: *Who will speak for JonBenét?* (2000)

Hodges, Andrew G., M.D.: *A mother gone bad* (1998)

Kendall, Elizabeth: *The phantom prince, my life with Ted Bundy* (1981)

Kolar, James A.: *Foreign Faction, who really kidnapped JonBénet* (2012)

McNichol, Andrea, and Nelson, Jeffrey A.: *Handwriting analysis, putting it to work for you* (1991,1994)

Miller, Patricia H: *Theories of Developmental Psychology* (2011)

Moir, Ann: *Brain Sex, the real difference between men and women* (1992)

Morris, Desmond: *Man watching* (1977)

Mullan, Usha: *Graphology and the Enneagram. Vol. III (2008)*

Newton, Michael: *The encyclopedia of serial killers, a study of the chilling criminal phenomenon* (2000)

Palmer, Helen: *The Enneagram, understanding yourself and the others in your life.* (1991)

Rabon, Don: *Investigative Discourse Analysis* (2003)

Ramsey, John and Patsy: *The death of innocence* (2001)

Rodger, Elliot: *My twisted world.* (Manifesto 2014)

Rhodes, Susan: *The positive Enneagram, a new approach to the nine personality types* (2009)

Roman, Klara G.: *Handwriting, a key to personality* (1952)

Rule, Ann: *The stranger beside me* (2001)

Schiller, Lawrence : *Perfect Town, Perfect Murder* (1999)

Seifer, Mark, Ph.D.: *The Definitive book of handwriting analysis* (2009)

Stone, Michael H: *The anatomy of evil* (2009)

Sue, David; Sue, Derald Wing, and Sue, Stanley: *Understanding abnormal behavior* 8th Edition (2006)

Vronsky, Peter: *Female serial killers, how and why women become monsters* (2007)

Wade, Carole, and Tavris, Carol: *Psychology, media and research update* 7th Edition (2005)

Zimbardo, Philip, Ph.D.: *The Lucifer Effect: Understanding how good people turn evil* (2008)

Index

Made in the USA
San Bernardino, CA
10 April 2015